Metaphysics

Dimensions of Philosophy Series

Norman Daniels and Keith Lehrer, Editors

Metaphysics, Peter van Inwagen

Philosophy of Biology, Elliott Sober

Philosophy of Physics, Lawrence Sklar

Theory of Knowledge, Keith Lehrer

Philosophy of Law: An Introduction to Jurisprudence,
Revised Edition, Jeffrie G. Murphy and Jules L. Coleman

Philosophy of Social Science, Alexander Rosenberg

Introduction to Marx and Engels: A Critical Reconstruction,
Richard Schmitt

FORTHCOMING

Philosophy of Science, Clark Glymour

Philosophy of Mind, Jaegwon Kim

Contemporary Continental Philosophy, Bernd Magnus

Political Philosophy, Jean Hampton

Normative Ethics, Shelly Kagan

Philosophy of Religion, Thomas V. Morris

Philosophy of Education, Nel Noddings

Philosophy of Language, Stephen Neale

Also by Peter van Inwagen

An Essay on Free Will

Material Beings

Metaphysics

Peter van Inwagen
SYRACUSE UNIVERSITY

Westview Press
BOULDER • SAN FRANCISCO

Dimensions of Philosophy Series

Copyright © 1993 by Westview Press, Inc.

Published in 1993 in the United States of America by Westview Press, Inc., 5500 Central Avenue, Boulder, Colorado 80301-2877

Library of Congress Cataloging-in-Publication Data
van Inwagen, Peter.
    Metaphysics / Peter van Inwagen.
        p.   cm. — (Dimensions of philosophy series)
    Includes bibliographical references and index.
    ISBN 0-8133-0634-5. — ISBN 0-8133-0635-3 (pbk.)
    1. Metaphysics.   I. Title.   II. Series.
BD111.V38   1993
110—dc20   92-28613
                                                                                      CIP

Printed and bound in the United States of America

The paper used in this publication meets the requirements
of the American National Standard for Permanence of Paper
for Printed Library Materials Z39.48-1984.

10   9   8   7   6   5   4   3   2   1

To my daughter,
ELIZABETH CORE VAN INWAGEN

Contents

Preface

THIS BOOK IS AN introduction to metaphysics that presupposes no prior ac-
quaintance with philosophy. It can be used either as an introductory textbook,
suitable for an upper-level undergraduate course in metaphysics (where it
would probably be supplemented by "readings" chosen by the instructor) or
as a book that the—I hope not mythical—"interested general reader" can pick
up and read without guidance from an instructor. It is primarily as an aid to
this interested general reader that I have included Suggestions for Further
Reading at the end of each chapter (but one).

Perhaps I should inform any interested general reader who is leafing
through this book in a shop or library that the word 'metaphysics' does not,
properly speaking, refer to the occult, to supernatural manifestations, to out-
of-body experiences, or to anything of that sort. (If you have taken it down
from a shelf labeled "metaphysics" in a shop or even in a small public library, I
am afraid that you may very well have found it in the company of books of
that sort.) What the word 'metaphysics' does properly refer to is dealt with at
length in the first chapter.

For the benefit of the instructor who is considering using the book as a text,
I list here the questions that the book addresses and some of the topics that are
considered in the course of addressing these questions:

- What is metaphysics? (Appearance and reality; which questions
  are metaphysical questions; comparison of the task and methods
  of metaphysics with those of science and theology; diagnoses of
  the failure of metaphysics to provide agreed-upon answers to any
  metaphysical questions, particularly the diagnoses of Kant and
  the logical positivists.)
- Is there a plurality of things, or is there only one thing? (Arguments for monism, particularly those of Spinoza and Bradley; the
  authority of mystical experiences.)
- Is there an external world, a world of things that exist independently of human thought and sensation? (Berkeley's arguments.)
- Is there such a thing as objective truth? (Realism and anti-
  realism.)
- Why is there something rather than nothing? (Necessary and contingent existence; the ontological and cosmological arguments;

the Principle of Sufficient Reason; dependent and independent beings; the relevance of scientific considerations to this question.)

- Why are there rational beings? (Design and purpose in nature; physical cosmology and "fine-tuning"; the teleological argument; the hypothesis of a Designer vs. the "many-worlds" hypothesis.)

- Are we physical or non-physical beings? (Dualism and physicalism; arguments for and against dualism and for physicalism; type-type physicalism and token-token physicalism; personal identity.)

- Have we free will? (Determinism and indeterminism; free choice; the apparent incompatibility of free choice with both determinism and indeterminism.)

It should be noted that this book is a "systematic" rather than an "historical" introduction to metaphysics. Although it contains discussions of arguments that have their origins in the works of various of the great philosophers, it does not pretend to present these arguments in a way that does scholarly justice to the form in which they were originally presented. And no attempt is made at a connected history of metaphysics.

It is also worthy of remark that some important topics that are often included in introductory books on metaphysics receive no treatment here. A draft of the book included brief discussions of the metaphysical problems raised by space, time, and causation. But the book had simply become too long, and I decided to delete this material rather than shorten other parts of the book.

At the end of each chapter (other than Chapter 12) are some suggestions for further reading. Publication information concerning the books and essays suggested is given in the Bibliography.

I wish to take this opportunity to thank (in two cases to remember) those philosophers who have taught me the most about metaphysics: William P. Alston, José Benardete, Jonathan Bennett, Mark Brown, Roderick M. Chisholm, James W. Cornman, Carl Ginet, Mark Heller, Frances Howard-Snyder, Keith Lehrer, David Lewis, Thomas J. McKay, Alvin Plantinga, Richard Taylor, Peter Unger, and Robert E. Whallon.

The treatment of type-type physicalism in Chapter 9 was influenced by Christopher S. Hill's recent book *Sensations: A Defence of Type Materialism* (Cambridge: Cambridge University Press, 1991).

John Martin Fischer and Mark Ravizza read a draft of the book and gave me the benefit of comments that have led to extensive revisions. I hope they will regard them as improvements. I am very grateful to them. I am also grateful to David Johnson for his comments on the first four chapters. Jonathan Bennett read the parts of the draft manuscript dealing with Spinoza and Berkeley. His extensive comments on this material contained many valuable suggestions (all of which, I believe, I have followed) and saved me from several embarrassing errors, thus increasing considerably my already great debt to him. Bennett also read and commented on a section of the manuscript dealing with animal intelligence. This part of the manuscript was, alas, eventually deleted. But *I* learned a great deal from his comments. As is customary, I hereby absolve Fischer, Ravizza, Johnson, and Bennett of responsibility for any defects that remain. These defects are due to my either ignoring their suggestions or dealing with them in a wrong-headed way.

I am grateful to Spencer Carr, senior editor and editorial director at Westview Press, the editorial staff of Westview (especially Martha Leggett, project editor, and Sarah Tomasek, copy editor), and to the Westview readers. The book has greatly benefited from the patient and untiring assistance of the editors and the comments of the readers.

I also wish to thank Alexander Rosenberg (I continue to hope that our not being departmental colleagues is a temporary aberration of the natural order of things) and Stewart Thau (that department chair than which no greater can be conceived) for friendship and encouragement, and, most of all, my wife, Lisette, for love, support, and pointing out that I had better finish this book because we need new storm doors.

Peter van Inwagen

1

Introduction

AN INTRODUCTORY TEXTBOOK of geology or tax law or music theory will probably begin with some sort of account of what geology or tax law or music theory is. Perhaps an introduction to almost any subject could be expected to begin with a general account of that subject, with something like a definition. Thus, an introduction to biology might begin with some such words as 'Biology is the scientific study of living organisms', and a textbook of sociology might begin by telling its readers that sociology is the study of how people live together. Nothing could be more natural than this, for the first thing the student of any subject wants to know is what that subject is. The need for a definition is especially acute in the case of metaphysics.

Most people have at least an inkling of what 'geology' and 'tax law' and 'music theory' mean, even if they would be hard put to it to provide dictionary-style definitions of these terms. But it is a near certainty that someone who has not actually studied metaphysics—formally, in a course of study at the university level—will have no inkling of what the word 'metaphysics' means. It seems obvious, therefore, that an introduction to metaphysics should begin with some sort of definition of metaphysics. Unfortunately, it is unlikely that a definition of metaphysics can convey anything useful.[1] The nature of metaphysics is best explained by example. When you have read this book you will have a tolerably good idea of what metaphysics is. But it hardly seems fair to leave the matter there. Anyone who opens a book has the right to some sort of preliminary account of what the book is about. This chapter is an attempt at this kind of account.

When I was introduced to metaphysics as an undergraduate, I was given the following definition: metaphysics is the study of ultimate reality. This still seems to me to be the best definition of metaphysics I have seen. Nevertheless, it is not as helpful and informative a definition as one might hope for. What, one might well ask, is meant by "reality," and what does the qualification "ultimate" mean? Our preliminary account of metaphysics will take the form of an attempt to answer these questions.

We know that appearances can be deceptive. That is, we know that the way things look (or sound or feel or smell or taste) can mislead us about the way those things are. We know that Jane may look healthy and nevertheless be dying. We know that Tom may sound honest and nevertheless be a confidence man. We know that if one has just withdrawn one's hand from very hot water, then a warm object may feel cool to one's touch. To take a more important example, we know that most people in the Middle Ages believed that the earth was at the center of the universe and that the stars and planets were embedded in invisible spheres that revolved around the stationary earth.

Let us concentrate on this last example. Why did the medievals believe this? Well, because that's how things felt (the earth beneath our feet feels as if it were not moving) and that's how things looked. Today we know that the astronomical system accepted by the medievals—and by the ancient Greeks from whom the medievals inherited it—is wrong. We know that the medievals, and the Greeks before them, were deceived by appearances. We know that while the solid earth beneath our feet may seem to be stationary, it in fact rotates on its axis once every twenty-four hours. (Of course, we also know that it revolves around the sun, but let's consider only its rotation on its axis.) Now suppose you were standing on a merry-go-round (in Britain, a roundabout) and were wearing a blindfold. Would you be able to tell whether the merry-go-round was turning or stationary? Certainly you would: passengers on a turning merry-go-round feel vibration and the rush of moving air and, in certain circumstances, a hard-to-describe sort of "pulling." (This last will be very evident to someone who tries to walk toward or away from the center of a turning merry-go-round.) These effects provide the "cues," other than visual cues, that we employ in everyday life to tell whether we are undergoing some sort of circular motion. The medievals and the ancient Greeks assumed that because they did not experience these cues when they were standing or walking about on the surface of the earth, the earth was therefore not rotating. Today we can see their mistake. "Passengers" on the earth do not experience vibration because the earth is spinning freely in what is essentially a vacuum. When they move about on the surface of the earth, they do not experience the "pulling" referred to above because this effect, while present, is not sufficiently great to be detected by the unaided human senses. And they do not experience a rush of moving air because the air is carried along with the moving surface of the earth and is thus not moving relative to them.

This example shows that it is sometimes possible to "get behind" the appearances that the world presents to us and discover how things really are: we have discovered that the earth is *really* rotating, despite the fact this it is *apparently* stationary.

Let us think for a moment about the two words 'really' and 'apparently'. These two words have little meaning in isolation from each other. When we say that something is *really* true, we imply that something else is *apparently* true. It is hard to imagine anyone saying that two plus two really equals four or that Abraham Lincoln was really a man. The reason is that in neither case is there an opposing "apparently." Two plus two does not apparently equal three or five, and Lincoln was not apparently a woman or a cat or a Martian.

The nouns 'appearance' and 'reality' are derived from 'apparently' and 'really' and are related to each other in the same way. We talk about *reality* only when there is a misleading appearance to be "got behind" or "seen through": the *reality* of the matter is that (despite appearances) the earth rotates on its axis; in *reality* (and despite appearances) the heavens do not revolve around the earth. But this may suggest that whenever we manage to get behind some misleading appearance, what we find there is something that we can call "reality" without any need for qualification. In fact, however, what we find behind appearance is often something that can be called "reality" only relative to that appearance. What we find behind appearance is often itself an appearance that hides a deeper reality. In the 1920s, for example, writers of books on popular science liked to astound their readers by telling them that science had discovered that what people had always thought were solid objects (things like tables and chairs) were in actuality "mostly empty space." And there was certainly a sense in which this was true. At the very time at which the popular science writers were proclaiming this revelation, however, physicists were beginning to discover that what had been called "empty space" was really very far from empty. In other words, no sooner had people begun to digest the idea that what are normally called solid objects contain a lot of what is normally called empty space than it was discovered that what is normally called empty space is actually very densely populated. This minor episode in the history of thought suggests a general question: Could it be that the reality behind every appearance is itself only a further appearance? If the answer to this question is No, then there is a reality that is not also an appearance. This final or "ultimate" reality is the subject-matter of metaphysics.

If there is no ultimate reality, then metaphysics is a study without a subject-matter. (It would not be the only one. Astrology, for example, is a study without a subject-matter, since the celestial influences on our lives that astrologers claim to study do not, as a matter of fact, exist.) It is, however, hard to see how there could be no ultimate reality. Suppose your friend Jane were to try to tell you that there was no ultimate reality. "It's all just appearances," says Jane. "Whenever you think you've found reality, what you've found is just another appearance. Oh, it may be a deeper appearance, or a *less* misleading appearance than the one you had before, but it will still be an appearance. And that's because there isn't any ultimate reality waiting to be found."

Let us look carefully at Jane's statement that there is no ultimate reality. Is this something that is really so or only something that is apparently so? It seems to be reasonably clear that Jane means to be telling us how things really are. Paradoxically, in telling us that there is no ultimate reality, Jane is telling us that ultimate reality consists of an endless series of appearances. In other words, the statement that there is no ultimate reality is, as we might say, self-refuting because it is a statement about ultimate reality and, if it is true, it is a *true* statement about ultimate reality. It does not seem to be possible, therefore, to avoid the conclusion that there is an ultimate reality and that metaphysics has a subject-matter. But, of course, we must concede that nothing we have said has any tendency to show that metaphysics has much more to say: perhaps nothing can be discovered about ultimate reality except that it exists.

Metaphysics, then, attempts to get behind appearances and to tell the ultimate truth about things. It will be convenient to have a collective name for "things"—for everything. Let us call "everything" collectively 'the World'. Since 'the World' is a name for everything, the World includes even God (if there is a God). We are therefore using the word in a more inclusive sense than that employed by the religious believer who says, "God created the world." If we should later decide that there is a God who created everything besides Himself, it will be easy enough to find another word to use as a collective name for all of the world besides God—'the universe', say.

Metaphysics attempts to tell the ultimate truth about the World, about everything. But what is it that we want to know about the World? What are the questions whose answers would be the ultimate truth about things? I suggest that there are three such questions:

1. What are the most general features of the World, and what sorts of things does it contain? What is the World *like?*
2. Why does a World exist—and, more specifically, why is there a World having the features and the content described in the answer to Question 1?
3. What is *our* place in the world? How do we human beings fit into it?

One way to get a feel for what is meant by a question is to look at possible answers to it. I will lay out two sets of answers to these questions, in the hope that they will make the questions clearer by showing what sorts of statements count as answers to them. The first set of answers, which was most widely accepted in the Middle Ages is this:

1. The World consists of God and all that He has made. God is infinite (that is, He is unlimited in knowledge, power, and goodness) and a spirit (that is, He is not material). He has made both spirits and material things, but all of the things he has made are finite or limited. God has always existed, and at a certain moment in the past He first made other things; before that, there had never been anything besides God. God will always exist, and there will always be things that He has made.
2. God has to exist, just as two and two have to equal four. But nothing else has this feature; everything besides God might not have existed. The things other than God exist only because God (who has the power to do anything) caused them to exist by an act of free will. He could just as well have chosen not to create anything, in which case there would never have been anything besides Himself. Moreover, God not only brought all other things into existence, but He also keeps them in existence at every moment. If God did not at every moment keep the sun and the moon and all other created things in existence, they would immediately cease to exist. Things other than God have no power to keep themselves in existence, any more

than heavy bodies have the power to keep themselves suspended in the air.

3. Human beings were created by God to love and serve Him forever. Thus, each of them has a purpose or function. In the same sense in which it is true of John's heart that its function is to pump blood, it is true of John that his function is to love and serve God forever. But, unlike a heart, which has no choice about whether to pump blood, a human being has free will and can refuse to do the thing for which it was made. What we call human history is nothing more than the working out of the consequences of the fact that some people have chosen not to do what they were made to do.

The second set of answers, which was most widely accepted in the nineteenth century, is this:

1. The World consists of matter in motion. There is nothing but matter, which operates according to the strict and invariable laws of physics. Every individual thing is made entirely of matter, and every aspect of its behavior is due to the workings of those laws.

2. Matter has always existed (and there has always been exactly the same amount of it), for matter can be neither created nor destroyed. For this reason, there is no "why" to the existence of the World. Because the World is wholly material, and because matter can be neither created nor destroyed, the World has always existed. The question 'Why does it exist?' is a question that can be asked only about a thing that has a beginning. It is a request for information about what it was that caused the thing to begin to exist. Since the World did not ever begin to exist, the question 'Why does the World exist?' is meaningless.

3. Human beings are complex configurations of matter. Since the World has always existed, it is not surprising that there should be complex configurations of matter, for in an infinite period of time, all possible configurations of matter will come to exist. Human beings are just one of those things that happen from time to time. There is no purpose that they serve, for their existence and their features are as much accidents as the existence and shape of a puddle of spilt milk. Their lives—*our* lives—have no meaning (beyond the purely subjective meaning that we choose to find in them), and they come to an end with physical death, since there is no soul. The only thing that can be said about the place of human beings in the World is that they are—very temporary—parts of it.

These two sets of answers are indeed radically opposed. Nevertheless, there is much that they have in common. For example, each set of answers assumes that individual things (things like you and me and Mount Everest) are real. Other sets of answers, however, would deny this and hold that all individuality is mere appearance and that, in reality, there are no "separate" objects at all. (Something like this would be said by the adherents of many Eastern religions like Hinduism and Buddhism.) Both sets of answers presuppose that *time* is real, but there are those who would say that both the order of events in time ("before" and "after") and the seeming movement or "passage" of time are mere appearances. And there are those who would say the same about *space:* that the familiar "here" and "there" of ordinary experience are no more than appearance. Both sets of answers assume that there is a material world, a world of non-mental objects, but there have been philosophers who have held that nothing exists outside the mind. And, finally, each set of answers—just by being a set of *answers*—presupposes that our three questions can be answered. As we shall see later in this chapter, however, there are philosophers who would maintain that our three "questions" were not really questions at all but only strings of words that have the superficial appearance of questions (and, of course, if they are not questions, they do not have answers).

If I am right in supposing that our three questions are the questions the answers to which would be the ultimate truth about the World, then we may define metaphysics as the study that proposes answers to these three questions and attempts to choose among the competing sets of answers to them. (This definition is reflected in the structure of the present book: each of the three parts of the book is an investigation of one of the three questions.)

Another sort of aid in understanding what is meant by 'metaphysics' is provided by distinguishing metaphysics from the things it might be confused with. First, metaphysics must be distinguished from the most general and all-embracing of the physical sciences: cosmology and the physics of elementary particles. (Cosmology is the part of astronomy that studies the physical universe or "cosmos" as a whole. The physics of elementary particles studies the basic building blocks of the physical universe and the laws by which they interact.) These two fields of study have turned out to be closely connected and have, since the 1960s, produced results that are of the deepest significance for metaphysics. Let us give the name "physical cosmology" to those scientific investigations that intimately involve both cosmology and the physics of elementary particles. Here is an example of the metaphysical significance of physical cosmology. Physical cosmology *seems* to show that the physical universe had a beginning in time (about fifteen thousand million years ago)—or at least that it does not have an infinite past throughout which it has been much the same as it is now. If this is correct, then all metaphysical speculations that presuppose an infinite past during which the components of a universe much like the present universe have been eternally rearranging themselves—our second set of answers to our three metaphysical questions provides one important example of speculations that make this presupposition—are incorrect. And this by itself is sufficient to show the relevance of physical cosmology to metaphysics.

But if physical cosmology is of the deepest significance for metaphysics, it nevertheless does not and cannot answer all of the questions that metaphysics poses. For one thing, it cannot answer the question, Why does the World exist?

(Or, at least, this seems evident to me. But there are many who hope that some day—perhaps very soon—physical cosmology *will* answer this question. This is in my view a false hope. We shall consider it in Chapter 6.) Physical cosmology, moreover, does not and cannot tell us whether the physical universe is all that there is—whether there is more to the World than the physical universe. Scientists sometimes assert that the World is identical with the physical universe, as the astronomer Carl Sagan did in the opening words of his popular television series *Cosmos*, but the assertion is a metaphysical, not a scientific, assertion. It is certainly possible to argue that science will someday explain all observable phenomena and that one should therefore believe that the World is identical with the physical universe, since one should believe that nothing exists beyond those things that science postulates in the course of giving its explanations. But this argument is—and any argument for the same conclusion will be—a metaphysical, not a scientific, argument.

Secondly, metaphysics must be distinguished from sacred or revealed theology. Theology is, by definition, the science or study of God. Theology partly overlaps metaphysics. What is common to theology and metaphysics is usually called *philosophical*, or *natural*, theology. It is the remaining part of theology that is called sacred, or revealed, theology. According to those religions that regard God as a conscious, purposive being who acts in history (the so-called Abrahamic religions: Judaism, Christianity, and Islam), God has revealed to human beings certain important truths that they could not have found out for themselves. Sacred, or revealed, theology is the systematic study of the truths that God has supposedly revealed. Many of these supposedly revealed truths are metaphysical, or partly metaphysical, in character. That is, they are theses of the right kind to be, or to imply, answers to one or more of our three metaphysical questions. Nevertheless, just as metaphysics must be distinguished from physical cosmology, metaphysics must be distinguished from revealed theology.

Physical cosmology and revealed theology have their own methods and their own histories, each of which differs from the method and history of metaphysics, although the histories of all three are hard to disentangle from one another in practice. Both physical cosmology and revealed theology, in addition to endorsing (in various ways and degrees) statements and theories that are unrelated to the business of metaphysics, endorse statements and theories that have important metaphysical implications. But it does not follow that the metaphysician[2] can make the same sort of use of physical cosmology and revealed theology. There are two important differences between physical cosmology and revealed theology that imply that the metaphysician must treat these two disciplines differently.

First, there is in a very straightforward sense only one science of physical cosmology, but each of the Abrahamic religions has its own revealed theology (since each has its own views about the content of God's revelation to humanity). It is worth noting that a unique science of physical cosmology is not an inevitable state of affairs. It would be easy enough to imagine a world in which there were a variety of religions and political ideologies each of which had its "own" science, including its own physical cosmology. Anyone who doubts that this is a possibility should reflect on the fact that it was not long ago that cosmological theories that implied that the physical universe had a beginning in time were discouraged in the Soviet Union, since this idea contradicted the teachings of the official Soviet philosophy, dialectical materialism.

The second important difference between physical cosmology and revealed theology is this: Although practically no one regards physical cosmology as a pseudo-science or a repository of illusion, there is a large and respectable body of opinion that holds that there have never been any divine revelations and that revealed theology is therefore entirely illusory. This view of revealed theology is certainly strengthened by the fact that believers in divine revelation do not speak with one voice as to its content. But even if there were complete unanimity as to the content of divine revelation (among those who believed that it occurred at all), there would no doubt still be a large body of respectable opinion that held that revelation was illusory. It is important to remember, in connection with these observations, that, like those who believe in revelation, those people who collectively constitute "respectable opinion" do not speak with one voice. It follows that respectable opinion must sometimes be in error. Indeed, respectable opinion is sometimes in very pernicious error. Respectable opinion has held that it was the sacred duty of Europe to impose its own style of civilization on the rest of the world; respectable opinion has held that Karl Marx had achieved a scientific understanding of history.

When these qualifications have been duly noted, however, it remains true that there is in fact only one science of physical cosmology (and many revealed theologies), and it remains true that a large body of respectable opinion holds that revealed theology is entirely illusory. It can therefore hardly be maintained that the metaphysician, even the metaphysician who accepts the reality of divine revelation, can make the same kind of use of physical cosmology and revealed theology. In this book I regard myself as free to appeal to any widely accepted cosmological theories. But, despite the fact that I believe in divine revelation and believe that many of the things that have been revealed by God have important metaphysical implications, I make no appeal to revelation. The reason is simple enough: by appealing to physical cosmology, I do not restrict my audience in any significant way, and if I were to appeal to what I believed to be divine revelation, I should no doubt restrict my audience to those who agreed with me about the content of divine revelation—and I do not wish so to restrict my audience.

Metaphysics, then, must be distinguished from physical cosmology and from sacred or revealed theology. But metaphysics is a part or branch of the more general field of *philosophy* and it must also be distinguished from other parts of philosophy.[3] Any distinction between metaphysics and the other parts of philosophy will, however, be to some degree artificial, for every part of philosophy raises metaphysical questions and therefore cannot be regarded as absolutely distinct from metaphysics. Let us look at an illustration. The branch of philosophy called ethics, or moral philosophy, is an inquiry into the nature of good and bad and right and wrong. Anyone who thinks about these topics will soon find that they raise metaphysical questions. Consider, for example, the statement that Hitler was an evil man. (Statements like this one are certainly a part of the subject-matter of ethics.) Many would consider this statement to be, in a quite straightforward sense, true. If it is true, then the person who makes this statement would seem to be correctly ascribing to Hitler a certain feature or property called *being evil*. But what sort of thing is this property? It is obviously not a physical property of Hitler like his height or his weight. And if it is not a physical property, and if it really does exist, then it would seem to follow that the World in some sense contains non-physical things—for if Hitler is evil, and if evil is something non-physical, then how can the World consist entirely of matter in motion?

For the sake of convenience of reference, I list here the most important branches of philosophy other than metaphysics and ethics. *Epistemology*, or *the theory of knowledge*, investigates the nature, scope, and conditions of human knowledge. *Logic* investigates the nature of valid reasoning and attempts to lay down rules that guarantee validity of reasoning. *Aesthetics* investigates the nature of works of art, the nature of their creation by the artist, and the nature of the act of viewing, listening to, or reading them. In addition to these branches of philosophy that have traditional one-word names, there is a long list of "philosophies of"—branches of philosophy that deal with very general and very puzzling questions (that is, philosophical questions) about important branches of human knowledge and important human characteristics and activities. Their names more or less explain themselves: the philosophy of mind, the philosophy of politics, the philosophy of science, the philosophy of mathematics, the philosophy of language, the philosophy of religion, the philosophy of history, the philosophy of law. No final list of "philosophies of" is possible, owing to the fact that no final list of important topics that can pose very general and very puzzling questions is possible. What the beginner in metaphysics should keep in mind is that while metaphysics is to be distinguished from all of these branches of philosophy, each of them, like ethics, poses important metaphysical questions and therefore cannot be regarded as entirely distinct from metaphysics.

Perhaps we have done all that can be done by way of giving a preliminary account of what is meant by 'metaphysics'. A deeper understanding of the concept of metaphysics can be achieved only by actually "doing" some metaphysics, and that is the task to which the remaining chapters of this book are devoted. Before we begin to do some metaphysics, however, we should be aware of a second way in which a textbook of metaphysics differs from a textbook of geology or tax law or music theory.

Textbooks in these three subjects—and in hundreds of other subjects—contain information. There are things you can learn from them: that the continents are in motion, or that corporations can be taxed, or that a diminished-seventh chord is put together in such-and-such a way. You can be required to take examinations on the content of these textbooks, and it is, unfortunately, quite possible that your answers will be wrong. If you write on your tax law examination that only individuals can be taxed, no one is going to praise your originality or independence of mind. You will just be marked wrong. Metaphysics is not like that. In metaphysics there is no information and there are no established facts to be learned.[4] More exactly, there is no information and there are no facts to be learned besides information and facts about what certain people think, or once thought, concerning various metaphysical questions. A history of metaphysics will contain much information about what Plato and Descartes and the other great metaphysicians of the past believed. The present book contains no information, other than a little incidental information about what famous and respected people—famous among philosophers and respected by the author of this book, at any rate—have said about certain topics in metaphysics.

One might well wonder why metaphysics is so different from geology and tax law and music theory. Why is there no such thing as metaphysical information? Why has the study of metaphysics yielded no established facts? (It has had about twenty-five hundred years to come up with some.) This question is really a special case of a more general question: Why is there no such thing as philosophical information? The situation that confronts the student of metaphysics is not any different from the situation that confronts the student of any part of philosophy. If we consider ethics, for example, we discover that there is no list of established facts that the student of ethics can be expected to learn (nor are there any accepted methods or theories that the specialist in ethics can apply to search out and test answers to unresolved ethical questions). And the same situation prevails in epistemology and the philosophy of mathematics and the philosophy of law and all other parts of philosophy.[5] Indeed, most people who have thought about the matter would take this to be one of the defining characteristics of philosophy. If some branch of philosophy were suddenly to undergo a revolutionary transformation and began, as a consequence, to yield real information, it would cease to be regarded as a branch of philosophy and would come to be regarded as one of the sciences.[6] It is, in fact, a very plausible thesis that this is just how "the sciences" began. At one time what we now call natural science was not clearly distinguished from what we now call philosophy—it was then called natural philosophy. (As late as the early nineteenth century, people occasionally used the word 'philosophical' to mean what 'scientific' now means,[7] and physics is still officially called 'natural philosophy' in the Scottish universities.) When the sciences, as we now call them, began to yield real information, they began to be perceived as something different from metaphysics and epistemology and ethics, and the word 'science', which comes from the Latin word for 'knowledge', was reserved for them. (The word already existed, but before that time a "science" was what we should call a "discipline" today.)

Well, *why* is there no philosophical information? Why is there no agreed-upon body of philosophical fact? Why is there no such thing as a philosophical discovery? Why are there not even philosophical theories that, although it is admitted that they are unsatisfactory in various respects, are at least universally agreed to be the best theories treating their particular subject-matter that we have at present?

It would not be the whole truth to say that it is true by definition that there is no body of philosophical fact because it is a defining characteristic of philosophy that it has no information to offer. A few onetime branches of philosophy (natural science and logic and psychology, say) may have, at a certain point in history, begun to be sources of information and thus, for that reason, have ceased to be called 'philosophy', but metaphysics and ethics and most other branches of philosophy have not been able to make the transition that natural science and logic and psychology have made. Why not?

This is an extremely interesting question to which I do not pretend to know the answer. A moment's thought will show that the question could have no uncontroversial answer, for the question is itself a philosophical question. It is a question that belongs to the philosophy of philosophy (for philosophy itself is one of the many human activities whose features raise very general and puzzling questions; the present question is one of them) or to *metaphilosophy*, as the philosophy of philosophy is sometimes called.

Philosophers have not been blind to the fact that philosophy has not been able to produce any uncontroversial results. Naturally enough, philosophers have not been inclined to blame themselves for this state of affairs. And it is hard to see how they could be to blame. It can't be that there is no body of established philosophical fact simply because philosophers are stupid. Despite hints occasionally dropped by a few scientists that this is the case, it would seem to be statistically unlikely that any given field of study should attract only stupid people. Besides, there have been philosophers who have demonstrated by their accomplishments outside philosophy that they were not only highly intelligent but were great geniuses. This was particularly true in the seventeenth century, when the philosopher Descartes invented analytical geometry and the philosopher Leibniz invented the infinitesimal calculus.[8] Despite these accomplishments, however, when Descartes and Leibniz turned their attention to philosophy, they produced work that was as controversial as any other philosophical work. Each of these men thought he had established certain philosophical facts. Each of them thought that he had made philosophical discoveries, discoveries that were discoveries in the same sense as, say, Harvey's discovery of the circulation of blood. But this has not been the judgment of history. In the end, their philosophical work convinced no one. Analytical geometry and the calculus are indispensable tools of scientific thought to this day, but the philosophical work of Descartes and Leibniz is simply a part of the history of philosophy.

If the lack of established results in philosophy is not the fault of the philosophers themselves, then what is its explanation? Philosophers who have thought about this question have given two sorts of answers. According to one point of view, it is a consequence of the nature of philosophy: philosophical questions are defective questions, in that they have no answers. According to the other point of view, it is a consequence of the nature of the human mind: there is something about the human mind that unfits it for investigating philosophical questions.

As an example of the first point of view, we may consider a school of philosophy called *logical positivism* that flourished between the two world wars.[9] According to the logical positivists, all metaphysical statements and questions are meaningless. And since almost all traditional philosophical statements and questions have (as we noted above) an important and essential metaphysical component, almost all traditional philosophical questions and statements are meaningless.

In saying that metaphysical questions and statements were meaningless, the logical positivists were not saying that these questions and statements were pointless or that they were divorced from the real concerns of human life. They were advancing a much more radical thesis. They were saying that these "statements" and "questions" were not really statements and questions at all, but merely sequences of words that had the superficial appearance of statements and questions. Thus, for a logical positivist, a metaphysical question like 'Why is there a World?' is a mere piece of articulate noise that, because it has the grammatical form of a question, has been mistaken for a question. It can be compared with such "questions" as 'How high is up?' and 'Where does your lap go when you stand up?' If metaphysical—and, more generally, philosophical—questions are in this sense meaningless, it is not surprising that philosophers have not been able to agree about how to "answer" them. If one stares into the fire long enough, one will see pictures there, and, since pictures seen in the fire are merely reflections of the psychology of the viewer, it is to be expected that different people will see different pictures.

Like the metaphysical systems of Descartes and Leibniz, logical positivism now belongs entirely to the history of philosophy. Like those systems it was unable to provide the basis for any kind of philosophical consensus. If, as the logical positivists maintained, the metaphysical systems of the past were so many pictures seen in the fire, logical positivism itself would appear to have been just one more picture: some philosophers saw things that way and some did not and those who saw things that way were unable to get the philosophical community as a whole to see things their way. (We could contrast this case with the case of a young employee of the Swiss patent office named Albert Einstein. In a series of papers published between 1905 and 1915, this hitherto unknown young man proposed a way of looking at the relations among motion, mass, energy, space, time, and gravity that was radically different from the received view of these relations. Within a few years, the community of physicists saw things his way.) The fate of logical positivism is the fate of all attempts to diagnose the failure of philosophy to produce a body of established fact or even a body of provisionally accepted theories. Such diagnoses are invariably "just more philosophy" and exhibit the very symptoms that they are supposed to explain: they are proposed, people argue about them, a few converts are made but only a few, and, in the end, they retire to occupy a place in the history of philosophy.

What of the other view that was mentioned above, the view that explains the failure of philosophy to produce a body of information as being due to the intrinsic incapacity of the human mind to find the answers to philosophical questions? The most famous example of a view of this sort was held by the eighteenth-century German philosopher Immanuel Kant. Kant held that metaphysical questions—such as 'Did the world have a beginning in time, or has it always existed?'—are meaningful but that human beings are not constructed the right way to be able to find out the answers to them; if they insist on trying to do so, they will lose themselves in contradictions. Kant did not base his position on some special feature of human beings, some feature that might be absent from Martians or intelligent dolphins. He held that his diagnosis of the human failure to achieve established metaphysical results applied to any possible beings that represent external reality to themselves by means of their internal states. (For example, if I know that there is a tree—an external thing, a thing that is not a part of myself—before me, this can only be because I have an internal, or mental, representation of a tree that is before me. If my mind were a blank, if there were no configuration within my mind whose meaning for me was "Here's a tree," I could not know that there was a tree before me.) This description is so abstract and general that it is hard to see what kind of being could fail to satisfy it. Perhaps only God could fail to satisfy it. If so, then, if Kant is right, only God could know the answer to any metaphysical question.

There could be more modest versions of the second view than Kant's. One might hold that the human failure to achieve established metaphysical results is due to some special quirk of the human mind, a quirk that could be absent from the minds of Martians or intelligent dolphins. Evolutionary biology suggests that human beings possess a very specific set of mental talents and that other intelligent or rational species might possess a different but equally specific set of talents. We, as a species, are very good at physics, and—all the evidence suggests this—very bad at metaphysics. Perhaps we shall one day discover among the stars a species that is very good at metaphysics and very bad at physics.[10] It may be that the best human metaphysicians are like acrobats. Acrobats are people who, in virtue of long training and arduous discipline, can do what arboreal apes do much better without any training at all. Acrobats achieve what they do achieve by taking capacities of hand, mind, and eye that were "designed" for purposes quite unrelated to swinging through the air and pushing these capacities to their limits. Perhaps human metaphysicians are like that: they work by taking human intellectual capacities that were designed for purposes quite unrelated to questions about ultimate reality and pushing these capacities to their limits. It may be that a comparison that Samuel Johnson used for a rather different purpose applies to the human metaphysician: such a person is like a dog walking on its hind legs. "It is not done well," said Dr. Johnson, "but you are surprised to find it done at all."

This latter, more modest, version of the second view is the one that I favor. I recognize, however, that this proposed explanation is, like the proposal of the logical positivists, "just more philosophy." In the end we must confess that we have no idea why there is no established body of metaphysical results. It cannot be denied that this is a fact, however, and the beginning student of metaphysics should keep this fact and its implications in mind. One of its implications is that neither the author of this book nor your instructor (if you are reading this book because it is an assigned text) is in a position in relation to you that is like the position of the author of your text (or your instructor) in geology or tax law or music theory. All of these people will be the masters of a certain body of knowledge, and, on many matters, if you disagree with them you will simply be wrong. In metaphysics, however, you are perfectly free to

disagree with anything the acknowledged experts say—other than their assertions about what philosophers have said in the past or are saying at present.[11]

Let us consider a concrete case. Alice has always believed that she has an
immortal soul. She enrolls in a course in metaphysics. Alfred, her instructor,
believes—as I do—that people do not have immortal souls. Several scenarios
are possible.

It is possible that Alfred will treat his position as instructor in the course as
a platform from which to make fun of the idea that there are immortal souls.
When it comes to affecting students' opinions, this is a remarkably effective
procedure. But Alice should not be impressed: that someone finds an idea ri-
diculous is not a reason to reject it.

It is possible that Alfred will treat the thesis that there are no immortal souls
as an established fact, as something that all educated people believe. This, too,
is a very effective procedure for affecting students' opinions. Again, however,
Alice should not be impressed. She should ask herself whether it is really true
that all educated people believe that there are no immortal souls. (Admittedly,
it may be difficult for her consciously to formulate this question, since Alfred
will probably not have said in so many words that educated people do not believe in immortal souls. He will simply have talked as if this were something
that everyone knew.) And she should ask herself whether, if it is true, all these
educated people have some good reason for their beliefs—after all, educated
people have believed in all sorts of things: the beneficence of colonial rule,
Freudian psychology, and Marxism, for example.[12]

It is possible that Alfred will give reasons for believing that there are no immortal souls. He will define his terms, make relevant distinctions, cite various
scientific facts, and, finally, use these terms, distinctions, and facts as the basis
for one or more *arguments* for the conclusion that there are no immortal souls.
Here, at last, is something that Alice's intellect can go to work on. She can examine the definitions and the distinctions and try to decide whether the arguments really do prove their point. (Perhaps she will also want to check out the
supposed scientific facts to see whether Alfred has indeed got them right.) If
there seems to her to be something wrong or dubious about the argument, she
can, and should, raise her hand.

But suppose that she can't find anything in the argument that seems to her
to be wrong. What shall she do then? Shall she abandon her belief that she has
an immortal soul? Well, she might. That's really up to her. In the end, it is Alice
who is responsible for what Alice believes. But she needn't abandon her beliefs. She may well reason as follows. "Look, if there were really an unanswerable argument for the conclusion that there was no immortal soul, everyone
would know about it, or at least all the experts would. If there were such an argument, then every philosopher would believe that there were no immortal
souls. Or at least practically every philosopher. But philosophers don't agree
about *anything*, so that can't be right. I'll bet there are lots of philosophers who
know all about these arguments and still believe in immortal souls. So there
must be lots of philosophers who think that there's something wrong with
these arguments. Chances are, some of them save *said* what they think is

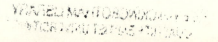

wrong with them. I think I'll ask the instructor how those philosophers who disagree with him would reply to his arguments." If Alice does take this course, she should realize that it is possible that Alfred may not know of the best arguments against his position. People are inclined to suppose that an expert in a certain field of study must be omniscient in that field, but this is wrong. Experts can be quite ignorant of things they really ought to know. She should also realize that Alfred may not represent the arguments that run counter to his position in their strongest or most convincing form. (It really is very hard to act the part of a convincing advocate for a position that one is unsympathetic with.) She should also remember that Alfred is much more experienced than she is in the art of metaphysical disputation, and the fact that he is able to "outmaneuver" her in debate is to be expected on that ground alone; it needn't mean that her position is indefensible.

All this is by way of practical advice to the beginning student of metaphysics. To sum up this advice, take anything said in this book (or in any other book about metaphysics) or by your instructor with a grain of salt. What you can hope to learn from an introductory textbook on metaphysics, or an introductory course in metaphysics, is what it is like to work out and defend a metaphysical position. And this is something that you should do for yourself.

In the following chapters, I am going to work out and defend metaphysical positions on a number of issues. That is, I am going to say what I think is true, and I am going to explain why I think that *these* things, and not various other things, are what is true. I am going to do this because that is the only way of writing a book that I am capable of. Because I have chosen to write the book this way, it may bear a certain superficial similarity to a text in geology or tax law or music theory. Remember, however, that there is nothing that will be said in this book that you are required to believe and that everything that will be said in this book would be disputed by many people whose qualifications to expound on metaphysics are at least as impressive as mine.

The reader of a textbook has the right to know its author's biases. This is particularly true of a subject like metaphysics, in which there is no body of established fact, for a textbook in such a subject must inevitably be very deeply influenced both as to form and to content by the opinions of the author. The nineteenth-century English metaphysician F. H. Bradley once said that metaphysics was an attempt to find bad reasons for what one was going to believe anyway. This is perhaps an unduly pessimistic statement. There have been cases of metaphysicians who have changed their minds, and perhaps some of the reasons that have been advanced by metaphysicians in support of various theses have been good reasons. Nevertheless, I have to admit that there is probably some truth in the charge that there are certain theses that I "was going to believe anyway"—theses that I would believe no matter what philosophical arguments I was presented with.

The reader will remember that earlier in the chapter I listed three questions and suggested that to know the answers to these three questions would be to know the ultimate truth about everything. And I put forward two possible sets of answers to these questions, in order to show what answers to them would look like. The first set of answers more or less expresses my beliefs concerning the ultimate truth about everything. These beliefs, moreover, are not ones that I hold in a tentative or halfhearted way. They are firm convictions about matters that I hold to be of the utmost importance, and it is almost certainly true that I should hold them no matter what metaphysical arguments I was presented with. While I have, of course, *tried* to be fair and objective in discussing points of view opposed to my own, it is unlikely that I have succeeded. Another firm conviction of mine is that the reader is unlikely to find a book about metaphysics whose author does not hold some view or other in just the firm and "non-negotiable" way in which the author of the present book holds the view represented by the first set of answers to our three metaphysical questions. I have seen books about metaphysics (and about other parts of philosophy) that give the impression that their authors reached the positions that they defend in those books solely on the basis of logical argument and the objective evaluation of carefully gathered data. The authors of these books write in such a way as to suggest that either they had no biases when they began to try to formulate their metaphysical opinions or else that they sternly set their biases aside and allowed themselves to be influenced only by evidence and argument. While I do not claim to be able to read minds, I doubt whether any metaphysician has actually proceeded this way.

What is much more likely to be true is this. There are many factors that are effective in forming people's opinions besides evidence and argument. Among these we may cite religion (and anti-religion), politics, loyalties to certain social groups, antipathy to other social groups, the desire for emotional comfort, the desire to be respected by one's peers, the desire to be thought original, the desire to shock, the desire to be in a position to force one's opinions upon others, the desire to belong to a like-minded group of people who flatter one another by making fun of people whose opinions differ from those of the group, and the desire to be one of a small group of enlightened ones who bravely struggle against the superstitions of the masses.

There are two senses in which one may be said to care about the answer to a question. First, one may want very much to know what the right answer to that question is. Secondly, one may desire very strongly that a certain answer to that question be the right one. Those who care deeply in the first sense about the answers to metaphysical questions (or any questions) will be moved by evidence and argument. Those who care deeply in the second sense about the answers to metaphysical questions (or any questions) will be moved by factors like those listed above. It is unlikely that anyone who has actually taken the trouble to write a book about metaphysics will be completely free of any desire that certain answers to metaphysical questions be the right ones. It is therefore likely that the author of a book about metaphysics will be subject to biases arising from factors like those listed in the preceding paragraph. Sociological investigations of scientific research strongly suggest that this is the case in the sciences, and it is unlikely that metaphysicians are any freer from bias than scientists.

In the sciences (and particularly in the "hard" sciences like physics and chemistry), the biases of investigators are to a large degree corrected—in the long run—by the responsibility of these sciences to the data of observation. A scientific theory is expected to make predictions about how experiments will go and what observations will reveal, and—again, in the long run—if a theory does not make the right predictions, it will be abandoned even if all sorts of factors like those listed above make it psychologically attractive to the members of the scientific community. But no such corrective exists in metaphysics. If two metaphysical theories are in competition, no experiment will decide between them. They will not differ about how the World will look to an observer, no matter how sophisticated the observer's instruments may be.[13] It is likely, therefore, that a metaphysician's position is going to be, to a significant degree, a reflection of certain biases, however much it may also owe to evidence and argument. It is likely that there will be certain theses that the metaphysician would have accepted no matter what evidence or what arguments had come to his or her attention. I have tried to forewarn the reader about what theses I bear this sort of allegiance to.

Suggestions for Further Reading

Very useful articles on almost every philosophical topic imaginable can be found in the monumental *Encyclopedia of Philosophy,* edited by Paul Edwards. The Encyclopedia was published in 1967, and thus no longer represents the "state of the art." Nevertheless, it remains an indispensable resource for the student of philosophy.

Kant's diagnosis of the failure of metaphysics to become a science in the sense in which mathematics and physics are sciences received its most complete and systematic expression in his *Critique of Pure Reason* (1781; second and considerably revised, edition, 1787). Unfortunately this book is impenetrable to the uninitiated. There are two "little" books on Kant's philosophy that generations of beginning students have found to be very helpful, despite the fact that some specialists in Kant's philosophy have reservations about them: Ewing's *A Short Commentary on Kant's Critique of Pure Reason* and Körner's *Kant.*

A. J. Ayer's *Language, Truth and Logic* (1936) is a classic popular exposition of logical positivism, written with the enthusiasm of a recent convert.

PART ONE

The Way the World Is

IN CHAPTERS 2 THROUGH 4, our topic will be the World. Or, rather, our topic will be most of the World, for human beings—who, like all other things, are parts of the World—will be the special topic of Part Three.

Ordinary people, the people you pass on the street every day, have widely differing conceptions of the World. A Roman Catholic or an Orthodox Jew will have one sort of conception of the World, an atheist a very different conception, and a Hindu yet a third conception, one that differs greatly from the conceptions of the Catholic and the Jew and from the conception of the atheist. Are these examples intended to imply that when we are talking about conceptions of the World we are talking about religion? Well, only accidentally. For one thing, the atheist will no doubt stoutly insist that atheism is not a religion. (Let us take the person we are calling "the atheist" to be a typical Western atheist—the sort of atheist you would be likely to encounter in Europe or one of the English-speaking countries—and not a Japanese Zen Buddhist or any such exotic atheist as that.) For another, most of the five billion or so people in the world practice some religion, and every religion involves some sort of conception of the World. As a consequence, most people get their conceptions of the World wholly or partly from their religions. But not everyone does, and views of the World can be discussed without any need to talk about many of the things that are typically involved in a religion—things such as ritual, the veneration of sacred objects or persons or places, and characteristically religious emotions.

The differences between the Catholic and the Jew, on the one hand, and the atheist, on the other, are obvious. The Catholic and the Jew both think that the basis of the World is personal: each believes that there is a Person—a conscious Being who acts for reasons and carries out plans—who caused everything besides Himself to exist. And the atheist does not. The atheist thinks that the World existed before there had ever been any persons, and that the first persons there ever were came to be as a by-product of various purposeless processes going on here and there in the World. One might suppose that there

19

could be no more profound disagreement about the nature of the World than this. And yet the atheist shares with the Catholic and the Jew many important metaphysical beliefs that would be rejected by the Hindu. All three of the "Westerners" believe that the things they see around them are real, and that these things have the features, or many of the features, that they seem to have. All three of them would probably give their assent to the following statement.

> Buildings and trees and grass and the sun and the stars are all real. Each building, each tree, each blade of grass, each star, is an object distinct from the others, and each has a certain set of properties. That building is one thing and that tree is another. The tree weighs a certain number of kilograms, even if no human being knows just how many kilograms that is. Each of them is at a certain *distance* from me. Either the three is forty meters away from me or it is some other perfectly definite distance away. And if it is forty meters away, then anyone who thinks it's thirty meters away from me is just wrong. If Jane insists that the tree is thirty meters away from me when it is really forty meters away, she is wrong because her beliefs do not match the way things are. The tree and its properties exist independently of Jane's beliefs and of anything else that belongs to her mind, and it is up to the contents of her mind to correspond to external reality, just as it is up to a map to correspond to the territory. If the contents of her mind do not match external reality, if they do not correspond with the independently existing facts, then she has a picture of the world that is at least partly false.
>
> The properties of the tree, moreover, are not exhausted by the properties it has at the present moment. The tree has a certain *age*. There is a certain time in the past at which it began to exist. Before that, for ages and ages, things came to be and flourished and passed away, and the tree did not yet exist. Although there was an all but unimaginably long (perhaps even an infinite) period during which the tree did not yet exist, it is nevertheless *now* true that the tree has existed for quite a long time: it was here yesterday, and it was here the day before, and the day before that and so on through a series of many thousands of days. And this is no mere manner of speaking. This use of the pronoun 'it' should be taken literally. The tree (this very tree) was here last year, even though it then had a slightly different set of properties from those it has now. (For example, it probably had a different number of leaves then.) But it was the *same* tree. And the tree can change its position as well as its properties. Not only is the tree being carried around the sun by the earth, but one could uproot the tree and carry it to the opposite side of the earth and re-plant it there, and it would be the same tree at every moment during this sequence of events.
>
> Furthermore, the tree and all of the other things we have mentioned exert influences on one another. The light of the sun falls on the grass and the tree and the building and me and warms us: it is no accident that an object gets warmer when it moves from shadow to sunlight; the warming happens because the sunlight has an *effect* on the object. And it is only

because these things have effects on me that I am able to perceive them. The perceptions I have of the tree or the building are due to influences that cross the space that separates me from those objects and cause changes in my sense-organs and my brain.

The Hindu—at least the well-educated Hindu who understands the full implications of Hinduism—will agree with none of this. The Hindu will insist that to say that this statement describes how things really are is to mistake appearance for reality. And it is not only a Hindu who would say this. This point of view is confined neither to religion nor to the Far East. Many Western philosophers, particularly in the nineteenth century, would have agreed with our Hindu and would have given philosophical arguments to back up their assertions. Many more Western philosophers would not go so far as to reject the entirety of this statement but would reject certain parts of it, particularly those having to do with space and time, the cause-and-effect relation, and perception.

Let us say that the above passage—the passage I said the Roman Catholic and the Orthodox Jew and the atheist would all give their assent to and the Hindu would not—represents the Common Western Metaphysic,[1] that is, the core of metaphysical belief that is common to most of the views of the World that are held by ordinary, unreflective people in Europe and the English-speaking countries.[2] Since most of the readers of this book will no doubt be Westerners, let us take the Common Western Metaphysic as a starting point for our discussion of the way the World is. Since most of us are Westerners, it is not surprising that most of us will find this metaphysic to be obviously right. But is it *really* right? Does the Common Western Metaphysic describe things as they really are or only as they apparently are?

We shall use this question to organize our discussion of the way the World is. It would require a work of many volumes even to touch briefly on all of the important metaphysical issues raised by the question whether a statement of the Common Western Metaphysic is a description of appearance or reality. We shall be able to discuss only three of these issues in detail. We shall discuss them under the three headings *Individuality, Externality,* and *Objectivity.*

2

Individuality

ACCORDING TO THE Common Western Metaphysic, the world contains many individual things. Each human being, each living thing, each star, each atom, each building, is an individual thing. Even God, if there is a God, is an individual thing. But what do we mean by calling all of these very different things "individual" things? As far as dictionary meaning goes, we may say that an individual thing is a *separate* thing, a thing that is distinct from the rest of the World, but this statement does not really tell us very much, and its use of the word 'separate' has at least one misleading implication.

Let us first deal with the misleading implication. We would not ordinarily say that an object and one of its parts—a tree and one of its leaves, say—were "separate" things. But a part of an individual thing may very well be itself an individual thing: a tree and one of its leaves, for example, are both individual things. The sense of 'separate' in which an individual thing must be a "separate" thing, therefore, is not the same as the sense of 'separate' in which a leaf is not "separate" from the tree it is a part of. A leaf that is still growing on a branch, a rabbit's foot (undetached), and the roof of a house are separate things in the required sense of 'separate'. But that sense is rather unclear. This unclarity is the reason why the dictionary sense of 'individual' is not very helpful in explaining the metaphysical concept of an individual thing. Perhaps the best way to say what is meant by 'individual thing' is to supplement our list of examples of individual things by giving some examples of things that are *not* individual things.

First, a thing is not an individual thing if it is a mere modification of something else. For example, a wrinkle in a carpet is not an individual thing because it is a mere modification of the carpet. This use of the word 'modification' is a metaphysician's term. It may be explained as follows. One way to "modify" (or change) something is to add to its parts, as when we modify a house by adding a room. But we may modify a thing without adding to its parts: I can modify my hand by making a fist, modify a piece of string by tying a knot in it—or modify a carpet by wrinkling it. If something comes into existence as the direct and inevitable result of modifying a thing x in the second way—without causing x to gain any new parts—then we call the thing that is thereby brought into existence a mere modification of x. Thus, a fist is a mere modification of a hand, a knot in a piece of string is a mere modification of the string, and a wrinkle in a carpet is a mere modification of the carpet.

Let us think about the wrinkle, this mere modification of the carpet, which we have said is not an individual thing like the carpet itself. It certainly seems in many ways to be like the things we *are* willing to call individual things. It has a certain location in space, it came into existence at a certain time, and it can influence other things—you could trip over it, and break your nose, which is a pretty robust case of influence. Is it different from the carpet in any important way?

Note that if the carpet is not in its accustomed place, it makes sense to ask what happened to it, since a carpet can move in relation to other things or be destroyed. If the wrinkle is not in its accustomed place, can we ask what happened to it? Can a wrinkle move in relation to other things? Well, a wrinkle in a carpet can move if the whole carpet moves, of course. But a carpet can move without the necessity of anything else's moving—other than the carpet's own parts and the things that have to get out of the carpet's path to make way for it. Can the wrinkle move like that? Anyone who has tried to "get a wrinkle out of a carpet," as the idiom has it, will perhaps be inclined to say that the answer is Yes. But is the wrinkle that seems in some sense to move across the carpet the *same* wrinkle throughout the whole frustrating procedure? If it is, then that one wrinkle has to be made of different carpet threads at different times as it moves, while the carpet can move without any necessity of changing its parts. It would seem that the question 'Does the wrinkle really move?' should either be answered No or else the question should be regarded as a pointless conundrum like 'Where does your lap go when you stand up?' The answer to the question 'Does the carpet really move?' however, is a very straightforward Yes—at least according to the Common Western Metaphysic.

The case is similar with the question whether the wrinkle can be destroyed. If a wrinkled carpet is straightened, the wrinkle in the carpet no longer exists, but it would be a joke to say that the wrinkle or anything else had been *destroyed* in this episode.

These differences between the wrinkle and the carpet suggest that (according to the Common Western Metaphysic) the carpet is a thing that exists "in its own right," whereas the wrinkle is only a sort of temporary complication in the shape of the carpet; it does not exist in its own right, but, as we might say, in the carpet's right. If this is true, then we must distinguish between the wrinkle and the particular part of the carpet that has been thrust up to form the wrinkle. The latter is what you trip over when you "trip over the wrinkle," and it *is* an individual thing, a thing that exists in its own right. There is a perfectly good answer to the question whether it is destroyed when the carpet is straightened: No; it is still right there. If you wanted to, you could bend over the now-flat carpet and cut it out of the carpet with a carpet knife, and you could then move it about in space in the same way you could have moved the whole carpet about.

Other examples of things that are not individual things because they exist only as modifications of other things are: the Cheshire Cat's grin (as opposed to the Cheshire Cat's lips and teeth), the point of a knife (as opposed to the first millimeter of the knife), and a hole in a piece of cheese (as opposed to the cheese that "lines" the hole).

Secondly, a thing is not an individual thing if it is a mere collection of things. If we say that the army is much larger than it was in 1935, and if we assume that any army is (in some sense) composed entirely of soldiers, then the thing—if indeed there is such a thing—of which we are saying that "it" is larger than "it" used to be, is not an individual thing but a mere collection of things. It is very hard to give any precise sense to the idea of a *mere* collection of things. After all, a cat is an individual thing, and yet in a way a cat is a collection of cells or of atoms. The intuitive reason for saying that the army is a *mere* collection of soldiers is that the army of 1935 and the army of today are supposed to be the same army (the U.S. Army or the British Army, or whatever), and yet not a single soldier is common to both. This suggests that there is really no individual thing "there" besides all the soldiers and that, therefore, the army is "nothing more than" the soldiers to such a striking degree that it seems appropriate to call it not only a collection but a *mere* collection. This consideration seems to have a certain amount of force, and yet it is hard to say why it does, since there are few if any atoms common to the cat of today and the cat of five years ago, despite the fact that—according to the Common Western Metaphysic—these are one and the same individual thing.

We could, of course, define a mere collection as a collection that is not an individual thing, but that would not help us to understand the notion of an individual thing. Perhaps the best we can do is to say that insofar as we understand the notion of a mere collection, no mere collection is an individual thing—or that, if we are inclined to think of a thing as a mere collection, then we should be disinclined to call it an individual thing.

Thirdly, a thing is not an individual thing if it is a stuff, like water or flesh or steel or hydrogen. The Walrus's famous list of topics for after-dinner conversation—shoes and ships and sealing wax and cabbages and kings—contains four kinds of individual things and one stuff. The Walrus says that his list comprises "many things," but a stuff like sealing wax is not a thing in the same sense as that in which shoes and cabbages are things. When we say that water is a chemical compound of hydrogen and oxygen or when we say that sealing wax is used for sealing envelopes, we are in a sense describing things called 'water' and 'sealing wax'. But these "things" are not individual things, and, more generally, stuffs are not individual things.[1]

Fourthly, a thing is not an individual thing if it is a "universal," a universal being a thing that can have "instances." For example, the novel *War and Peace* is not an individual thing, although my *copy* of *War and Peace* and your *copy* of *War and Peace* are both individual things. Each of these two copies of the novel is, in the language of metaphysics, an "instance" of the novel, which is a universal. Other examples of universals are numbers and properties and relations. The number four has as instances any things that are four in number: the points of the compass, the Gospels, or the Stuart kings of England. A property, such as wisdom, aridity, or the color white, has as instances those things that possess it: each of the three wise men is an instance of wisdom; Arizona and New Mexico are both instances of aridity; the Taj Mahal and the Washington Monument are both instances of the color white. Instances of a relation like 'to the north of' are things standing in that relation: Montreal and New York stand in the relation 'to the north of', as do Edinburgh and London. The problem of the nature of universals is an important problem in the history of metaphysics, but it is not a problem addressed in this book.

Finally, an individual thing is not an event or process, like the death of Caesar or the Second World War or the industrialization of Japan. Events and processes *start* and *end* and *happen* (or *take place* or *occur*), while individual things *come into existence* and *go out of existence* and *endure* (or *last* or *get older*).

Perhaps we now have some notion of what is meant by an individual thing. According to the Common Western Metaphysic, the World consists of individual things. (Does that mean that the World is itself an individual thing? Not necessarily. Many metaphysicians who have held that the World consists of individual things have also held that the World is a mere collection of individual things. The question whether the World is an individual thing will become important in Chapter 6.) Moreover, the Common Western Metaphysic holds that there are *many* individual things. As we have seen, there are metaphysicians who deny this. But what do people who deny this believe instead? What are the alternatives to believing in many individual things? The following three alternatives are exclusive and exhaustive (that is, they are inconsistent with each other and they cover all the remaining possible cases):

- There are no individual things (Nihilism).
- There is one individual thing (Monism).
- There is more than one individual thing, but there are not many.

The third alternative has no name because it has not had any adherents. Metaphysicians who reject the thesis that there are many individual things are either Nihilists or Monists. (The word 'dualism' is the name of several metaphysical positions involving the number two, but it has never been used for the position that there are two and only two *individual* things. "Dualists" believe that there are two *kinds* of things—mental things and physical things are the usual ones—or that the World embodies two fundamental and opposed *principles*, such as Order and Disorder or Good and Evil.) This is in a way surprising, because metaphysicians are as fond of the numbers two and three as they are of the numbers zero and one. We have seen, for example, that metaphysicians are perfectly willing to say that there are two kinds of things. Whatever the explanation may be, it appears that the unanimous opinion of the metaphysicians is that once real diversity among individual things has been admitted to exist, the question how many of them there are is not a philosophical question. Let us not struggle against this remarkable consensus (any consensus among metaphysicians is remarkable). Let us rather turn to and examine Nihilism and Monism.

The word 'nihilism' comes from a Latin word that means 'nothing'.[2] Does this imply that the Nihilist believes that nothing exists? Not necessarily, for there are other things than individual things. It is, for example, consistent with Nihilism to say that there are universals, such as numbers or properties. But it does not seem very plausible to say that there are no things but universals. If there are only universals, what is "this" that we see all around us? If there were no things but universals, then we—leaving aside the question what "we" should be if there were no things but universals—should see nothing at all. Can Nihilists believe in anything besides universals?

What about mere modifications and mere collections? Could those things exist in the absence of individual things? Could it be that A is a mere modification of B, and B a mere modification of C, and C a mere modification of D, and so on forever? Or could it be that A is a mere modification of B, and B a mere modification of C, and C a mere modification of A—or, more briefly, that A and B are mere modifications of each other? I can only record my conviction that, while it may well be that there are "second-order" mere modifications (mere modifications of mere modifications) or even third- or higher-order mere modifications, any chain of mere modifications must terminate in something that is not a mere modification of anything but exists in its own right. It seems reasonable to adopt the convention that any member of a chain of mere modifications, however long, that terminates in an individual thing is itself a mere modification of that individual thing. Thus, if a crimp in a wrinkle in a carpet is a mere modification of the wrinkle, and the wrinkle is a mere modification of the carpet, then the crimp is a mere modification not only of the wrinkle but of the carpet as well. The principle that any chain of mere modifications must terminate in an individual thing may then be put this way: anything that is a mere modification of something is a mere modification of an individual thing.

The case for there being nothing but mere collections seems even more implausible. Could there be a collection each of whose members was a collection and which, moreover, was such that each of the members of its members was a collection, and so on forever? Or could A be a collection whose members were B and C, B a collection whose members were A and C, and C a collection whose members were A and B? The answer to both of these questions is plainly No. While there may well be second- and higher-order collections (perhaps the phrase 'the armies of South America' designates a collection of collections), there must be things that are not collections if there are to be collections at all. Otherwise the collections "couldn't get started," so to speak.

What about events? It would seem that there cannot be an event unless there is something that is not an event. An event is a change in something or a change in the relations that hold among two or more things. If there were no things "there" to undergo change, there could be no events. It may be that events themselves can change (a war that had been confined to Europe might spread to the Far East, and that sounds like a change in an event), but it is very hard to see how there could be events "in the first place" if there were no things of other kinds that were capable of change.

This is not to say that Nihilists cannot believe in mere modifications or mere collections or events. But Nihilists who do believe in those things must also believe in things that are neither universals nor modifications nor collections nor events. What sort of thing might there be for them to believe in that fills this bill? We have seen only one sort of thing that is neither an individual thing nor a universal nor a mere modification nor a mere collection nor an event: stuffs. A Nihilist who believed in stuffs would believe that there was stone but nothing made of stone, butter but nothing made of butter, steel but nothing made of steel, and so on. Such a Nihilist would believe in stone but not in stones, butter but not in pats of butter, and in steel but not in battleships. Such a Nihilist would believe that various stuffs are spread out in space, just as any adherent of the Common Western Metaphysic does: in this region of space there is only air, in that region there is only water, in the other there is only marble … and so on. (And such a Nihilist might maintain that in some regions of space there is no stuff at all, only emptiness.) According to this Nihilist, the stuffs that are spread out in space never add up to or compose or constitute anything. And it might be that this Nihilist would say that there were things that were mere modifications of various stuffs and collections of mere modifications of stuffs and events that consisted in changes in stuffs.

Is this a tenable theory? It would certainly seem to face grave difficulties. It would have been easier for an ancient Greek to hold this theory than it would be for someone today. It was possible for an ancient Greek to believe that matter was continuous and that all stuffs were "homoeomerous," that is, that any stuff was that stuff "all the way through" or "all the way down." If bronze, for example, is homoeomerous, and if a certain region of space is filled with bronze, then any smaller region within that region must also be filled with bronze. Today we know that bronze is not homoeomerous: within any region of space that is entirely filled with bronze there are smaller regions that have no bronze in them.[3] There are, for example, regions that contain single tin atoms, regions that contain single copper atoms (bronze is a copper-tin alloy), and regions that contain only empty space, or space that is as nearly empty as modern physics allows. And we know that bronze is in no way special in this respect. Every stuff that is visible to the naked eye arises from an arrangement of atoms that are not themselves made of that stuff.

This failure of visible stuffs to be homoeomerous does not by itself refute the form of Nihilism that holds that there is nothing but various stuffs, for it might be that *atoms* are made of some stuff or stuffs. If that were true, the Nihilist could say that there were really no atoms—just as there are really no stones or pats of butter or battleships. Rather, the Nihilist could say, there is just "atom-stuff" spread out in space in a certain way. Unfortunately for the Nihilist, atoms are not made of any kind of stuff. There is no answer to the question 'What is an atom made of?' that is like 'stone' or 'butter' or 'steel'. There is no such thing as "atom-stuff." It is true that an atom is made out of smaller particles. Atoms are made out of electrons, protons, and neutrons, and the protons and neutrons in their turn are made out of still smaller particles called quarks. And, at least if current physics is right, the electrons and quarks are not made out of anything, whether it be smaller particles or some kind of stuff. The most obvious conclusion to draw from this is that all stuffs are ulti-mately arrangements of quarks and electrons: for a region of space to be filled with stone is for the region to contain quarks and electrons arranged in one way; for a region of space to be filled with butter is for it to contain quarks and electrons arranged in another way, and so on. And it would seem that quarks and electrons are individual things. (But this is not beyond dispute. According to one of the versions of Monism that we shall later consider, quarks and elec-trons are mere modifications of the one individual thing.) If this is correct, then, in an obvious sense individual things are more "basic" than stuffs: to have stuffs, you have to have individual things, but you can have individual things without having stuffs. And in that case the Nihilist who says that there are no individual things but only stuffs is in the unenviable position of hold-ing a theory that is inconsistent with modern physics.

This is not a knockdown, irrefutable argument against the thesis that there are only stuffs. (For one thing, what we now call "modern physics" may be su-perseded. Perhaps the physicists will some day decide that quarks and elec-trons are made of some homoeomerous stuff.) There are no knockdown, irrefutable arguments in metaphysics. But it has sufficient force that it would seem that we should not accept the thesis that there are only stuffs unless there is a good reply to this argument. And since the thesis that there are only stuffs is the only form of Nihilism that seems even plausible,[4] let us, tentatively, re-ject Nihilism and turn to Monism.

The word 'monism' comes from a Greek word that means 'alone' or 'sin-gle'.[5] As we have said, Monism is the thesis that there is only one individual thing. But this statement of Monism raises an interesting question. If there is only one individual thing, what is meant by calling it an *individual* thing? We have seen that an individual thing is a thing that is in some not-too-well-defined sense a *separate* thing. But if there is only one individual thing, what is it "separate" from? It can't be its own parts that it is separate from, for, if it had parts, those parts would themselves be individual things: an individual thing with parts would "automatically" not be the only individual thing.[6] (For ex-ample, if the World consisted of a single chair, there would be many individ-ual things. There would be the legs of the chair, the back of the chair, various carbon and oxygen atoms that were parts of the chair, and so on.)

It might be suggested that the one individual thing was separate, at least potentially, from other things that might have been. A theist (someone who believes in God), for example, might argue as follows. "Suppose God—who has no parts—had never created anything. Then Monism would have been true: there would have been only one individual thing, God. But God would have known that He could have created, say, Eve, and that if He had created her, she would have been separate from Him, another individual thing. Thus, He would know that He was at least potentially separate from other things. And that's really all that is needed for something to be an individual thing: for it to be potentially separate from other things."

The trouble with this suggestion is that it seems to misrepresent the inten-tions of the Monist, although that is perhaps the fault of our statement of Mo-nism. The serious Monist does not think of Monism as something that

happens to be true but might have been false—or as something that potentially has the following feature: it happens to be false but it might have been
true. The serious Monist thinks of Monism as a doctrine about the way things
have to be—a doctrine that, if true, couldn't possibly have been false and, if
false, couldn't possibly have been true. The serious Monist does not think that
there are *even potentially* separate things. The serious Monist thinks that the
idea of there being two or more individual things does not represent a possible
state of affairs.

Let us therefore understand Monism as the thesis that there is a single individual thing and that, moreover, this thing could not possibly have coexisted
with any other individual thing. And let us say that it is a part of the thesis of
Monism that that is the way the World *has* to be: the World must consist of a
single individual thing that could not possibly coexist with any other individual thing. When Monism is so stated, it is indeed difficult to see what the Monist could mean by saying that there is only one individual thing, for it is
difficult to see in what sense the word 'separate' could be applied to a thing
that not only does not but could not coexist with other individual things, and
it is therefore difficult to see what is meant by applying the word 'individual'
to the thing that is supposed to be the one individual thing.

Perhaps the best thing to say is the following: Monists believe that there is
only one thing that is at all like the things that those who believe that there are
many individual things (people like the proponents of the Common Western
Metaphysic) call individual things. Monists believe that there is, and could be,
only one non-universal that exists in its own right. More exactly, they believe
that there is only one thing that is not a universal or a stuff or a mere modification of something else or a mere collection of things or an event. Let us call this
thing the One. The Monist's thesis, then, is that everything there is is either a
universal or a stuff or an event or the One or a mere modification of the One or
a mere collection of mere modifications of the One.

Ordinary people think that Julius Caesar and the Taj Mahal and the sun are
three distinct things, each of which exists in its own right. Monists say that
there is only one thing that exists in its own right. The ordinary people and the
Monists therefore disagree. But what is the exact point on which the ordinary
people and the Monists are disagreed? There are actually several points at
which the disagreement between the ordinary people and the Monists might
be located, each of which corresponds to a possible "version" of Monism.

First, a Monist might say that the ordinary people are wrong to think that
Julius Caesar and the Taj Mahal and the sun are things that exist in their own
right. The Monist might say that these three things are mere modifications of
the One—three *different* modifications, to be sure, but nevertheless only modifications. They are thus related to the One in somewhat the same way as the
way in which three wrinkles in a carpet are related to the carpet. But this analogy is imperfect. For one thing, each wrinkle in a carpet involves a particular
part of the carpet, and the One has no parts. (If the One did have parts, each of
its parts would be a thing that existed in its own right, just as—according to
the Common Western Metaphysic—every part of a carpet, including those
parts that happen to be thrust up to form wrinkles, is a thing that exists in its

own right.) Thus it cannot be that the sun is a modification of one part of the One and Julius Caesar a modification of another part of the One. The differences between Caesar and the sun (and the differences between Caesar and Brutus) must, according to this version of Monism, arise from the fact that Caesar and the sun are different kinds of modification of the One. This version of Monism was held by the seventeenth-century Dutch philosopher Benedict Spinoza.

Secondly, a Monist might say that Caesar and the Taj Majal and the sun do not really exist at all, not even as mere modifications of the One. According to this version of Monism, a belief in these things, or any things like them, is an illusion, the result of taking what is mere appearance for reality. The first version of Monism holds that ordinary people are right to think that Caesar and the Taj Mahal and the sun exist but wrong to think of them as things that exist in their own right. The second holds that individuality is a complete illusion: individuality does not exist even at the level of mere modification. According to this version of Monism, the One cannot have a plurality of modifications; it must have either one modification or none.

This second version of Monism was adopted by those nineteenth-century Western philosophers who were mentioned above in passing as opponents of the Common Western Metaphysic. (These philosophers were called Absolute Idealists. They were called idealists not because they professed high ideals but because they believed that no reality existed apart from the mind and its ideas. The eighteenth-century Irish philosopher George Berkeley, whose metaphysic we shall examine at some length in the following chapter, also believed this and is also called an idealist. But Berkeley believed in individuality. He believed that minds were individual things and that ideas were mere modifications of these individual minds. The nineteenth-century idealists, however, believed that the only thing that existed in reality, the only thing that was not mere appearance, was a sort of mind or idea—the distinction between a mind and the ideas or thoughts of that mind, they held, is a distinction that is valid only at the level of appearance—which they called the Absolute Mind or the Absolute Idea or simply the Absolute. The Absolute is, of course, their name for what we have been calling the One.) It may be that the second form of Monism is held by some Buddhists, but I am not prepared to say this with any confidence.

Thirdly, a Monist may believe that Caesar and the Taj Mahal and the sun really do exist and are not mere modifications of the One. According to the third form of Monism, Caesar and the Taj Mahal and the sun are all the very same thing, that is to say, each of them is the only thing there is: each of them is the One. According to this view, the One presents itself to people (that is, to itself, for, of course, there is nothing special about Julius Caesar: you and I and Madame Curie and "everyone else" are also the One) in various guises, sometimes as Caesar, sometimes as the sun, and so on. The third form of Monism, like the second, therefore entails that individuality is a complete illusion, an illusion that arises from mistaking the various guises of the One, which exist only at the level of appearance, for reality. I am not sure whether anyone really holds the third form of Monism. I have often hea. 1 it said that this is the form of Monism accepted by the Hindus, but I've never heard this from anyone I regard as a reliable source. While it is certainly true that Hindus accept some form of Monism, it is possible that my informants have failed to distinguish the three forms of Monism with sufficient care and that Hindus really accept the first or the second form of Monism.[7]

All three forms of Monism agree in affirming the doctrine that individuality is, if not an illusion, not fully real, either. Even the most "liberal" form of Monism, the first, consigns individuality to the realm of things that exist only as mere modifications of something else.

The question naturally arises why anyone accepts this metaphysic. It seems most natural to accept individuality as a real feature of the World. The Monists themselves concede this—even the "hard-line" Monists of the second and third varieties—when they describe individuality as belonging to the level of appearance, for what that means is that there is *apparently* such a thing as individuality. Normally, we believe that what is apparently the case is really the case unless there is some known reason to believe that what is apparently the case is not really the case after all. For example, as we saw in Chapter 1, people once believed that the earth was stationary and that the rest of the universe revolved around it, and they believed this because it was apparently true. Later, when new evidence came to light that not only showed that the earth revolved around the sun and rotated on its polar axis but which also showed how it could be apparently true but really false that the earth was stationary, people revised their opinion and came to accept what was apparently true as being really false. This would seem to be the best procedure. It is obvious that we human beings do not have any infallible way of knowing the truth. The best we can do is to believe what seems to us to be true unless we have some good reason to reject it. What, after all, is the alternative? To believe what does not even *seem* to be true when we know of *no* good reason to accept it? Or even to believe what seems to be *false* when we know of no good reason to accept it? One could, of course, be so impressed by the fallibility of our accepted procedures for finding out the truth that one decided to believe nothing at all or to believe very little. (Philosophers who take this option are called "skeptics.") But this is not the decision of the Monists, who do believe something, and, in fact, something that one would expect would be (if true) very hard to find out.

There seem to be two kinds of reasons that Monists have given for rejecting individuality: some Monists have appealed to metaphysical argument and some have appealed to a kind of direct experience or "vision" of the World as a whole that supposedly unmasks individuality as an illusion.

We earlier cited Spinoza as an example of a philosopher who accepted the first form of Monism. In his great book the *Ethics*,[8] he presents an extended argument for the conclusion that all of the things that we should normally take to be individual things are mere modifications of the One, which he variously calls, depending on context, 'Substance' (see note 1), 'God', and 'Nature'. It would be beyond the scope of a book like this to present a serious and historically adequate discussion of Spinoza's argument for this conclusion. I will remark, however, that Spinoza's argument appears to rest on the following premise:

If a thing is not absolutely independent of everything else, then it must be a mere modification of something that is absolutely independent of everything else.[9]

To say that a thing is absolutely independent of everything else (here 'everything else' means 'everything else besides its own parts and modifications'—everything "external" to it, we might say) is to say at least that it could exist without there being anything else. In an example we used earlier, we considered the possibility that there be nothing besides (i.e., nothing external to) a single chair. But is that really a possibility? One might argue that a being of unlimited intellect who examined a chair would see that its existence implied the existence of other things. For example, if the chair were made of wood, this being might be able to deduce the existence of trees and go on to deduce the existence of soil, air, water, and the sun. One might therefore argue that the hypothesis that a chair could exist "all by itself" is impossible, a chair being a thing that in effect carries a label that reads 'this thing can exist only as a result of the action of other things.' Even if God—not Spinoza's God, but the traditional God of Judaism and Christianity—were to "short-circuit" the usual processes by which wood is produced and create a wooden chair without first creating trees, soil, air, water, and the sun, the chair would still owe its existence to the action of something other than itself, namely God. If these speculations are correct, then it is not possible for a chair to exist all by itself, and a chair is not in the required sense absolutely independent of everything else. If Spinoza's premise is correct, therefore, it follows that if there are chairs, they must be mere modifications of something that *is* absolutely independent of everything else.

Spinoza applies this premise in the following way. He presents arguments that are supposed to show, first, that there must exist a being that is absolutely independent of everything else and, secondly, that there could not be *two* beings each of which was absolutely independent of everything else. It follows that there is exactly one being that is absolutely independent of everything else. From this result and the premise, it follows that all other things are mere modifications of this one "independent" being. It is by this argument—or rather by a very complicated argument of which this is a highly simplified version—that Spinoza claims to establish Monism.

It is not clear to me, however, why one should accept Spinoza's premise.[10] Why should one believe that anything that is not an absolutely independent being is a mere modification of some absolutely independent being? This premise has been denied both by theists and by typical atheists.[11]

Most theists would maintain that there is exactly one absolutely independent being, God. They would maintain that everything besides God depends upon God for its existence and that this is the way things have to be: that there could not possibly be a thing (other than God Himself) that did not depend upon God for its existence. And yet, they would maintain, chairs and tables and the Taj Mahal and Julius Caesar and the sun are not mere modifications of God. To say that they were—theists maintain—would be a form of *pantheism*. (Monists who apply the term 'God' to the One are called pantheists, 'pan' being Greek for 'all'. Spinoza is thus a pantheist. Two other forms of pantheism are possible; they correspond to the two other forms of Monism.) Theists have generally regarded theism as a middle ground between two extremes: atheism, which holds that the term 'God' applies to nothing, and pantheism, which holds that the term 'God' applies to everything. Theism, by contrast, holds that the term 'God' applies to one thing and not to any of the others.[12] Theists, therefore, are no more kindly disposed to pantheism than they are to atheism (they are in fact inclined to regard pantheism as a disguised form of atheism, since they believe that what pantheists apply the term 'God' to is not properly called 'God'), and they would reject Spinoza's premise.

Typical atheists regard the physical universe as the World, as all that there is. As to the existence of absolutely independent beings, they divide into several camps. Some say that there are no absolutely independent beings, that everything depends on something else, the World being a mere collection of such "dependent" beings. Others say that there are many independent beings—elementary particles, perhaps—and that the World is either itself an independent being that is made of these "small" independent beings or else is a mere collection of them. Still others say that there is one independent being, the World or physical universe itself, tables and chairs and such being *parts* of the one independent being. The differences among these theories are important for the student of metaphysics, but all of the theories agree that tables and chairs and the Taj Mahal and Julius Caesar and the sun are not mere modifications.

Since, therefore, many people reject Spinoza's premise, it can hardly be regarded as being so obvious that it requires no argument. (He himself seems to have regarded it as just that obvious. He in effect builds it into one of his definitions.) And since he has given no argument for it, there would seem to be no compelling reason to believe it. We must conclude that Spinoza has given us no compelling reason to accept Monism.

Spinoza's argument was an argument for the first form of Monism. The Absolute Idealists argued for the second form. They accepted the second form of Monism because they thought that the idea of there being two or more things could be seen to be self-contradictory. They were, of course, willing to concede that we cannot get along in everyday life without talking as if there were many things, but they believed that if one made a serious attempt to think through the idea of there being two or more things *in reality*, one would see that this idea was incoherent. The most celebrated argument for this conclusion was due to the late-nineteenth-century English philosopher F. H. Bradley. In his book *Appearance and Reality*, Bradley argued for this astonishing conclusion on the basis of a distinction between "internal" and "external" relations. I am not at all sure that I have been able to follow Bradley's reasoning. What follows is my own reconstruction of that reasoning, a reconstruction that may very well misrepresent Bradley's intent. The argument requires a little stage-setting.

We begin with a distinction between "intrinsic" and "relational" properties. A relational property is a property that a thing has only in virtue of the ways in which it is related to other things. Some examples of relational properties are: being fifty miles north of a burning barn; once having met the Canadian prime minister; being a widow. All properties that are not relational are intrinsic. Some examples of intrinsic properties are: being spherical; being male; being bright green; having a mass of fourteen kilograms. The distinction between intrinsic and relational properties is sometimes explained in terms of the concept of a "real change in a thing": if the gain or loss of a property would be a real change in a thing, then that property is intrinsic; otherwise, it is relational. Suppose, for example, that a barn fifty miles to the south of you catches fire. At that moment you acquire the property "being fifty miles to the north of a burning barn." But there seems to be an obvious sense in which the acquisition of this property does not constitute a "real change" in you. For all you know—unless geographical considerations render it impossible—you *did* acquire this property a moment ago, and you never noticed a thing. And if you had been undergoing, say, a complete physical examination at the moment, the physician conducting the examination wouldn't have noticed a thing either.

If we restrict our attention to the properties of physical objects, there is a useful, but fallible, test for a property's being "intrinsic." The test involves the idea of a "perfect duplicating machine." Readers of science fiction will be familiar with that idea: one places any sort of physical object one likes in the "in" tray of this useful device, and a perfect atom-for-atom duplicate of the object appears in its "out" tray. If a property of the original object is intrinsic, it will be reproduced by the machine; that is, it will be a property of the duplicate. Or, what is the same thing, if a property is *not* reproduced by the machine, it is not intrinsic but relational. Thus, if one makes a perfect duplicate of, say, a woman who has met the Canadian prime minister, the duplicate will not have met the prime minister (although she will no doubt think she has); the property of having met the Canadian prime minister is therefore a relational property. But the property of having a mass of fourteen kilograms passes the test because if an object has a mass of fourteen kilograms, so will a perfect duplicate of the object. It does not, alas, follow that this property is intrinsic, for there are relational properties that will pass the test: being the same color as the thing in the "in" tray, for example, or being in contact with a perfect duplicating machine. I call the test "useful" for two reasons. First, failure is conclusive: a property that fails the test has to be relational. Secondly, the relational properties that pass the test are rather contrived. "If a property passes the test, it is intrinsic" is a good rule of thumb.

We are now ready to explain the central idea employed in Bradley's argument, the distinction between internal and external relations. An internal relation is a relation that holds between objects just because of their intrinsic properties; a relation is internal if the intrinsic properties of two (or more) objects *settle the question whether* that relation holds between (or among) them. Thus, the relation "being the same color as" is an internal relation because for any two objects, the intrinsic properties of those objects settle the question whether that relation holds between them—which is not surprising, since color is an intrinsic property. But spatial relations, relations like "being between," are external. For consider three objects, *x*, *y*, and *z*, each of which has a spatial location. No matter how much you know about the intrinsic properties of these three objects, this knowledge will not enable you to tell whether x is between y and z, for more or less the same reason that aerial photographs of New York, Chicago, and San Francisco will not enable you to tell whether Chicago is between New York and San Francisco.

Bradley's argument has two main premises:

1. If there are two or more things, then there are external relations.
2. All relations are internal.

The first of these premises is at least somewhat plausible. This may be seen if we try to imagine a World in which there are no external relations but which nevertheless contain two or more things. Suppose that one of these things has the properties A, B, C, ... , and that the other has the properties X, Y, Z, ... What would make it the case that these were indeed *two* things having these two sets of properties rather than *one* thing having the properties A, B, C, ... , X, Y, Z, ... ? If the World had the features that the Common Western Metaphysics ascribes to the real World, and if the two things were, say, chairs, it is clear enough what the answer to this question would be: the chair having A, B, C, ... is over *here*, and the chair having X, Y, Z, ... is over *there*, and, therefore, what has A, B, C, ... is one thing, and what has X, Y, Z, ... is another. (Some philosophers think that, in addition to the two chairs, there is a larger object that is "made out of" the two chairs, the so-called *sum* of the chairs. Assuming that this thing does exist, however, it certainly does not have the properties A, B, C, ... , X, Y, Z, ... If, for example, A is the property of having a mass of fifteen kilograms, and X is the property of having a mass of twenty kilograms, the sum of the two chairs will not have either A or X; it will instead have the property of having a mass of thirty-five kilograms.)

As far as physical things like chairs go, therefore, it seems plausible to suppose that it is only because there are—or so we normally suppose—external relations like spatial and temporal relations that the World can be "split up into" separate things each with its own set of properties. And perhaps it is even plausible to suppose that this principle also applies to non-physical things, although in that case it might be hard to say what the external relations were. But let us assume for the sake of argument that this principle applies to all possible things; that is, let us suppose that the first premise of Bradley's argument is true.

What about the second premise? Why is it supposed to be true that there are only internal relations? Bradley has an argument for this thesis, an argument that is celebrated both for its influence and for its obscurity. The argument goes like this:

Suppose for the sake of argument that two things, x and y, are related by or stand in a certain external relation, R. (For example, if R is the relation " ... is ten meters from ... ," then any two things that are ten meters apart are "related by" or "stand in" R.) Since R is external, the fact that x and y stand in R does not depend on the intrinsic properties of x and y. But then *why* do these two things stand in that relation? What *makes it true* that they do? Or, to put the question another way, what makes it true that x, y, and R stand in the relation "the two things ... and ... stand in the external relation ... "? (Let us call this second relation R*.) The fact that x, y, and R stand in R* cannot depend on the intrinsic properties of x, y, and R, for if it did, x and y would stand in R just because of the intrinsic properties of x and y. Therefore, the second relation, R*, is also an external relation. But if R* is an external relation, what makes it true that x, y, and R stand in R*? Or, to put the question another way, what makes it true that x, y, R, and R* stand in the relation "the two things ... and ... and the external relation ... stand in the external relation ... "? (Let us call this third relation R**.) The fact that x, y, R, and R* stand in R** cannot depend on the intrinsic properties of x, y, R, and R*, for if it did, x, y, and R would stand in R* just because of the intrinsic properties of x, y, and R. Therefore, the third relation, R**, is an external relation.

It should be clear at this point that this style of argument can be carried on without limit. No matter how far we go, some further *external* relation will be "needed" to relate the things (the objects and earlier external relations) we have previously considered. No matter how far we go, we shall never come to an internal relation whose holding makes it true that all of the previously considered external relations hold.

Bradley's reasoning so far is very complex and very abstract, but it seems to be correct. But what is the point of it? The point depends on a further premise: that the fact that a certain set of things stand in a given relation must somehow be grounded in or explained by the intrinsic properties of those things. Bradley argues that the "infinite regress of external relations" that he has shown to exist—the series the first few members of which we constructed above—shows that this condition can never be satisfied by any external relation and that it is therefore impossible for there to be external relations.

All of this reasoning seems to me to be plausible—with the crucial exception of the premise that was introduced in the preceding paragraph. This premise seems to be just a way of saying that there are no external relations, for what is an external relation if not a relation that things can stand in without the fact that they stand in it being grounded in their intrinsic properties?

Nevertheless, there *is* something puzzling about the idea of an external relation. To get an intuitive sense of what is puzzling about external relations, let us consider spatial relations, which are clear and easily visualizable examples of external relations.

Suppose that the objects A and B are ten meters apart. What is it that makes it true that A and B are ten meters apart? What factor is it that allows a relation of spatial separation like "being ten meters apart" to attach itself—so to speak—to one pair of objects and yet not attach itself to another pair of apparently equally suitable objects? As we have seen, this factor cannot be a function of the intrinsic properties of A and B, for there might be perfect duplicates of A and B that were not ten meters apart. And it cannot be a function of their relational properties, for the only relevant ones are spatial properties, and these cannot explain themselves; it cannot be that A and B are ten meters apart because A and B are ten meters apart—and it's not much more helpful to say that A and B are ten meters apart because (say) each is five meters from an object that is halfway between them. It is, moreover, no answer to say that A and B are ten meters apart because they occupy points or regions in space that are ten meters apart. If there really are such things as points or regions in space, the relations of distance that hold between them are as much external relations as the relations of distance that hold between material things like tables and chairs. (And there is a further problem: the relation "is located at" that holds between a material thing and a certain point or region in space would also be an external relation.)

Spatial and other external relations would therefore seem to raise the following puzzle: it seems that there is nothing about the objects that they hold between that could explain the fact that such relations hold between them. The fact that a given external relation holds between two objects, therefore, has to be a kind of "brute" or ultimate fact. The fact that two things are the same color can be explained; one object is, say, red and the other is red, too. The fact that two things are ten meters apart, however, can have no explanation at all; it just *is* a fact and that's all there is to be said about it.

In the preceding paragraph, I have tried to give some sense of what it is that the Absolute Idealist may have found puzzling about the idea of external relations. Perhaps Bradley's elaborate argument was an attempt at an articulation of this intuitive sense of the existence of a puzzle. But is there really a puzzle here? Suppose that the fact that a certain external relation holds between two objects *is* a brute fact. What's so bad about brute facts? Surely there must be some brute facts somewhere in the World? If we are determined to be puzzled by brute facts, we shall find that *internal* relations and the intrinsic properties in which they are grounded also present us with problems about brute facts. The fact that A is the same shape as B is explained by the properties of A and B. But what explains the fact that A is the shape it is—spherical, say. Let us call the relation that holds between a thing and its properties 'having'. So the thing A has the property of sphericality or being spherical. But what explains the fact that the thing and the property stand in that relation? There does not seem to be anything we can point to. The only fact about A that we can point to that seems at all relevant is the fact that A is spherical. And the only fact about sphericality that we can point to is that it is one of the properties of A. But these facts yield no explanation. The fact that A is spherical does not explain the fact that A has the property of being spherical, and the fact that the property of being spherical is one of the properties of A does not explain the fact that A has the property of being spherical.

It seems, therefore, that if Bradley's enormously complicated argument for the conclusion that there are no external relations is of any value, a much simpler argument that appeals to some of the same principles can be used to show that there are not even any intrinsic properties—and, of course, if there are no intrinsic properties, then there are no internal relations, because internal relations are by definition relations that are grounded in intrinsic properties.

This conclusion, however, is very hard to accept. If it is right, it is hard to see how one could be even a Monist. Even a Monist must believe that the One exists (whatever the Monist's favorite name for the One may be) and that it has some intrinsic properties. The Monist may indeed insist—many Monists have insisted—that none of the properties of the One can be known to the finite human intellect. The Monist may insist that none of the properties of the One is in any way even remotely analogous to the properties that ordinary people mistakenly believe belong to the individual objects of the world of appearance. But the conclusion we reached in the preceding paragraph by reasoning that seems to be just as convincing as Bradley's is much stronger than this. This conclusion is not that there are no properties that can be grasped by the finite human intellect. It is not that there are only properties that are not even remotely analogous to the properties that ordinary people believe in. It is that there are no properties at all. And this is inconsistent with Monism. We mentioned a moment ago those Monists who hold that none of the properties of the One can be known to the finite human intellect. And there are indeed Monists who say things like that. But their position is not coherent, for in the very act of saying this they ascribe a property to the One, a property that their own finite human intellects are perfectly capable of grasping: the property "being a thing that has no properties the finite human intellect can grasp." And there are certainly lots of properties that all Monists agree that the One has. The property "being the only thing that exists in reality," for example, belongs to the One by definition. It is not my purpose to make much of this incoherency into which some Monists have fallen; I wish only to point out that, whatever they may say in an incautious moment, all Monists really believe that the One has certain intrinsic properties and that, therefore, any argument that shows that there are no intrinsic properties refutes Monism.

The bottom line is this: Bradley's argument for the conclusion that there cannot be, in reality, two or more things depends on his argument for the conclusion that there are no external relations. And if this very complicated argument is correct, then a much simpler argument that claims to show that there are no intrinsic properties is correct. But if there are no intrinsic properties, then not even the One can exist. Thus, the principles of reasoning that Bradley uses in his attempt to refute the existence of a plurality of things, if valid, refute even the existence of the One.

We have looked at two philosophical arguments for Monism. It is impossible to establish a negative conclusion by examining two or three cases: one cannot establish that there are no black swans by examining two swans and seeing that they are white. And, similarly, one cannot establish that there are no satisfactory arguments for Monism by examining two arguments for Monism and showing that they are unsatisfactory. Still, the prospects for establishing Monism by philosophical argument at this point appear bleak, if only because the two arguments we have examined (those of Spinoza and Bradley) are the two best-known and most influential arguments for that conclusion.

What other reasons than philosophical argument might one have for accepting Monism? I know of only one other reason that people have had for being Monists: some people have been Monists because they claim to have had a certain sort of *experience* that shows that individuality is an illusion. Obviously, the experience they appeal to cannot be ordinary sense experience, because ordinary sense experience (sight and hearing and so on) represents the World to us as composed of a multitude of individual things. The experience they appeal to is rather what is usually called *religious* or *mystical* experience. Some people claim to have had experiences—extraordinary experiences, quite unlike anything that occurs in everyday life—in which it has been revealed to them that the World has the features that we have ascribed to the One. These experiences may simply *happen* to a person, "out of a clear blue sky," so to speak, or they may be the result of taking drugs, or they may be achieved only after long training in various spiritual disciplines that are especially associated with certain Eastern religious traditions. Whatever the occasion for them, however, the people who have them are convinced that they are sources of knowledge and that one of the most important pieces of knowledge that one gains from them is that individuality is an illusion.

While those who have such experiences are generally agreed that the experiences are *ineffable*—that it is absolutely impossible to describe either what it is like to have them or to give an adequate description of the knowledge that one gains by having them—it is also generally agreed that certain very abstract statements can be made about them. And one of these descriptions is that these experiences reveal that individuality is an illusion, that our belief that there are individual things is like the belief of our ancestors that the heavens revolve about the earth: these beliefs have their origins in the way the World appears to us and not in the way the World really is. Thus, according to these claims, certain experiences have revealed to certain human beings that there is no such thing as the sun and no such thing as the Taj Mahal, or else they have revealed that the sun and the Taj Mahal are the very same thing, the One. The following quotation from Williams James's *The Varieties of Religious Experience* contains several examples of the kind of language that is used by those who believe that the truth of some form of Monism has been revealed to them in mystical experience:

> That art Thou! say the Upanishads, and the Vedantists add: 'Not a part, nor a mode of That, but identically That, that absolute Spirit of the World.' "As pure water poured into pure water remains the same, thus, O Gautama, is the Self of a thinker who knows. Water in water, fire in fire, ether in ether, no one can distinguish them; likewise a man whose mind has entered into the self." 'Every man,' says the Sufi Gulshan-Râz, whose heart is no longer shaken by any doubt, knows with certainty that there is no being save only One. ... In his divine majesty the *me*, the *we*, the *thou* are not found, for in the One there can be no distinction. Every being who is annulled and entirely separated from himself, hears resound outside of him this voice and this echo: *I am God.*'[13]

Most of the readers of this book (like its author) will not have had experiences that have convinced them that there is no individuality. The question naturally arises, What should those of us who have not had mystical experiences conclude on the basis of the claims of those who have? This is a large question, and it cannot be adequately investigated in a book about metaphysics. I will mention only that it is not the unanimous verdict of those who have claimed to have mystical experiences that there are no individual things. This is illustrated in the following quotation, which is from the writings of Saint Teresa of Avila, a sixteenth-century Spanish nun, who was one of the great Christian mystics:

> One day, being in orison [meditation], it was granted to me to perceive in one instant how all things are seen and contained in God. I did not perceive them in their proper form, and nevertheless the view I had of them was of a sovereign clearness and has remained vividly impressed upon my soul. It is one of the most signal of the graces which the Lord has granted me.

While it may not be absolutely clear in every respect what Saint Teresa means to convey in this passage, it seems evident that her words imply that although "all things" may be "seen and contained in" God they nevertheless exist and are what we have been calling individual things. And there would seem to be no reason to suppose that her visions are of any less authority than those of any Eastern mystic whose visions supposedly reveal that there are no individual things. Therefore, since mystical experiences do not give unanimous witness to Monism, we cannot appeal to them to show that Monism gives the true account of ultimate reality. That the Eastern mystics nevertheless know, on the basis of their experiences, that there is no individuality certainly remains a possibility, but there does not seem to be any way for those of us who do not have such experiences to investigate this question further.

Neither philosophical argument nor mystical experience (or, rather, the written accounts of mystical experiences that are available to those of us who do not have such experiences) has given us any reason to reject the thesis, central to the Common Western Metaphysic, that individuality is a real feature of the way the World is. Let us therefore tentatively conclude that one feature of ultimate reality is that there are individual things. We should note that this conclusion is rather weak; it is not a part of this conclusion that the individual things that really exist are the individual things that we ordinarily believe in. We have not concluded that Julius Caesar or the sun or the Taj Mahal exist but only that some individual things or other exist.

Suggestions for Further Reading

Spinoza's *Ethics* is printed in its entirety in *Spinoza: Selections*. This collection is easily available and inexpensive, but some scholars are unhappy with the Stirling and White Translation of the *Ethics* that Wild has used. E. M. Curley's recent translation of the *Ethics* (included in Curley's *The Collected Works of Spinoza*) is highly thought of. Spinoza's argument for Monism occurs in Part 1 of the *Ethics*. As is the case with Kant, the beginning student of Spinoza needs a guide. Bennett's *A Study of Spinoza's Ethics* is recommended. An excellent discussion of the argument for monism can be found in Chapter 3.

Blackman's *Classics of Analytical Metaphysics* contains a very useful selection of writings related to Bradley's argument for the conclusion that all relations are internal: Chapters II and III of Bradley's *Appearance and Reality* ("Substantive and Adjective" and "Relation and Quality"), Bradley's "On Appearance, Error and Contradiction" (a criticism of the "pluralistic" position that had recently been taken by Bertrand Russell in his *Principles of Mathematics*), Russell's reply, "Some Explanations in Reply to Mr. Bradley," and Bradley's rejoinder, "Reply to Mr. Russell's Explanations."

There are a great many excellent textbooks that are devoted wholly or partly to Eastern religions and Eastern philosophy. I have found Hutchinson's *Paths of Faith* to be very useful. William James's *The Varieties of Religious Experience* is a classic treatment of the question whether we can learn metaphysical truths from mystical or religious experience. Readers of this book will find Lectures XVI and XVII particularly interesting.

3

Externality

One of the most important features of the Common Western Metaphysic is its thesis that the sun and the Taj Mahal and Caesar (or, at any rate, Caesar's body) are not only individual things but are also things that exist independently of the mind. It is a part of the Common Western Metaphysic that there exist objects that are in no sense mental, that not everything that exists or occurs exists or occurs within the mind. This thesis is sometimes expressed by the statement that there exists "an external world"—that is, a world of individual things external to the mind. But not all philosophers have accepted the existence of an external world, and of those who have, many have thought that the existence of an external world was sufficiently unobvious that it would be a good idea to have some sort of proof of or strong argument for its existence.[1] Why have philosophers not simply regarded the existence of an external world as something that was so obvious that it need never be called into question? The answer seems to be that most philosophers—or at least most European philosophers of the seventeenth and eighteenth centuries—have been certain of the existence of an "internal world," of the world of the mind. And they have observed that the factors that made them certain of the existence of the mind and its contents did not apply in the case of external objects. Let us examine the sources of this certainty and this observation.

Suppose that you find yourself with a persistent sharp pain in your left shoulder. You go to a doctor, who, after some examination, is unable to find any organic cause for the pain. The doctor says to you, "There doesn't seem to be anything wrong with your shoulder. Are you sure you're in pain?" The natural response to this question would be indignation; you would assume that the doctor was accusing you—using a somewhat ironic turn of phrase—of *pretending* to be in pain. But suppose the doctor disclaimed any such intent. Suppose the doctor went on to say, "No, no, I'm sure you're perfectly sincere. I just thought you might be making an honest error. Nobody's perfect, after all. We all make mistakes. Maybe you're not really in pain." These words make no sense at all. Although a person may be mistaken about the *intensity* of a certain

42

pain—the coward may describe as excruciating a level of pain that the stoic will say is all in a day's work—no one can say sincerely, "There's a pain in my shoulder," and be mistaken. Whether one is in pain is one of the few things that one can be absolutely certain about. Why this is true is an interesting question, but it is not one we need to go into at present. The fact to note at present is that one cannot be mistaken about one's own pain or about any other sort of feeling: one cannot be mistaken about whether one is feeling warm or cold or nauseated or elated or depressed. And what holds for feelings holds for thoughts. If a friend asks you what you are thinking about, and you reply that you are thinking about the meaning of life, your friend cannot sensibly ask, "Are you sure? Isn't it possible that you're really thinking about whether to buy a new car?" Or rather, your friend can ask this, but only as a way of questioning your truthfulness. (In that case, the question would be a way of saying, "Come on, you can't fool me. Tell me what you're really thinking about. It's buying a car, isn't it?")

What is common to thoughts and feelings is that both are in the mind. The general lesson of our examples is that one cannot be mistaken about the present content of one's own mind.[2] It is for this reason that many of the philosophers who have believed in individual things have taken it for granted that at least some of them are mental. The reasoning that underlies this conviction may be spelled out in detail as follows. One cannot be mistaken about one's feelings and thoughts, and, therefore, since we all believe that we *have* feelings and thoughts, it must be that feelings and thoughts exist. And these feelings and thoughts must either themselves be individual things or else be modifications of individual things. If they are modifications of individual things, the things of which they are modifications must be mental. (A feeling or thought couldn't be a modification of something that was *material* or *physical*, could it?—any more than a knot or a wrinkle could be a modification of something that *wasn't* physical?) Therefore—given that individual things exist at all—at least some of them must be mental.

It is clear that any argument to show that at least some individual things must be non-mental must be of a very different sort from this argument, for we do not have grounds for claiming to be absolutely certain that non-mental things exist that are at all similar to our grounds for being certain about the contents of our own minds. If there is any doubt about this, it may be dispelled by considering a famous argument invented by the seventeenth-century French philosopher René Descartes. Descartes pointed out that it would be quite possible for some immensely powerful spirit—he calls it an "evil genius"—to deceive us about the existence of the external world. (The phrase 'evil genius' may suggest to the present-day reader that Descartes was imagining a mad scientist. But the original meaning of the word 'genius' was 'spirit'.) We could conceive of the evil genius as being powerful and clever enough to be able to supply us with sensations just like the ones we should be receiving from external objects if those objects existed, even though there are in fact no such objects. If there were indeed an evil genius engaged in this activity, then things would look and feel to us exactly as if there were an external world—things would look and feel exactly as they do now—and we should therefore believe that there was an external world when there was no such thing. The evil genius would thus be able to *deceive* us about the existence of an external world. And yet even the evil genius would be unable to deceive us about what was going on in our own minds. (Imagine, for example, the task the evil genius would be faced with if it had to deceive Tom—who is not experiencing any pain—into believing that he has an intense pain in his chest; or imagine the task of deceiving Jane—who is a convinced atheist—into believing that she is a devout Mormon.)

It would seem therefore to be certain that at least some individual things are mental and less certain that any individual things are non-mental. Might it be that *all* individual things are mental? The thesis that all things are mental—that nothing exists apart from the mind and its contents—is, as we saw in Chapter 2, called idealism ('idea' being a word that some philosophers have found convenient to use for thoughts and feelings and any other things that exist only as contents of the mind). As we have seen, some idealists, the Absolute Idealists, have rejected individuality. Others—the eighteenth-century Anglo-Irish philosopher George Berkeley, Bishop of Cloyne, is the most famous example—have accepted the existence of individual things. If Berkeley is right, then all individual things are mental, a thesis that would certainly seem to be inconsistent with what ordinary people believe. Interestingly enough, however, Berkeley claimed *not* to be offering a theory inconsistent with the beliefs of ordinary people but rather to be giving a careful account of what it was that ordinary people believed.

A great many philosophers have found this claim that Berkeley made for his philosophy highly implausible. They would contend that ordinary people believe in an external world, a world of external things, a world of things that are in no sense mental—things such as trees and buildings and snowballs and stars. Berkeley would reply that this contention misrepresents what ordinary people believe. If you had asked Berkeley what, say, a snowball was, he would have told you, first, that it was nothing apart from its properties (for example, its roundness, hardness, whiteness, and coldness) and that all of its properties were modifications of the mind. That is, Berkeley would have denied that there was anything "to" the snowball but its properties, and he would have denied that any of its properties could exist apart from the mind. And this is just what ordinary people believe, Berkeley maintains. Only a metaphysician, Berkeley tells us, could believe that there is an unperceivable "something" that is somehow present together with the perceivable roundness, the perceivable hardness, the perceivable whiteness, and the perceivable coldness. We all believe that we can see and feel snowballs. No ordinary person would say that a snowball was invisible or intangible, after all. But, in the strict sense, all we ever see are colors and shapes, and the only things that are ever detected by the sense of touch are shapes and tactile qualities like hardness. Therefore, a snowball (or any other object present to the senses) must be composed of colors and shapes and tactile qualities. And colors and shapes and tactile qualities cannot exist apart from the mind.

Proponents of the Common Western Metaphysic will reply by disputing Berkeley's thesis that there is nothing "to" an object present to the senses but its properties or qualities. They will argue that in addition to the roundness, hardness, whiteness, and coldness of the snowball, there must be something "there" that is not itself a property but which *has* the properties of roundness, hardness, whiteness, and coldness. And they will add that both this thing *and* its properties could exist apart from the mind: even if there were no human beings or other creatures with minds, there could still be round, hard, white, cold objects.[3] That is to say, they will affirm against Berkeley the existence of an external world.[4]

What reasons might there be for rejecting, with Berkeley, the existence of an external world? Berkeley gives many arguments for the absurdity (as he sees it) of believing in things independent of the mind, but perhaps the simplest and most appealing is based on this simple question: If there is an external world, how do we know anything about what it is like or whether it exists? Consider the snowball that we perceive—the round, hard, white, cold thing. If in addition to the perceived snowball there is an "external" snowball, a thing that is the common cause of the roundness, the hardness, the whiteness, and the coldness that we perceive, what is it like? We cannot say that it is round or hard or white or cold, for these are properties that exist only in the mind.

At this point the reader may want to break in and protest that it seems absurd to say that roundness is a property that exists only in the mind. As we have noted, it may be somewhat plausible to say that colors exist only in the mind, but it seems much less plausible to say this about shapes. Berkeley's defense of the thesis that roundness and other shapes exist only in the mind is sufficiently interesting to be worth a brief digression. Berkeley argues that there is not just one kind of roundness but two: "visual" roundness and "tactile" roundness. If one looks at a snowball that one is not touching, one perceives a certain sort of property that one reports by saying, "It's round." If one handles a snowball in the dark, one perceives an entirely different property that one reports by saying, "It's round." One uses the same word for both properties only because they are always found together; more exactly, experience shows that when one is having both visual and tactile sensations of the same object, one perceives either both properties together or else perceives neither. Nevertheless, when we stop to think about it, when we turn our gaze inward, as it were, and carefully examine our sensations, we see that these two properties in no way resemble each other. Therefore, there is, strictly speaking, no such property as roundness. There are only the *two* properties "visual roundness" and "tactile roundness." And each of these two properties, considered by itself, is obviously something that cannot exist apart from the mind. The fact that visual "roundness" exists independently of touch and the fact that tactile "roundness" exists independently of vision conspire to produce the illusion that there is *one* property called 'roundness' that exists independently of both touch and vision. And this point may be generalized. Each of our words for a shape ('triangular', 'cubical', and so on) really stands for two properties, a visual property and a tactile property. This fact misleads us into thinking that shapes are a kind of thing that can exist independently of the mind.

If, therefore, there were a "real" snowball, a thing that existed independently of the mind, it could not have a color or a shape or any tactile property. Nor, says Berkeley, could it have properties that in any way *resembled* roundness or hardness or whiteness or coldness, for "nothing but an idea can resemble another idea"—that is, a thing that exists in the mind (which is where hardness, whiteness, coldness, and both kinds of roundness exist) can resemble only other things that exist in the mind. The nature of a mind-independent thing, what it was *like*, would therefore be completely unknowable to us.

And not only could we have no idea of what such things were like, but we could have no reason to believe they existed. After all, there is no way for us to "get behind" our sensations and observe the (by definition) unobservable things that are supposedly causing them. It is true that we can sometimes infer the existence of things we cannot observe from the features of things we can observe. Robinson Crusoe, for example, can infer the existence of a person he cannot see from a footprint he finds in the sand. But this is possible only because we sometimes do observe people and we sometimes observe them leaving footprints. The hypothetical external things that cause our sensations, however, are things that we in principle cannot observe, and whatever properties they have are properties that correspond to nothing in our experience. Berkeley concludes that if the objects we think about and talk about in everyday life (snowballs, chairs, trees, and so on) were really mind-independent objects, then we should have to be thoroughgoing skeptics about them: we should have to admit that we had no reason to believe that they existed and that we could say nothing about what they might be like if they did exist. The wages of belief in a external world is skepticism.

If Berkeley had said nothing but what we have so far represented him as saying, there would be a very obvious objection to his argument: He has told us nothing about where our sensations come from. And, because our sensations come to us in coherent order, this is a question that requires some sort of answer. If I am carried blindfolded to a certain spot, and my blindfold is then removed and I see a rose garden, what is the cause of the visual sensations (the colors and shapes) I then experience? Could they somehow come from within me? Am I their *source?* The solipsist (see note 4) thinks this, but Berkeley denies it, and it does seem rather implausible. In dreams I experience colors and shapes, and for all I know these colors and shapes arise from some source inside myself. But dreams are fragmentary and incoherent and vague, whereas the series of experiences I have as I observe the rose garden, and perhaps not only see stationary rose bushes but also watch gardeners and rose fanciers and dogs going about their lawful occasions, are integrated and coherent and sharp. Nothing could be more unlike a dream. When I think about it, it seems inconceivable to me that I have within myself the resources to fabricate (without any awareness that that is what I am doing) this very undreamlike series of experiences. And if I consider the whole body of my experiences, from the earliest time I can remember to the present, it seems, if possible, even more inconceivable that I am their author.

Very well then, the solipsists are wrong. My sensations—my experiences of colors and shapes and textures and sounds and tastes and smells—come from a source outside myself. What is this source? The Common Western Metaphysic has an answer to this question. Their source is the external world, the world of mind-independent physical objects like rose bushes and dogs and (the bodies of) gardeners and rose-fanciers. (The postulation of an external world also explains why it is that the sensations of two people can be coordinated in such a way that communication about what they are observing is possible: they are observing the same objects from different perspectives.) But what is Berkeley's answer?

Since Berkeley admits the existence of nothing but minds and their modifications, it is clear that he must say that the cause of my experiences lies within some mind, or minds, besides my own. And this is just what he does say: the cause of my experiences is God. God, like you and me, is a mind—the Supreme Mind. Since He is the source of all being, He has created everything besides Himself and at every moment holds everything besides Himself in existence—"everything besides Himself" being just all the minds besides Himself, since minds and their modifications are the only things that exist. As a part of His general activity of creating other minds and holding them in existence from moment to moment, God supplies them with modifications and, in particular, with sensations. Moreover, He *coordinates* the series of sensations that come to different minds. If you and I are standing side by side and together enjoying the view of a rose garden and talking about the roses, the visual sensations that the two of us have will be very similar but, owing to our slightly different perspectives, not quite the same. And they will not only be similar, but similar in a very precise way. They will "fit together," as we might say, like adjacent pieces of jigsaw puzzle. If this were not so, the fact would very quickly become evident to us. ("What do you mean, 'That's an interesting variety'? There are no roses there. You're pointing at a trash bin.")

According to Berkeley, this is just how God creates rose gardens: by precisely coordinating the series of sensations that come to certain minds, the ones that we call observers of rose gardens. More generally, this is how God creates what Berkeley in a famous phrase calls "all the furniture of earth" (i.e., all of the things that are usually called physical objects; in Berkeley's day the word 'furniture' was not yet tied down to domestic movables). He carefully coordinates the sensations that come to all human minds in such a way that a common world is available to these minds.

Berkeley would stoutly deny the charge that his theory represents God as creating the *illusion* of a world of snowballs and rose bushes and trash bins. No, says Berkeley, in causing sensations of roundness and hardness and whiteness and coldness to be present in a carefully coordinated way in the minds of various people, God thereby causes a round, hard, white, cold thing really to exist—the coordinated presence of roundness, hardness, whiteness, and coldness in various minds is what it *is* for a round, hard, white, cold thing really to exist[5]—and, therefore, those of us who report the presence of a round, hard, white, cold thing when God puts certain sensations into our minds are under no illusion.

There is a further role that the activity of God plays in Berkeley's metaphysic. This activity makes the existence of unobserved objects possible—or,

rather, makes possible the existence of objects unobserved by any human being, for nothing is unobserved by God. This role for the activity of God has
been celebrated in two well-known limericks:

> There was once a man who said, "God
> Must think it exceedingly odd
> If he finds that this tree
> Continues to be
> When there's no one about in the Quad."

> Dear Sir,

> Your astonishment's odd:
> *I* am always about in the Quad.
> And that's why the tree
> Will continue to be,
> Since observed by

> Yours faithfully,
> God.[6]

There does not seem to be any other way for an idealist to account for the
order in which our sensations come to us than to follow Berkeley's lead and
ascribe this order to the activity of God. A person who accepts the existence of
an external world can (at least as far as anything we have said so far goes) be a
theist or an atheist or an agnostic. But someone who rejects the existence of the
external world has no real option but belief in a Supreme Mind. (It is worth
noting that Berkeley gave the following subtitle to his *Principles of Human
Knowledge:* "An Antidote Against Scepticism and Atheism.") It is better to say
"a Supreme Mind" in this context than "God," because the mind that idealism
requires in order to account for the order of our sensations need not have all of
the attributes that have traditionally been ascribed to God.[7] But let us continue
to use the word 'God' for the Supreme Mind, and let us call the thesis that
there is a Supreme Mind 'theism'.

It will be convenient at this point to introduce some additional terminology. Let us call the doctrine that there exists an external world 'externalism'.
(Externalism, as we have seen, is an important component of the Common
Western Metaphysic.) And let us call the doctrine that the external world is the
cause of the order in which our sensations come to us 'realism'. Is realism or
idealism the more reasonable thesis? It might be argued that realism is the
more reasonable since idealism requires those who accept it also to accept a
very strong and far-reaching thesis (theism) while realism requires only that
those who accept it also accept the relatively weak thesis of externalism.

The general principle that this argument appeals to is sound enough. (It is
called Occam's Razor, in honor of the medieval philosopher William of
Ockham, who is usually credited with having first explicitly formulated it.)
Suppose, for example, that there are two theories about a certain murder that
account equally well for the evidence that the police have collected. One theory is that the murder was the work of a robber who was surprised by the vic-

tim in the act of committing a robbery. The other is that the murder was the work of a vast (and hitherto completely unknown) international conspiracy. Clearly the former theory is preferable to the latter, and it is preferable just because it accounts for the available evidence on the basis of an assumption that is much weaker than the assumption that the latter theory requires. Given the premise that externalism is a weaker assumption than theism, we should accept realism and reject idealism. But is this premise in fact true?

The idealist (if we may judge from Berkeley's conduct of the idealist's case) will reject this premise and argue as follows.

> We already know that there exist minds. We know from our own case what minds are like, since each of us *is* a mind. Theism requires only that we postulate an additional mind, an additional thing of a sort that we already understand. Externalism, on the other hand, requires us to postulate the existence of something that bears no relation to anything in our experience: we must postulate a whole world of "some things we know not what." For, as we have seen, this hypothetical "external world" is not only composed of things having properties that we can form no conception of, but of things whose properties can in no way resemble any property that we can conceive of. God may be vastly, even infinitely, greater than ourselves, and our understanding of Him may fall far short of His reality, but at least the fact that He is a mind like ourselves allows our understanding to get some sort of foothold in His nature. The so-called external world, however, if it existed, would provide us no such foothold. It would be *entirely* mysterious and unknowable to us. To assume the existence of an entity that is in this sense entirely mysterious and unknowable to us is certainly to make a very strong assumption, stronger than the assumption of the existence of something of the same sort as ourselves, even if that thing is infinitely greater than ourselves. (And let us not forget that many who believe in an external world assert that the external world is infinite—and hence, presumably, is infinitely greater than ourselves.)

This reply rests on Berkeley's analysis of what it would be for there to be an external world, and it is plausible to just the degree that that analysis is plausible. Up to this point, our presentation of Berkeley's metaphysic has been sympathetic and uncritical. It is time to raise the question of what can be said against Berkeley's analysis of what it would be for there to be an external world.

Berkeley's analysis of what it would be for there to be an external world is determined by his analysis of the nature of what he calls the furniture of earth; if the nature of the furniture of earth is what he says it is, then his analysis of the external world follows almost automatically: the external world is a hypothetical "something" in addition to the furniture of earth. Let us devise a less poetical and more descriptive name for the furniture of earth: we shall call the items it comprises 'objects of our common perception and discourse'—or 'common objects', for short. This phrase is meant to call attention to the following feature of certain objects: more than one human being can perceive them (unlike, say, the pain in my shoulder or the colors and shapes that I am aware of in immediate conscious experience, which I alone can perceive), and they are the objects that we talk about to one another and call one another's attention to as we conduct the ordinary business of life.[8]

We have already given many examples of such objects: the sun, the Taj Mahal, trees, chairs, rosebushes, dogs.... Both the idealist and the realist believe in common objects; idealists and realists differ about the *nature* of common objects, about what they *are*. In this respect, they may be compared with two travelers who are arguing about whether the dark mass on the horizon is a mountain range or a bank of clouds; each can perceive the dark mass, and each can refer to it and speak of it to the other. (Although the two travelers have very different opinions about its nature, there is nevertheless *one thing* that they are arguing about. It is not as if one of them were saying of one thing that it was a mountain range and the other were saying of something else that it was a cloud bank.) If Berkeley and his fellow idealists are right about the nature of common objects, the external world (the world of non-mental objects) is "something, we know not what" in addition to the totality of common objects. If, however, the realists are right about the nature of common objects, the external world (the world of non-mental objects) just *is* the totality of common objects.

I venture to suggest that Berkeley's analysis of the nature of common objects is based on two very doubtful assumptions. It will be easier to state these assumptions if we first define the notion of a sensible property of a common object. By sensible properties of common objects we mean those properties of common objects, or of the stuffs they are made of, that are closely related to sensation. A property is a sensible property of a common object if one can tell, without making use of any special knowledge, whether something possesses that property by looking at the object or touching it or listening to it or smelling it or tasting it. (Someone might be able to tell by its taste that a certain mixture contained quinine. But this ability would require special knowledge: knowledge of how quinine tastes.) Thus, roundness and hardness and whiteness and coldness are sensible properties, but electrical conductivity and chemical valence are not. The two assumptions are

1. A common object is nothing more than (or nothing apart from) its sensible properties.
2. The sensible properties of common objects are the same things as the sensations we have when we see or touch (or hear or taste or smell) common objects.

As to the first assumption, what does the statement that a common object is nothing more than its sensible properties mean? One question that this statement immediately suggests is this: What about the *non-sensible* properties of common objects? What about properties like electrical conductivity, whose presence in an object cannot be detected by looking at or touching or listening to or tasting or smelling the object? Common objects *have* non-sensible properties, don't they? And if they do, then it can hardly be said that the sensible properties of an object exhaust the being of that object. How then can the idealist say that a common object is nothing apart from its sensible properties? Idealists have, for the most part, been aware of the seriousness of this question and have given some very interesting answers to it. Let us, however, ignore this question, which raises some very difficult and technical philosophical problems, and let us pretend that common objects have only sensible properties. We assume, for example, that a snowball has only such properties as roundness, hardness, whiteness, and coldness.

What, then, is meant by saying that the snowball is "nothing more than," or "nothing apart from," roundness, hardness, whiteness, and coldness? It is certainly possible for roundness, hardness, whiteness, and coldness to exist without the snowball's existing. But then what is it for a snowball to exist? What is it for there to be a round, hard, white, cold thing? Berkeley, as we have seen, has an answer to this question: it is for these properties to be coordinated in a certain way in various minds. The Common Western Metaphysic also has an answer: it is for there to be a thing that is not itself a property but *has* the properties roundness, hardness, whiteness, and coldness. This, says the proponent of the Common Western Metaphysic, is a trivial statement, one that wouldn't be worth making if it were not for the fact that idealists like Berkeley deny it. The statement is trivial because it is in the very nature of properties (or features, characteristics, qualities, or attributes) to be *had*. A property just is something that can be had by, or be possessed by, or belong to something. Berkeley and the other idealists like to try to give the impression that if a snowball were a non-property that had the properties of roundness, hardness, whiteness, and coldness, then it would be a wholly mysterious thing—a thing that we should be unable to describe. But this is a piece of misdirection. We can easily describe it: it is round, hard, white, and cold. We have already said that it has these properties, and what is it to describe a thing but to say what properties the thing has? Again this is trivial. It would not be worth saying if the idealists had not denied it.

One argument that is sometimes used against this position goes as follows. "As your question implies, to describe a thing is to say what properties it has. It follows that to give a *complete* description of a thing is simply to give a *complete* list of its properties. Therefore, once you have listed all of the properties of a thing, you have said everything there is to say about it. And, therefore, there can't be anything more to a thing than its properties."

This is mere playing with words. If we assume for the sake of the illustration that 'roundness, hardness, whiteness, and coldness' is a complete list of the properties of the snowball, it does not follow from this assumption that 'roundness, hardness, whiteness, and coldness' is a complete description of the snowball. All that follows is that 'a *thing* that has the properties roundness, hardness, whiteness, and coldness' is a complete description of the snowball. The slogan, 'to give a complete description of a thing is simply to give a complete list of its properties', is true only if it is understood in the following sense: to give a complete description of a thing is to follow the phrase 'a thing that has the properties' with a complete list of the properties of the thing.

"Ah," replies Berkeley, the spokesman for the idealists, "but you are forgetting the arguments I gave to show that sensible properties of common objects—properties like roundness, hardness, whiteness, and coldness—can exist only in the mind. If these properties exist only in the mind, then how can a *non*-mental thing, which is what you say the snowball is, *have* them? Do you really want to say that a thing that is supposed to be wholly independent of the mind can be such that all of its properties exist wholly within the mind?" This reply brings us to the second of Berkeley's assumptions.

Suppose that I look at a blank sheet of white paper. When I do this, I have a certain sensation—a sensation of whiteness. And the paper, everyone agrees, is white, or has the property of whiteness. The word 'whiteness' occurs both in my description of my sensation and in my description of the piece of paper. It seems, therefore, to designate something that is both a property of the paper and is present in my mind. That it does designate something that has both these features is the burden of Berkeley's second assumption.

But is this right? Isn't it far more plausible to suppose that the word 'whiteness' designates two different things when we are talking about my sensation and when we are talking about the piece of paper? When we use the words 'white' and 'whiteness' to talk about sensations, we are talking about something that can exist only as a part of some person's conscious experience. When we use these words to talk about a piece of paper, however, we are using them to talk about a feature of the piece of paper, a feature of the paper that it would have even if it were locked up in a dark room. (Suppose you were to ask me whether there was any white paper in the storeroom and I were to reply, "No, of course not. The lights are off in the storeroom, and the door is shut." This would be rather a strange reply to your question, would it not?) The feature or property of the paper that we call 'whiteness' does not vanish from the paper when no one is experiencing the paper; the paper can lose this feature only if it is dyed or undergoes some other treatment of the kind that we—of course—describe as "changing the paper's color."

This is not to say there are two unrelated things that we just happen to use the same word for, as is the case with the "bank" of a river and the "bank" where you deposit your savings. Here is an analogy that may help. We may say both that Jane is "healthy" and that her diet is "healthy." Obviously, we who say this are using the word 'healthy' to designate two different things: one of them is a feature of some but not all human beings, and the other is a feature of some but not all patterns of eating and drinking. Nevertheless, it is not a mere accident of the English language that we use the same word in both cases, as it is with the two uses of 'bank': a healthy diet is a diet that is conducive to health in a person who follows that diet. The two things that are designated by the word 'whiteness' are connected in a similar way. A person experiences sensations of whiteness when that person looks at an object that has the property whiteness—at least if the person's eyes, optic nerve, and brain are in good working order and if the object is being viewed under normal conditions (someone who looks at a white piece of paper that has been placed under an intense green spotlight will experience sensations of greenness, not whiteness).

The idealist is likely to argue at this point that this supposed "whiteness" that belongs to external objects is a property that lies wholly outside our experience and is therefore a property that we can form no conception of. But it is hard to see what these words could mean—unless it is that the property is not a sensation, which is exactly the position that we are putting forward. We do experience the property whiteness, or at least we experience objects that have it, and experience them *as* having it. We experience the property whiteness *by* having sensations of whiteness (provided that these sensations are caused by the presence of a white object and are caused in the normal way). We could say that these sensations represent to us the presence of an object that has the property. And we can easily form a conception of this property: it is the property of common objects that (in appropriate circumstances) causes observers of the objects to experience sensations of whiteness.

The thesis that our sensations of "whiteness" and the "whiteness" that is a property of common objects are not the same can be strengthened if we imagine a race of beings who have different sensations from ours when they perceive the common objects that we perceive. Let us look at an example of this. In order to make the example as simple as possible, let us pretend that we perceive the world of common objects in black and white. It is easy to imagine a pair of spectacles that reverses black and white: when you put them on, the world (which had looked like a black-and-white photograph) looks like a photographic negative. Imagine that Alfred is wearing a pair of these spectacles. Now imagine that something that is a living part of Alfred has the same effect on the rest of Alfred's perceptual apparatus as the spectacles. Now imagine a whole race of "Alfreds," the Alfredians, a race of people who, as a natural feature of their species, have the kind of perceptual apparatus that we have imagined Alfred to have. It seems fairly obvious that we should say that the Alfredians see black where we see white and see white where we see black: when they look at a photograph, they have sensations like those we have when we look at the negative from which that photograph was made.

Now consider this question: Do the Alfredians *misperceive* the world of common objects? Do we human beings see the world as it is, while the poor Alfredians see it as it isn't? We should note that if a human being, Alice, and an Alfredian, Ecila, were exchanged in their cradles, no one would notice a thing. Ecila, raised by human English-speakers, would be taught to apply the word 'black' to charcoal and 'white' to salt, and no one would ever know that her sensations of black and white were our sensations of white and black—for she would apply the words 'white' and 'black' just as the rest of us do. And, of course, the same thing would be true of Alice among the Alfredians, but in reverse, as it were. It seems obvious enough that the Alfredians do not misperceive the world. Their sensations are, so to speak, just as good as ours, just as suitable for representing the whiteness (and blackness) of common objects. And, therefore, our sensations of whiteness and the property whiteness of common objects cannot be the same thing.[9]

I must warn the reader that the argument of the preceding several paragraphs depends on a picture of the perception of the colors of common objects that embodies two simplifying assumptions, one of which is questionable and the other of which is almost certainly false. The questionable assumption is that when two members of our species look at the same common object under the same conditions they will have the same sensations of color. The assumption that is almost certainly false is that there is just *one* property of common objects that produces a given color sensation—that when I look at the object x under appropriate conditions and experience, say, greenness, and when I look at the object y under the same conditions and experience greenness, the property of x that causes my sensation of greenness is the property of y that causes my sensation of greenness. But neither of these assumptions is really necessary to the argument of the preceding paragraphs; it's just that without these assumptions the statements made in the course of the presentation of the argument would have required so many qualifications that the argument would have been hard to follow. The important point to note is that it is at least a tenable position that we need not accept Berkeley's identification of the sensible properties of common objects with the sensations we have when we experience common objects.

Does this mean that we have refuted Berkeley's metaphysic? By no means. If Berkeley were in a position to read the above words, he would have a great deal to say in response to them.

Consider, for example, our argument that the concept of a property is the concept of something that can be had or possessed by a "thing," a non-property, and that, as a consequence, it cannot be that there is nothing more "to" a common object than its properties. Berkeley has a well-worked-out theory about how we acquire our concepts, and he would argue, on the basis of this theory, that we could not possibly have any concept that corresponds to the words 'a "thing" that is not a property but has or possesses properties'. And I should reply by arguing that his theory about how we acquire our concepts is false and unworkable. He would have a rejoinder to my reply. And so it would go.

Let us remember that it was not our object to try to refute Berkeley. Our object was rather to defend the Common Western Metaphysic and its allegiance to the reality of an external world against the criticisms of Berkeley and his fellow idealists. Whatever Berkeley may say, it seems clear that before we come to study metaphysics, we believe that there exist objects external to the mind. And this is not something that we just happen to believe. We believe this because it *seems* to us to be true. Our visual and tactile sensations are not mere colored shapes and feelings of pressure, like those we experience if we press hard with our fingers on our eyeballs. Rather, they seem to "tell" us about a world of non-mental objects. Seeming, of course, does not imply truth. After all, the earth *seems* to be at the center of the universe, and the heavens *seem* to revolve about it. If we were indeed being deceived by Descartes's evil genius, then this seeming would be mere seeming. It would, nevertheless, be seeming. If it were not, then what the evil genius was doing would not be deception. If our sensations did not "tell" us that there was a world of external objects, they would not tell us that falsely and there would be no deception. Let us recall something we said in our discussion of Monism:

It is obvious that human beings do not have any infallible way of knowing the truth. The best we can do is to believe what seems to us to be true unless we have some good reason to reject it. What, after all, is the alternative? To believe what does not even *seem* to be true when we know of *no* good reason to accept it? Or even to believe what seems to be *false* when we know of no good reason to accept it?

I suggest that idealism does not seem to us to be true and that, in fact, idealism seems to us to be false. And I suggest that our critique of Berkeley's two assumptions is strong enough to show that Berkeley has not presented any good reason to accept idealism. If this is correct then the best course is for us to accept realism—that is, unless we wish to be skeptics and say that the resources of the human mind for investigating the questions raised by the realism-idealism debate are wholly inadequate and that we should therefore conclude that we cannot say whether realism or idealism is the true metaphysic. At any rate it seems clear that we should not be idealists. (Of course, it may well be that the idealists have a better case than the one I have attributed to them. Students of metaphysics are hereby encouraged to investigate this possibility for themselves.)

Suggestions for Further Reading

The best introduction to Berkeley's philosophy is his *Three Dialogues between Hylas and Philonous* (1713). The R. M. Adams edition is recommended. For an excellent exposition of Berkeley's philosophy, and valuable commentary and criticism, see the relevant section of Bennett's *Locke, Berkeley, Hume: Central Themes.*

4

Objectivity

ONE IMPORTANT COMPONENT of the Common Western Metaphysic is the thesis that there is such a thing as objective truth. This thesis itself has two components. First, our beliefs and our assertions are either true or false; each of our beliefs and assertions represents the World as being a certain way, and the belief or assertion is true if the World is that way, and false if the World is not that way. It is, as one might put it, up to our beliefs and assertions to get the World right; if they don't, they're not doing their job, and that's their fault and no fault of the World's. Our beliefs and assertions are thus related to the World as a map is related to the territory: it is up to the map to get the territory right, and if the map doesn't get the territory right, that's the fault of the map and no fault of the territory.

The second component of the thesis that there is such a thing as objective truth is this: the World exists and has the features it does in large part independently of our beliefs and our assertions. (I say 'in large part' because our beliefs and assertions are themselves parts—very minor parts, it would seem—of the World. And, of course, our beliefs and assertions may *affect* other parts of the World, as when my false belief that the traffic light is green causes an accident. But even the totality of all of the parts of the physical universe affected by the beliefs and assertions of all human beings would seem to be a very small part of the universe: if we learn nothing else from astronomy and geology, we learn that the physical universe as a whole would be pretty much the way it is if there had never been any human beings.) The truth or falsity of our beliefs and assertions is therefore "objective" in the sense that truth and falsity are conferred on those beliefs and assertions by their objects, by the things they are *about*.

And how do the objects of our beliefs and assertions confer truth on them? The idea that the objects of our beliefs and assertions have this power may seem mysterious if we think about it in the abstract, but the mystery vanishes if we look at one or two concrete examples. If I assert that Albany is the capital of New York State, then what I have asserted is true if and only if Albany *is* the capital of New York State and is false if and only if Albany *is not* the capital of New York State. If Berkeley believes that nothing exists independently of the mind, then what he believes is true if and only if nothing exists independently of the mind, and what he believes is false if and only if something exists independently of the mind. If two people, you and I, say, have the same belief about something—perhaps we both believe that Albany is the capital of New York State—then truth or falsity is conferred on our common belief by the features of that one object. Truth is therefore "one"; there is no such thing as a belief or assertion being "true for me" but "not true for you." If your friend Alfred responds to something you have said with the words, "That may be true for you, but it isn't true for me," his words can only be regarded as a rather misleading way of saying, "That may be what you think, but it's not what I think."

Before we go further, it will be necessary to clear up a possible confusion. Many fair-minded people seem to object to the notion of objective truth and falsity because they believe that it implies some sort of dogmatism. They seem to think that if Mary says that all of our beliefs and assertions are either objectively true or objectively false, then Mary must be setting herself up as an arbiter of that objective truth and falsity. "Who's to say what's true and what's false?" they ask. But Mary is not committed by her belief in the objectivity of truth and falsity to the claim that she is in a position to lay down the law about what's true and what's false. Indeed, she is not committed to the thesis that *anyone* is in the position to lay down the law about what's true and what's false. She is committed only to the thesis that truth and falsity exist and are (in general) conferred on beliefs and assertions independently of what is going on in the minds of the people who have those beliefs and make those assertions. One example should suffice to make this clear. Consider the question whether there is intelligent life on other planets. "Who's to say whether there's intelligent life on other planets?" Who, indeed? In my view, no human being at this point in history is in a position to lay down the law on this question. But saying that is perfectly consistent with saying that either there is intelligent life on other planets or there isn't and that the statement that there is intelligent life on other planets is made true (if it is true) or made false (if it is false) by objective facts about the way things are on distant planets.

The thesis that each of our beliefs and assertions is either true or false, if it is to be at all plausible, requires two qualifications, qualifications that most adherents of the Common Western Metaphysic will be willing to make. The first is that it may well be that some of our utterances are meaningless, although they do not seem to us to be meaningless when we make them—otherwise, we should no doubt not make them. (We have seen, for example, that the logical positivists held that all metaphysical utterances were meaningless. But they did not hold that metaphysical utterances seemed to the metaphysicians who made them to be meaningless.) In the works of the nineteenth-century American Absolute Idealist Josiah Royce, there occurs the following sentence: 'The world is a progressively self-realizing community of interpretation.' Perhaps these words mean nothing at all—perhaps, as we say, they are "just words"—despite the fact that many people have thought that they meant something true and important. If this sentence is indeed meaningless, then the thesis that each of our beliefs and assertions is either true or false does not, properly understood, mean that someone who utters this sentence says something that is either true or false, for that person says nothing at all.

The second qualification that is needed has to do with vagueness. Many, perhaps almost all, of the words that we use in everyday life are vague. That is, there will be possible—and usually actual—cases in which it is not clear whether a certain word can be correctly applied. For example, if a man is 181.5 centimeters (5 feet 11-1/2 inches) tall, there is perhaps no definite answer to the question whether he is "tall." The word 'tall' is therefore vague, and the statement that Alfred (who is 181.5 centimeters tall) is tall cannot be said to be either true or false. The thesis that each of our beliefs and assertions is either true or false therefore requires this qualification: because some of the words and phrases that we use in making our assertions or formulating our beliefs are vague, there will sometimes be no definite yes-or-no answer to the question whether these words and phrases apply to the things we are talking about. As a consequence, some of our beliefs and assertions will be neither true nor false. Let us call these beliefs and assertions *indeterminate*. Believers in objective truth and falsity do not deny the existence of indeterminate beliefs and assertions. They simply insist that the status "indeterminate" is as much an objective status of certain beliefs and assertions as "truth" and "falsity" are of certain others. If, for example, Alfred's hero-worshiping ten-year-old brother believes that Alfred is tall, facts that exist independently of the boy's mind confer the status "indeterminate" on his belief. In the remainder of this chapter, I will simplify the discussion by ignoring the status "indeterminate"; I will talk as if the thesis of the objectivity of truth implied that every belief and assertion was either true or false. That is, I will ignore the existence of vagueness, which is not really germane to the questions we shall be considering.

Before leaving the topic of vagueness and what it implies about truth and falsity, however, I want to make just one more point. The fact that our language contains vague words and phrases does not entail that a given assertion (or belief) cannot be true or false unless it can be made (or formulated) without the use of vague terms. If that were so, few if any of our assertions or beliefs would be either true or false, owing to the fact that all or most of the terms that we use in our daily speech are vague. Most of the assertions that we make using vague terms manage to be either true or false, owing to the fact that for just about any vague term there are perfectly clear cases of things that that term applies to, and people do not normally use a term if they are in any doubt about whether that term applies to whatever they are talking about. While there are certainly cases of people who cannot be clearly said to be "tall" and cannot be clearly said to be "not tall," there are also many cases in which the term clearly applies or clearly does not apply—for example, men who are 200 centimeters tall, or men who are 150 centimeters tall. Thus, anyone who says that Bertram (who is 200 centimeters [6 feet 7 inches] tall) is tall says something true, and anyone who says that Charles (who is 150 centimeters [4 feet 11 inches] tall) is tall says something false.

With these two qualifications of the thesis that each of our assertions and beliefs is either true or false in mind, let us return to our discussion of the question of objective truth.

The most interesting thing about objective truth is that there are people who deny that it exists. One might wonder how anyone could deny that there is such a thing as objective truth. At least I might. In fact, I often have. For some people, I am fairly sure, the explanation is something like this. They are deeply hostile to the thought of anything that in any sense stands in judgment over them. The idea toward which they are most hostile is, of course, the idea of there being a God. But they are almost as hostile to the idea of there being an objective universe that doesn't care what they think and could make their most cherished beliefs false without even consulting them. (But this cannot be the whole story, since there are people who deny that objective truth exists and who also believe in God. What motivates these people is a *complete* mystery to me.) Let the reader be warned. It must be evident that I am unable to enter into the smallest degree of imaginative sympathy with those who deny that there is such a thing as objective truth. I am therefore probably not a reliable guide to their views. Perhaps, indeed, I do not understand these views. I would prefer to believe this. I would prefer to believe that no one actually believes what, on the surface, at least, it very much looks as if some people believe.

Philosophers who deny the existence of objective truth are today usually called "anti-realists"—in opposition, of course, to "realists," who affirm the existence of objective truth. This is confusing, because, in our discussion of the external world, we have opposed realism to *idealism,* to the thesis that everything that exists is a mind or a modification of a mind. (And it was no arbitrary decision on my part to use the term 'realism' this way. In opposing "realism" to idealism, I was following customary usage.) It could be argued that it is not entirely misleading to use the word 'realism' both for the thesis that is opposed to idealism and for the thesis that is opposed to "anti-realism." Is not idealism essentially the thesis that there is no mind-independent world "out there" for our sensations to be correct or incorrect representations of? And is not anti-realism the thesis that there is no mind-independent world "out there" for our assertions to be true or false statements about? Since the two theses are both rejections of a mind-independent world, is it so very misleading to oppose both of them to "realism," the thesis that there is a so-called real—that is, mind-independent—world?

This plausible-sounding argument depends on confusing two different senses of 'mind-independent'. The idealist who says that nothing is independent of the mind means that the nature of everything there is is mental: everything is either a mind or a modification of a mind or a collection of modifications of various minds. Nevertheless, according to the idealist, the general nature of reality, the way the World is, *how things are,* is something that does not depend on the mind. (Not even on the mind of God, although, of course, vast ranges of particular fact depend on His decisions—just as much smaller ranges of particular fact depend on your decisions and mine.) The anti-realist who says that nothing is independent of the mind, however, really does mean something very much like this: the collective activity of all minds is somehow determinative of the general nature of reality. What exactly the anti-realist does mean is a question we shall have to turn to in a moment. For the present, we must simply note that although the idealist and the anti-realist may both use the words 'nothing is independent of the mind', they mean something very different by these words. It is therefore misleading to oppose "realism" to both idealism and anti-realism.

Let us respect both the traditional opposition of realism and idealism and the current tendency to use 'realism' for the thesis that there is an objective truth; we can carry out this resolution by the simple expedient of retaining the traditional opposition of 'realism' and 'idealism' and calling the thesis that there is an objective truth 'Realism' with a capital R. (The thesis that there is no objective truth, or that the way the World is is mind-dependent, will, of course, be called anti-Realism.)

What, then, *is* the thesis of anti-Realism? I confess that I have had a very hard time finding a statement of this thesis that I can understand. I find, in fact, that I am much better at understanding examples of how particular "truths" or "facts" that would be supposed by most people to be independent of the mind are in fact (according to the anti-Realists) mind-dependent than I am at understanding formulations of anti-Realism as a general doctrine. Let us look at an example of such a particular truth and see what light it can give us. Here is an example of a fact that most people would say was in no way dependent upon the existence of the human mind or any activity of or fact about the human mind:

Mount Everest is 8,847.7 meters high.

Let us call this fact 'F'. F would seem to be a pretty good example of a fact that most people would take to be in any reasonable sense independent of human mental activity. The reasons that underlie this conviction might be articulated and presented in the form of an argument in the following way. This argument, while it may appeal to some scientific facts that not everyone is familiar with (and some people will reject the assumption it contains that human beings are the product of an evolutionary process), can certainly be said—scientific details aside—to represent the metaphysical point of view of the ordinary person:

The forces that cause mountains to rise have never been in the smallest degree influenced by the evolutionary processes that produced human beings. If no human beings had ever evolved, and if no other intelligent beings inhabited the earth, the vast, slow collision of the Indian subcontinent with the continent of Asia, which is what caused (and is still causing) the rise of the Himalayan Mountains, would have occurred in exactly the fashion that it did. And, as a consequence, if there had never been any intelligent beings on the earth, Mount Everest would, despite the absence of intelligence from the terrestrial scene, have exactly the size and shape it has in fact. If you think about it, this conclusion is presupposed by most explanations that geologists give of the present-day features of the earth, for these explanations presuppose that the processes that shaped these features had been going on for unimaginably long periods during which there were no intelligent beings to observe them or to think about them. Now since Mount Everest would be of exactly the size and shape it actually is even if there had never been any minds, it is obvious that the fact F is entirely independent of all human mental activity. If there were no beings with minds, there would be no one to observe or grasp or be aware of this fact, but the fact would still *be there.*

This argument, it will be noted, presupposes that common objects can exist independently of the mind and therefore presupposes the falsity of idealism, and the idealists, as we have said, are no friends of anti-Realism. Still, we have found reason to reject idealism, and there seems to be no reason to restrict ourselves to the use of arguments that would be acceptable to idealists. (I am tempted to say: Let the idealists find their own arguments against anti-Realism.) There is, however, one argument that Berkeley has used against this kind of reasoning, an argument that an anti-Realist might want to appropriate, and we had better take a moment to examine it. It is this: it is impossible to imagine geological processes—or anything else—going on independently of the mind, for if you try, you will find that you have to imagine *yourself* (or at least *someone*) present and watching the processes take place; therefore, you do not succeed in your attempt to imagine the processes in question going on independently of the mind. (Most undergraduates will probably have heard the similar argument for the conclusion that it is impossible for one to imagine one's own funeral: one would have to imagine oneself there, watching what was going on, so one would not really be imagining oneself *dead*, so one would not really be imagining one's funeral.)

This argument is without force, however. Even if we grant the point that one cannot imagine, in the sense of "form a mental image of," an event that no one is observing, the argument is without force. (But that point is very doubtful. Isn't it like saying that a painter can never paint a picture of someone who is alone, since any attempt to do so represents the figure in the painting as being observed by someone who is occupying a certain point of view—the point of view that the viewer of the painting is invited, in imagination, to share?) The above argument for the mind-independence of F does not require that those to whom the argument is addressed form a *mental image* of unobserved geological processes but only that they understand certain verbal descriptions of those processes.

What does the anti-Realist say about F? How can the anti-Realist continue to maintain that the way the World is is dependent on human mental activity in the face of the fact that the size and shape of Mount Everest were determined by geological processes that operated mostly before and always independently of the biological processes that produced intelligent life? The argument goes something like this:

Mountains and height are human social constructs. Let us first consider mountains. It is a human fiction, one that has gained currency because it serves certain social needs, that a certain portion of the earth's topography can be marked off and called a "mountain." What are the boundaries of Mount Everest? If you look at the place where these boundaries are supposed to be, you will not find any line on the surface of the earth; you will find only homogeneous rock. If you want to find out where Mount Everest begins and ends, you will discover that you have to apply to certain social institutions for your answer—the International Geographical Union or some such. And the answer you get will not be dictated by some "reality" that is independent of the activities of human beings. The International Geographical Union—or whoever is responsible for such decisions—might just as well ("just as well" as far as any mind-independent reality enters into the matter) have decided that a "mountain" began at the tree line, and they might have decided to call what we call the part of the mountain that is below the tree line the 'mountain base'. The fact that they made the decision they did about the boundaries of mountains and not some other decision has a social explanation, like any other social fact. Perhaps it is this: some people want to or have to climb mountains, and it serves their purposes to draw the boundaries around "mountains" at the place where the specifically human activity called climbing has to start. (Intelligent birds would not have that particular purpose; they might well draw the boundaries around "mountains" differently—if, indeed, they drew any such boundaries at all.) Mountains, therefore, are social constructs. So is height. You can't drop a weighted rope from the peak of Mount Everest to the ground and then measure the rope with a meter stick and call the result the height of Mount Everest. We therefore have to use a special instrument called a theodolite to measure the height of Mount Everest. But why do we call the figure that a certain procedure involving a theodolite gives us with respect to Mount Everest *and* the figure that measuring a weighted rope gives us with respect to a certain tower in each case the "height" of the thing in question? The answer is that we do this because we have found it socially useful to establish a convention to the effect that there is a single quality that is measured by these two very different procedures. Height is therefore a social construct. (It is true that if we used the theodolite to measure the "height" of the tower, it would give the same figure as the weighted rope. But that's not a reflection of some fact about an extra-social reality called height; it's rather a reflection of a certain social fact, namely the procedure we use for calibrating theodolites. If the theodolite did not give the same result as the weighted rope, we would recalibrate the theodolite.) Both mountains and height, therefore, are social constructs, and it follows that "facts" about the height of mountains are social facts. Facts about the height of mountains before there were any people (or facts about what the height of certain mountains would have been if there had never been any people) are no less social facts. They are simply facts about the way in which we apply social constructs retrospectively (or hypothetically). If we wanted, we could adopt quite different conventions about how to apply those constructs in discourse about the distant past.

We could adopt the convention that before, say, 1,000,000 B.C., everything was just one-half the size things were before that date according to our present system of conventions. We don't do this because it would make our geological and evolutionary and astronomical theories harder to state and harder to use. But ease of statement and use is a requirement that we impose on our theories because of our interests. If we were to meet Martians who did adopt such a convention because it satisfied *their* interests—aesthetic interests, perhaps, or interests that we couldn't understand at all—nothing but human chauvinism could lead us to say that they were wrong. Who are we to dictate their interests?

This is, or so I maintain, a fair sample of the way in which anti-Realists argue. (Their argument for the general thesis of anti-Realism would simply be an application of what has been said in this passage about the supposedly mind-independent fact F to all supposedly mind-independent facts.) If this is the extent of the anti-Realists' case, then I do not find it very impressive, for the reason that, in my opinion, it does not establish the mind-dependence of facts like F.

Let us first consider the case of Mount Everest. Let us grant for the sake of argument everything our imaginary anti-Realist has said about the social interests that are served by our drawing the boundaries around the things we call "mountains" the way we do. Let us grant that we might have drawn these boundaries differently if we had had different interests. Still, we *have* drawn these boundaries in a certain way, and—or so it would seem—in drawing them this way we have picked out certain objects as the objects designated by names like 'Mount Everest', 'Pikes Peak', 'the Matterhorn', and so on, and there are certain properties that *these* objects will turn out to have when we get round to examining them. They will turn out to have these properties because they already have them, for these properties belong to these objects independently of the human mind and human conventions and human interests and human social activities. If we had adopted different conventions about where to draw the boundaries of mountains, then 'Mount Everest', which in fact designates the object x, an object that is 8,847.7 meters high, would have designated some other object y, an object that presumably has some other height. But this is merely a fact about the names things have or might have had, and the height of a thing is not affected by what people call it or by whether they call it anything. No matter how we had chosen to use 'Mount Everest', the objects x and y would still be there, and x would still be 8,847.7 meters high, and the object y would still have whatever height it does have.

But doesn't this line of reasoning neglect the contention of the anti-Realists that properties like height, as well as physical objects like mountains, are "social constructs"? The same points apply to this contention. Height is a "social construct" only in the sense that it is a matter of social convention what property (if any) is assigned to the word 'height' as its meaning. (No doubt the fact that a certain property is chosen to be the meaning of some abstract noun like 'height' is best explained by the fact that it answers to some social interest to have a word whose meaning is that property. The Realist will concede this rather obvious thesis, which is in no way damaging to Realism.)

The social convention that assigns a particular property to the word 'height' is simply a social convention to the effect that the word 'height' is to be used as a name for what is measured by a certain set of procedures. The word 'height' might have been used as a name for what is measured by some different set of procedures. For example, what we call the 'height' of a mountain is measured in meters (or whatever) above sea level. Sea level was chosen as our benchmark because the system of measurement so established satisfies certain of our interests. Other benchmarks could have been used, however. If we had chosen to employ one of these other benchmarks, we might have had not only different *figures* for the heights of various mountains (perhaps 8,773.12 meters instead of 8,847.7 meters for the height of Mount Everest) but different answers to questions of the form 'Is Mount A or Mount B the higher mountain?'

But it does not follow that it is a matter of social convention what the height of Mount Everest is or whether Mount Alfred is higher than Mount Beatrice. All that follows is a fact about English usage: given the actual conventions for using the word 'height' (and related phrases like 'higher than'), the string of English words 'Mount Alfred is higher than Mount Beatrice' expresses a certain thesis x; if a certain different convention governed the usage of English-speakers, this string of English words would express the distinct thesis y. And it is consistent with these facts about the conventions that govern (or might have governed) English usage to suppose that x is true and y is false, the respective truth and falsity of these two theses being a thing that is not determined by our social conventions, since it depends only on the way in which masses of rock have been molded over the aeons by geological forces—forces that operate in serene indifference to social convention. Here is another way to express what is essentially the same point. Suppose we invent a word to designate the property that 'height' would have designated if we had adopted the other conventional benchmark we have been imagining. Let the word be 'schmeight'. (And we have the related verbal inventions 'schmigh' and 'schmigher than'.) Then all of the following statements may well be simultaneously true (*objectively* true):

- Mount Everest is 8,847.7 meters high.
- Mount Everest is 8,773.12 meters schmigh.
- Mount Alfred is higher than Mount Beatrice.
- Mount Beatrice is schmigher than Mount Alfred.

All that the impressive-sounding thesis that "height is a social construct" really comes to, therefore, is this: if we had adopted a certain different set of conventions for using the words 'height' and 'high', then the first sentence in the above list would mean what the second means, and the third sentence would mean what the fourth means. This harmless thesis—which is, of course, perfectly acceptable to the Realist—is not a premise from which anti-Realism can be deduced.

Not only does the "social construct" argument fail to establish any thesis that could reasonably be called anti-Realism, but our application of this argument to the case of the fact F (which certainly looks like a mind-independent fact) fails to provide us with any clue as to what thesis anti-Realism *is*. What the proponent of the "social construct" argument says about the fact F turns out to be, when it is properly understood, something that is perfectly consistent with Realism. And, therefore, anti-Realism cannot simply be a generalization to all facts of what the proponent of the "social construct" argument is represented above as saying about the fact F.

I am of the opinion that we can do more than simply show that a certain argument for anti-Realism fails to establish that thesis. (That, after all, is a very weak result, for there might be other arguments for anti-Realism.) We can present a very strong argument against anti-Realism. Now one might wonder how I could promise a strong argument against a thesis when, by my own testimony, I not really know what that thesis is. But nothing mysterious is being proposed. I do not fully understand anti-Realism, but I do understand some of the features that anti-Realism is supposed to have. The anti-Realists have ascribed various features to anti-Realism, and many of these features are clearly taken by the anti-Realists to be essential to anti-Realism: any thesis that did not have those features would not be anti-Realism. I shall argue that any thesis that combines these features must be incoherent.

In order to see this, let us consider some brief statement of anti-Realism. It will make no real difference what brief statement we choose or how well we understand it. Let us choose the following statement, which we shall call AR:

Objective truth and falsity do not exist.

Now let us enquire about the status of AR itself—according to AR. AR is a statement about all statements, and it is therefore a statement about itself. What does it say about itself? Well, just what it says about all other statements: that it is neither objectively true nor objectively false. And, of course, it follows from this that it is not objectively true. If it is not objectively true, if it is not true in virtue of corresponding to a reality that is independent of human mental activity, what is it—according to the anti-Realists? What status do they accord to it? No doubt the anti-Realists will say that they accord to it the same status that they accord to statements like '17 + 18 = 35' and 'Lions are carnivorous' and deny to statements like '14 ÷ 12 = 7' and 'Snails are aquatic mammals'. And what status is that? "Well," says the anti-Realist—at least many anti-Realists say something like this—"these statements fit in with our experience, and their denials go against our experience. For example, I have seen lions eating meat, I have never seen any eating vegetables, their teeth are obviously fitted for meat and not for vegetables, all the lion experts *say* that lions are carnivorous, and so on. You Realists admit that there is such a status as this. It's just the status that leads you to accept or believe certain statements. And you concede that there are statements that have this status and are nevertheless not what you call 'objectively true', since you concede that a misleading series of experiences could cause someone to accept, say, the statement that lions are herbivorous, which you regard as 'objectively false'. Well, we anti-Realists simply don't see the need for these two additional statuses that you call 'objectively true' and 'objectively false'. We are content with the statuses 'fits in with our experience' and 'goes against our experience'. To answer your question, it is the former of these two statuses that I assign to AR: it fits in with our experience."

But what does the anti-Realist mean by saying, "AR fits in with our experience"? What is this "fitting in"? The way AR fits in with our experience cannot be much like the way 'Lions are carnivorous' fits in with our experience. If one were to reject the latter statement and were to proceed on the assumption that lions were herbivorous, one might get eaten. This fact, and many others like it, provide a fairly robust sense in which the statement that lions are carnivorous "fits in with" our experience and in which its denial "goes against" our experience: if one does not accept this statement, and particularly if one accepts its denial, one may very well get into serious trouble, trouble that one's experiences will make it very clear to one that one is in. The same is true of highly theoretical scientific statements like 'Many of the important properties of water are due to hydrogen bonding' and 'Gravity is a function of the curvature of spacetime', although in the case of such statements, the "trouble" will typically reveal itself only in very special circumstances (just the circumstances that laboratories are designed to produce and astronomical observatories are designed to search out in the heavens). Mathematical statements, too, can be said to fit in with our experience in this sense; if we accept the wrong mathematical statements, our checks will bounce and our bridges will fall down.

But in what sense can a very abstract philosophical statement like AR be said to fit in with our experience? Suppose that Andrew is an anti-Realist and Rachel is a Realist. Are there any possible circumstances in which Rachel will get in trouble because she rejects AR and in which Andrew will avoid trouble because he accepts AR? It is absurd to suppose that Andrew is less likely than Rachel to be eaten by a lion or to propose a scientific theory that is refuted by experiment or to design a bridge that falls down. Andrew may say that he will produce better philosophical theories than Rachel will, but this statement would not seem to be consistent with his account of what is "good" about some statements and "bad" about others—theories are, after all, special kinds of statements—unless the qualities of his theories that make them "better" than Rachel's theories somehow reveal themselves to our experience. And this—making predictions about how our experiences will go—is just what philosophical theories, unlike scientific theories, notoriously do not do.

Or, at any rate, that is what philosophical theories notoriously do not do if by experience we mean sense-experience. Perhaps, however, the anti-Realist is thinking of experience in a broader sense than this. If there were some knockdown argument for AR, that fact might establish the anti-Realist's contention that this statement fits in with our experience, for one sort of experience we have is the experience of examining arguments and finding them compelling. Whether or not this would do the trick, however, it is not something that we have. There are, as we have observed, no knockdown arguments in philosophy. There are no philosophical arguments that all qualified philosophers regard as compelling.

If there were arguments for AR that seemed to the majority of the philosophical community definitely to outweigh all of the known arguments against AR, that fact might be enough to establish the anti-Realist's contention that AR fits in with our experience. But, again, whether or not this would do the trick, it is not something we have, for, as matters stand, this is not how things seem to the majority of the philosophical community.

It seems, therefore, that there is no clear sense in which AR can be said to "fit in with our experience." Suppose, then, that the anti-Realist were to give up on "us" and retreat to "me"; suppose that the anti-Realist were to say something like "The 'good' feature that I ascribe to statements like 'Lions are carnivorous' and AR and deny to others like 'Snails are aquatic mammals' and 'Objective truth and falsity exist' is just this: fitting in with *my* experience." Suppose our anti-Realist, Andrew, does say this. What can Rachel the Realist say in reply? Here is one possibility.

A. Objective truth and falsity do not exist.

R. If I understand your theory, when you make that statement you are claiming no more for it than that it fits in with your own experience. Well, you should know. Apparently, when you consider the arguments for AR, you find them convincing: you have that experience. I shouldn't dream of disputing your claim to find those arguments convincing. And you shouldn't dream of disputing *my* claim to have the experience of finding the arguments *against* AR compelling. So you can have no objection to my saying, as I do: Objective truth and falsity exist.

A. But that statement goes against my experience.

R. According to your theory, that would be a ground for objecting if *you* made the statement, "Objective truth and falsity exist." But why should you regard it as a ground for objecting when *I* make that statement?—unless you think I'm lying when I assure you that when I consider the philosophical arguments against AR I have the experience of finding them compelling. Whatever one may say against Realism, it at least makes disagreement intelligible: according to Realism, when two people disagree about a statement, one of them says it has the "good" feature *objective truth* and the other says that it lacks it. But, according to you, when you say "Objective truth and falsity do not exist" and I say "Objective truth and falsity exist," each of those statements has the only "good" feature whose existence you admit: each of them fits in with the experience of the person who made it. Or did you really mean that there is just one "good" feature that can belong to any statement, no matter who makes it—namely, fitting in with *your* experience? If you do mean that, I'm afraid that your theory isn't going to win many adherents beyond the one it already has.

Rachel, I believe, has an excellent point. If Andrew can find no "replacement" for truth but "fits in with my own, personal experience," then (assuming that Andrew isn't really proposing that everyone use "fits in with *Andrew's* experience" as a replacement for truth), he is proposing a theory according to which the philosopher who says "Objective truth and falsity exist" and the philosopher who says "Objective truth and falsity do not exist" are not in disagreement. And this is an absurd consequence. The avenue we have been exploring, therefore, the avenue opened by the suggestion that each individual person has a "private" substitute for truth, has turned out to be a dead end. Let us suppose, therefore, that anti-Realism must postulate a single substitute for truth, one that is the same for everyone.

In that case, however, it seems that anti-Realism is self-refuting: anti-Realism seems to tell us not to accept AR—that is, not to accept anti-Realism. The anti-Realists, if they are to make a convincing case for anti-Realism, must propose a substitute for objective truth; they must specify a feature that "good" statements like 'Lions are carnivorous' have and "bad" statements like 'Snails are aquatic mammals' lack. But they have conspicuously failed to find a substitute for truth that satisfies the following two conditions: (a) all of the uncontroversially "good" statements have it and all of the uncontroversially "bad" statements lack it and (b) anti-Realism has it.

In the preceding discussion, we considered one such substitute for truth: fitting in with our experiences and having a denial that goes against our experiences. Anti-Realists have offered other substitutes for truth than this, but I am convinced that my general criticism holds: it always seems that anti-Realism itself lacks the anti-Realist's proposed substitute for truth. (One famous—or notorious—anti-Realist has proposed the following substitute: a statement is one of the "good" ones if one's peers will let one get away with making it. Most of his peers have greeted this proposal with expressions of outrage or amusement, depending on their temperaments, which would seem to be a pretty clear example of not letting someone get away with something.) Realists face no such problem. Their position is simply that Realism is objectively true and that anti-Realism is objectively false. Whatever other problems Realism may face, it does not say of itself that it should not be accepted.

Our argument against anti-Realism is in some ways similar to the argument that was advanced in Chapter 1 for the conclusion that there is such a thing as ultimate reality, a reality that lies behind all appearances. This is no accident, for one consequence of anti-Realism is that the distinction between appearance and reality is a distinction that can be applied only in certain limited contexts and that, therefore, the notion of an ultimate reality—a reality whose status as reality is independent of context—is incoherent. If there were such a context-independent reality, then there would be such a thing as objective truth: those statements would be objectively true that correctly described the ultimate or context-independent reality. It is therefore misleading to think of anti-Realism as a metaphysic, in the sense in which idealism or lowercase-r realism is a metaphysic. Anti-Realism, rather, is a denial of the possibility of metaphysics, since the very enterprise of metaphysics is the attempt to discover the nature of ultimate reality. And Realism is a metaphysic only in the sense that it is a thesis that is common to all metaphysical theories.

I propose that, given the very plausible "geological" arguments for Realism, and given the apparently self-refuting nature of anti-Realism, we should be Realists.

Before we leave the topic of Realism and anti-Realism, however, I should like to direct the reader's attention to the greatest of all attacks on anti-Realism, George Orwell's novel *1984*. Anyone who is interested in Realism and anti-Realism should be steeped in the message of this book. The reader is particularly directed to the debate between the Realist Winston Smith and the anti-Realist O'Brien that is the climax of the novel. In the end, there is only one question that can be addressed to the anti-Realist: How does your position differ from O'Brien's?

This completes our promised discussion of three important issues raised by the question whether a statement of the Common Western Metaphysic is a description of appearance or reality. As we remarked earlier, there are many other issues that are raised by this question, issues that have bulked large in the history of metaphysics. Some of these issues will be addressed in later chapters. There is, for example, the issue of what metaphysicians call "persistence through time" or "the identity of an object across time," the problem of whether one and the same object can (as the Common Western Metaphysic alleges) exist at two different times. We shall discuss that problem in connection with our discussion of human beings, since it is human beings whose persistence through time we care most deeply about; because of this concern we have about the persistence of human beings, it will be important to examine the consequences of any theory of persistence for the special case of human beings, and, for that reason, we postpone discussion of persistence till Chapter 10.

Suggestions for Further Reading

It is very hard to find anything about the Realism/anti-Realism debate to recommend to the beginning student of metaphysics. Almost everything that has been written on this topic is either forbiddingly technical or else forbiddingly obscure (or both). With some reservations, I recommend the following four works. The first is rather on the technical side. The remaining three, although they contain many sections that are clear enough, are rather unclear on the matter of exactly what it is that the authors believe. Alston's "Yes, Virginia, There Is a Real World" is a defense of Realism. Putnam's *Reason, Truth and History* (see particularly the first three chapters) and *The Many Faces of Realism* see particularly Lectures I and II) represent the anti-Realist point of view, as does Rorty's *Philosophy and the Mirror of Nature*.

PART TWO

Why the World Is

IN PART ONE, we considered various arguments and speculations concerning the features of the World. But why is there a World at all? Why is anything *there* to have the features we argued and speculated about—or any other features, any features at all? Why is there something rather than nothing? One cannot plausibly argue that this is an illegitimate question owing to the fact that if there were nothing we should not be here to ask it. After all, essentially the same argument could be addressed to the astronomer who asked why the sun had planets or to the biologist who inquired into the origin of life, and everyone agrees that questions about the origin of the planets or of life are legitimate questions. It does not follow, however, that the question, Why is there something rather than nothing? *is* a legitimate question, and it is undeniable that in some respects it is strikingly unlike questions about the origin of the planets or of life.

The philosopher who asks why there is anything at all faces a difficulty to which nothing in the inquiries of our astronomer and our biologist corresponds. Before there was life, before there were planets, there were already lots of things, and the problem of explaining the origin of the planets or the origin of life is just the problem of explaining how those already existing things interacted to produce the planets or to produce life. But before there was anything—if indeed the world 'before' makes any sense in this context—there was, of course, nothing. And how can "nothing" serve as the basis of an explanation? If nothing exists then nothing is going on. If nothing exists, then there is nothing that has any properties that can be used in giving an explanation—as can the properties of a "pre-planetary" nebula surrounding the sun or the properties of the "pre-biotic soup" that some have said was the arena within which life developed. "Nothing" has no parts that could interact with one another or display contrasting properties. For that matter, "nothing" has no parts that could fail to interact with one another or fail to display contrasting properties.

In fact, the word 'nothing' is not a name at all, although our use of the word in double quotes in the last few sentences might suggest that it is something like a name. Surrounding the word 'nothing' with double quotes makes the word look as if it were supposed to function as a sort of nickname for a vast emptiness or an enormous vacuum. But to regard the word 'nothing' as functioning in that way would be to misunderstand it. To say that there is nothing is to say that there isn't *anything*, not even a vast emptiness. If there were a vast emptiness, there would be no material objects—no atoms or elementary particles or anything made of them—but there would nevertheless be something: the vast emptiness.

If it seems inplausible to suppose that an emptiness is something, a thing, consider the fact that we have qualified this emptiness with an adjective: 'vast'. To say of something that it is vast is to say that it has a size, and only a *thing* can have a size—or any other property or feature or characteristic. One can of course see why someone would say that if there were only a vast emptiness there would be nothing. For that matter, one can see why someone would say that if there were no furniture or other large, solid objects in a room the room "contained nothing" or there was "nothing in" the room. When we talk about what is in a room, it is generally furniture and other large, solid objects that interest us. And if you said, "Well, we could move all of that stuff into Janice's old bedroom. There's nothing in there now. It's completely empty," you would probably regard it as a tedious joke if someone replied that you were mistaken because the room contained lots of air and water vapor and millions of dust motes. Nevertheless, what the tedious humorist said would be *true*. And the same applies to the vast emptiness. If we said, "If there were only a vast emptiness, there would be nothing," we should no doubt mean that there would be nothing of the sort that we are usually interested in— things made out of atoms or elementary particles—and the statement that there would still be a vast emptiness would be regarded as a tedious joke. Nevertheless, it would be *true* that there was still a vast emptiness, for spatial extent would still exist, and there couldn't even be spatial extent if there were really *nothing*.

When it is fully appreciated what 'There is nothing' means when these words are taken in the strictest sense, it becomes evident how strange and difficult the question 'Why is there anything at all?' is. The question 'Why is there life on the earth?' may be difficult, but it is easy enough to see in a very general way what sort of thing would count as an answer to it. The question would be answered by someone's showing how a state of affairs in which there were no living things but lots of non-living things developed into a state of affairs in which there were both non-living and living things. The person who answered the question would show how non-living things interacted and came together and arranged themselves to produce living things. But no one is going to show how a state of affairs in which there were no things of any sort developed into a state of affairs in which there were things. No one is going to show how non-existent things interacted and came together and rearranged themselves to produce existent things. To undertake such an explanation would be to undertake nonsense, for, just as 'nothing' is not a name of a thing, so 'non-existent thing' is not a name of a kind of thing. Words like 'dragon' and 'unicorn' are not names for kinds of non-existent things. Rather, they are not names for anything of any sort, for there are no dragons or unicorns for them to name.

The strangeness of our question, if not its difficulty, doubtless explains why it has occurred only to philosophers. One might expect that the religions of the world would have offered various explanations of why there was something rather than nothing. But it is in fact only under the impetus provided by philosophical speculation that any religion has provided an explanation, be it profound or silly, plausible or implausible, of the fact that there is something rather than nothing. It is true that the adherents of many religions tell stories that our culture describes as "creation myths"; it is often said that these stories are primitive attempts to explain the beginnings of things. I am doubtful about whether these stories really were attempts to *explain* the beginnings of things, but I do not propose to go into that question. The point I want to make is that none of these stories even pretends to answer the question, Why should there be anything at all? This is immediately evident when we read them with this question in mind. Here is a story that is typical of a large range of "creation myths," despite the fact that I have made it up.

> Once there was nothing but a great sea of mud. The god Unwit rose in this sea of mud like a bubble. When he had reached the surface, he gave birth to the god Um from his mouth and the goddess Usk from his navel. Um and Usk fell upon their father and devoured his flesh, but his bones they did not eat. Then Um lay with Usk and she bore him seven gods and seven goddesses, whom Um and Usk commanded to build a great palace for them. But the gods and goddesses grew weary of this task and they begged Um and Usk to make servants for them to help them in their labors. Um and Usk had pity on their children, and from the bones of their father Unwit they made Ea, the first man, and Iwa, the first woman.

We may note that this story says nothing about where the great sea of mud came from or how long it had been there or what lay outside its borders or why a god should rise in it like a bubble. The story does not begin with there being nothing. It does not even begin with a vast emptiness. When the curtain rises, there is already something on the stage. It might be objected that this grotesque little tale is modeled on very primitive creation stories. But if we look at "purer" or "more highly developed" traditional creation stories, we still find the stage occupied when the curtain rises:

> The god Tagaloa lived in the far spaces. He created all things, He was alone, there was no heaven, no earth. He was alone and wandered about in space.[1]

> In the beginning God created the heaven and the earth. And the earth was without form, and void; and darkness was upon the face of the deep. And the Spirit of God moved upon the face of the waters. And God said, Let there be light: and there was light.[2]

In the Samoan story, the god Tagaloa is on stage when the curtain rises. And there seems to be a fair amount of empty space as well, since Tagaloa is able to move about. In the Hebrew story, God, at least, is on stage when the play begins. If the alternative translation mentioned in the note is correct, a "heaven" and a formless, empty, watery "earth" are also present. It is clear, therefore, that if all of the creation stories that any religion tells are like these, none of these stories addresses the question why there should be anything at all. This does not mean that no religion has ever had anything to say about why there is something rather than nothing, for it may be that some religion has had something to say about this question that is unrelated to or goes beyond the creation story it tells. And in a sense—but only in a sense—this is the case. It is the case because many religions have co-existed with philosophical speculation and have absorbed some of the ways of thinking generated by philosophical speculation.

In Christian Europe, for example, there was an intimate relation between philosophy and the Christian religion, a relation that lasted in one form or another from almost the beginnings of Christianity till the eighteenth century. And many of the Christian philosophers belonging to one strand or another of this tradition were aware of the question 'Why should there be anything at all?' and attempted to answer this question from a Christian perspective. Or perhaps it would be more accurate to say that these philosophers gave answers to this question that incorporated many Christian elements, even if they were never simply dictated by Christianity.[3] Nevertheless, the investigations of these philosophers were philosophical investigations and stemmed at least in large part from philosophical motives: the discussion of the question may have belonged to Christian philosophy, but it certainly belonged to Christian *philosophy* and not to any other aspect of the Christian religion.

The same point could be made in relation to Jewish and Muslim philosophy. The philosophical traditions on which Christian, Jewish, and Muslim philosophy have drawn are Greek in origin and antedate Christianity and Islam. And if these roots do not antedate Judaism, they certainly antedate any Jewish concern with speculative philosophical questions. It would be a task far beyond the scope of this book to examine all of these roots. I will instead discuss two metaphysical arguments that are products of the appropriation by the three Middle Eastern or "Abrahamic" religions of the tradition of philosophical reflection that began in Greece. These two arguments are of central importance in any investigation of the question, Why is there a World? Their central importance in the investigation of this question is due to the fact that they turn on the concept of a "necessary being." As we shall see, any answer to the question, Why is there a World? must somehow involve this notion.

5

Necessary Being:
The Ontological Argument

LATE IN THE ELEVENTH CENTURY, an archbishop of Canterbury named Anselm wrote a book called the *Proslogium*, which was largely devoted to the exposition of a certain argument for the existence of God. The interesting thing about this argument was that it claimed to show that the non-existence of God was impossible, owing to the fact that any assertion of the non-existence of God must be self-contradictory. This is a very strong claim indeed. To see how strong it is, imagine an atheist named Athelred who is fond of proclaiming to all and sundry that there is no God. If Anselm is right, then every time Athelred issues this proclamation, he contradicts himself; he contradicts himself in just as strong a sense as he would have if he had said, "There is no God ... *and* there is a God" or "My house is rectangular and has six sides." Anselm did not, of course, contend that the contradiction involved in saying that there is no God is quite as blatant as the contradictions involved in these two statements. (If the contradiction were that easy to spot, no argument would be needed to show that it exists.) But he did contend that this contradiction, though hidden and requiring an argument for its exposure, was a contradiction in the same strong sense as the contradictions involved in these two statements.

It should be obvious that if Anselm is right in his claims for his argument, then this argument provides an answer for the question, Why should there be anything at all? For if the thesis that there is no God is self-contradictory, then it cannot be true. And if there were nothing at all, then that thesis would be true. If Anselm's argument shows that there has to be a God, then it shows that there cannot be nothing at all. It is true that it does not show that there has to be a physical universe like the one we observe around us, and thus it does not answer the question why there should be such a universe. But the question, Why should there be anything at all? is not the same question as, Why should there be a physical universe? The conclusion of Saint Anselm's argument, moreover, is not irrelevant to the latter question, since, if there is a God, then this God no doubt has a great deal to do with the fact that there is a physical universe.

Anselm's argument was almost immediately attacked by one Gaunilo, a Benedictine monk, and theologians and philosophers have been attacking it ever since. About two hundred years after Anselm's time, in the late thirteenth century, the argument was declared invalid by Saint Thomas Aquinas, and almost everyone has followed his lead in declaring it invalid. Indeed, philosophers and theologians have not only mostly regarded the argument as invalid but have also mostly regarded it as obviously, scandalously, and embarrassingly invalid. This judgment was nicely summed up by the nineteenth-century German philosopher Arthur Schopenhauer, who called the argument a "charming joke."

And what is this notorious argument? Actually, rather than examine Anselm's argument, we shall render our task considerably easier if we look at an argument devised about five hundred years later—at roughly the time the Pilgrims were landing at Plymouth Rock—by Descartes. Descartes's argument (which is much easier to state and to follow than Anselm's) and Anselm's argument are generally considered to be different "versions" of the same argument: each is customarily described as a version of "the ontological argument."[1]

Descartes's argument goes something like this:

> If we look within ourselves, we find that we possess the concept of a perfect being. [Descartes identifies the concept of a perfect being with the concept of God and therefore regards his argument as a proof of the existence of God. But since the existence of God is not our primary concern at the moment—our primary concern is the question why there is anything at all—let us ignore this aspect of Descartes's argument. We shall simply avoid the word 'God' and the question whether the concept of a perfect being is the same as the concept that we customarily associate with this word.] That is, we find the concept of a being that is perfect in every respect or, as we may say, possesses all perfections. But existence itself is a perfection, since a thing is better if it exists than if it does not exist. But then a perfect being has to *exist*; it simply wouldn't be perfect if it didn't.
> Existence is a part of the *concept* of a perfect being; anyone who denied that a perfect being had the property existence would be like someone who denied that a triangle had the property three-sidedness. Just as three-sidedness is a part of the concept of a triangle—the mind cannot conceive of triangularity without also conceiving of three-sidedness—existence is a part of the concept of a perfect being: the mind cannot conceive of perfection without also conceiving of existence.

Now if this argument of Descartes's is correct, then it provides us with an answer to the question, Why is there anything at all? If Descartes is right, then it is impossible for there to be no perfect being, just as it is impossible for there to be a triangle that does not have three sides. And if it is impossible for there to be no perfect being, then it is impossible for there to be nothing at all, since the existence of a perfect being is the existence of something.

The faults that have been ascribed to the ontological argument are many and various. One might, for example, raise the question why existence should be regarded as a "perfection." What's so wonderful about existence? one might wonder. After all, many people seem to think that they can improve their lot by suicide—that is, by electing non-existence. But it is generally conceded, or was until rather recently, that one of the faults of the ontological argument is so grievous that it is the only one that the critic of the argument need mention. This fault, or alleged fault, is best known in the formulation of Immanuel Kant. Kant's diagnosis of the argument's chief fault can be stated as follows:

Whatever else a perfection may be, any perfection must be a property—or feature, attribute, or characteristic—of things. But existence is not a property of things. 'Existence' is not one item in the list of the properties of (for example) the Taj Mahal, an item that occurs in addition to such items as 'white', 'famous for its beauty', 'located in the city of Agra', and so on. Rather, when we specify certain properties and say that something having those properties *exists,* all we are saying is that something has those properties. Suppose, for example, that the following are the properties that everyone agrees the poet Homer had if he existed: he was a blind, male Ionian poet of the eighth century B.C. who wrote all or most of the epic poems we know as the *Iliad* and the *Odyssey.* Call this collection of properties H. Now suppose that there are two classical scholars, one of whom thinks that Homer existed and one of whom thinks Homer was legendary (the two great epics that are supposedly his compositions having been pieced together over a long period from the work of many anonymous poets). It would be wrong—in fact, it would be absurd—to describe the disagreement of these two scholars by saying that the former thinks that someone had the collection of properties H and, in addition, the property of existence while the latter agrees that someone had the collection of properties H but goes on to assert that this person lacked the property of existence. No, it's just that the former scholar thinks that someone had all of (or at least most of) the properties in the set H and that the latter thinks that no one had all of (or even very many of) them. This case illustrates the sense in which existence is not a property.[2] But if existence is not a property, it cannot be an ingredient in a concept. A concept is really no more than a list of properties, the properties that a thing must have to fall under that concept. For example, the concept of a dog is just the list of properties that a thing must have to count as a dog. (The list of properties enumerated a few sentences back spells out the concept associated with the description 'the poet Homer'.) What Descartes has done is to treat existence as if it were the kind of thing that could be an ingredient in a concept. If one does this, however, one opens the door to all sorts of evident absurdities. Here is an example of such an absurdity. Define an 'egmount' as an existent mountain made entirely of gold: to be an egmount, a thing must (a) be a mountain, (b) be made entirely of gold, and (c) exist. It is obviously a part of the concept of an egmount that an egmount *exists*: it says so on the label, as it were. But, as everyone knows, there are no egmounts. The ontological argument is this same absurdity in a (thinly) disguised form.

Although this refutation of the ontological argument was "standard" for almost two hundred years, it cannot be regarded as satisfactory. The problem is not so much that Kant says anything that is definitely wrong. The difficulty is rather as follows. It is possible to construct an argument very similar to Descartes's argument—an argument that just obviously ought to be invalid for the same reason as Descartes's argument—that does not treat existence as a property. And it is possible to point to a rather obvious defect that is shared by the two arguments. It will be obvious when we have done this that the shared defect is what is really or fundamentally wrong with Descartes's argument and that the Kantian refutation of the argument is at best a point about a peripheral fault in the argument.

Let us consider the idea of *necessary existence*. A thing has necessary existence if it would have existed no matter what, if it would have existed under any possible circumstances. An equivalent definition is this: A thing has necessary existence if its non-existence would have been impossible. And by 'impossible' we mean *absolutely* impossible: if x is a necessary being, then the non-existence of x is as impossible as a round square or a liquid wine bottle. It is obvious that you and I do not possess necessary existence: we should never have existed if our respective sets of parents happened never to have met, and that is certainly a "possible circumstance." Moreover, it is clear that the same point applies to Julius Caesar and the Taj Mahal. As to the latter, it would not have existed if the beloved wife of a certain Mogul emperor had not died young. And even an object that has, by everyday standards, a really impressive grip on existence—Mount Everest, say—lacks necessary existence: Mount Everest would not have existed if the Indian subcontinent had not drifted into contact with Asia. The very sun would not have existed if certain random density distributions in the pre-stellar nebulae had not led to the gravitational contraction of a particular grouping of hydrogen atoms into a radiating body. For all we know, even the physical universe might not have existed—either because whatever it was that caused the universe to come into existence ten or fifteen thousand million years ago failed to produce any universe at all or because this unknown factor produced some different universe.

These reflections make it clear that necessary existence is a property, in just the sense that mere existence is not (if Kant is right) a property. It is true that it may not be a *possible* property. Perhaps it is a property like *being both round and square* or *being a liquid wine bottle* or *being a prime number that is larger than all other prime numbers* that nothing could possibly have. (It is certainly hard to think of an uncontroversial example of something that has necessary existence.) The important point for present purposes is that necessary existence cannot be said not to be a property at all or at least not because of considerations like those that Kant adduces to show that existence is not a property. It seems clear that whatever may be the case with mere existence, necessary existence *can* be an ingredient in a concept. In fact, many philosophers and theologians have held that necessary existence is a part of the concept of God—and other philosophers and theologians have denied that necessary existence is a part of the concept of God. Now let us consider an argument that is like Descartes's ontological argument, except that 'necessary existence' is substituted for 'existence' throughout. The argument would look something like this:

- A perfect being has all perfections.
- Necessary existence is a perfection.
  Hence, A perfect being has necessary existence.
- Whatever has necessary existence has existence.
  Hence, A perfect being has existence.
- Whatever has existence exists.
  Hence, A perfect being exists.

It is interesting to note that in one way, at least, this argument is more plausible than Descartes's actual argument. We saw above that it is not quite clear why one should assume that existence is a perfection. But there seems to be no such problem about necessary existence. A being (like you and me and Caesar and the Taj Mahal and the sun and perhaps even the physical universe) that lacks necessary existence will typically depend for its own existence on the prior operations of other beings, and probably these operations will involve a large element of sheer *chance*. But a being that has necessary existence is not dependent on the vagaries of chance, for its existence is absolutely inevitable. Necessary existence is, therefore, a most impressive property—the same can hardly be said for existence: the lowliest worm and the most ephemeral subnuclear resonance *exist*—and anything that possesses it is a most impressive being. It is for this very reason that many philosophers and theologians have wanted to include necessary existence among the attributes of God. It therefore seems very plausible to hold that necessary existence should be an item in any list of "perfections."

Be that as it may, the new version of Descartes's argument is obviously invalid, and it looks very much as if it were invalid for much the same reason as the original version. Recall the example of the egmount. We can easily construct a similar example that is addressed to the revised argument. Let us define a "negmount" as a *necessarily* existent golden mountain. If the revised version of the argument is valid, then (or so it would seem) so is the following argument. Let us call the three properties that occur in this definition (necessary existence, being made of gold, and being a mountain) the "negmontanic properties." We may now argue:

- A negmount has all negmontanic properties.
- Necessary existence is a negmontanic property.
  Hence, A negmount has necessary existence.

- Whatever has necessary existence has existence.

  Hence, A negmount has existence.
- Whatever has existence exists.

  Hence, A negmount exists.

But the conclusion of this argument is obviously false. There is no negmount. In fact, it can plausibly be argued that not only is the conclusion false but it couldn't *possibly* be true. A mountain, whatever it may be made of, is a physical object, and it is very hard to see how a physical object could possibly be necessarily existent. Even if necessary existence is possible for some sorts of things, a physical object is composed of parts, and it would not have existed if those parts had never come together. But there is no need to argue about this subtle point. The same conclusion can be reached in a way that allows no evasion. Let a "nousquare" be a necessarily existent round square. If the above argument is valid, then an exactly parallel argument proves the existence of a necessarily existent round square—and hence of a round square.

It is clear, therefore, that the above argument is *not* valid. But wherein does its invalidity lie? Not, apparently, where Kant says, for the argument does not assume that existence is a property, and Kant has provided no reason that should lead us to say that necessary existence cannot figure as an ingredient in a concept. (The concept of a negmount seems to me to be a perfectly good example of a concept, albeit it is not a very useful concept.) What is wrong with the negmount argument is very simple: its first premise—'A negmount has all negmontanic properties'—is ambiguous. That is, it could have either of two meanings:

- Anything that is a negmount has all of the negmontanic properties.
- There is a negmount that has all of the negmontanic properties.

(The former of these statements is true whether or not there are negmounts. It simply says that a thing does not count as a negmount unless it has all of the negmontanic properties. The latter statement, of course, cannot be true unless there is a negmount.) The ambiguity is rooted in two quite different functions performed by the indefinite article. To say "A public official is sworn to uphold the law" is to say that anyone who is a public official is sworn to uphold the law, an assertion that, in principle, could be true even if there were no public officials. To say "A public official was arraigned in Superior Court today" is to say that there *is* a public official who was arraigned in Superior Court today. (Descartes's original statement of his argument was in Latin, which has no word corresponding to 'a' and 'an'. But there is a corresponding ambiguity in Latin.)

Because the first premise of the negmount argument is ambiguous, "it" is not really one argument at all, but two arguments jumbled together. When we disentangle the jumble, we find that one of these arguments proceeds from the premise that anything that is a negmount has all of the negmontanic properties to the conclusion that anything that is a negmount exists; the other proceeds from the premise that there is a negmount having all of the negmontanic properties to the conclusion that there is a negmount that exists. Neither of these two arguments should convince anyone that there is a negmount.

As to the first argument, its premise is clearly true, but its conclusion—anything that is a negmount exists—is true whether or not any negmounts exist (just as 'Anything that is a unicorn has a single horn' is true whether or not there are any unicorns). As to the second argument, its conclusion obviously implies that there is a negmount (an existent negmount, if that adds anything to the assertion that there is a negmount), but this was asserted by the premise—there is a negmount that has all of the negmontanic properties—and it is no news that one can derive the conclusion that there is a negmount from the assumption that there is a negmount. Such plausibility as the original negmount argument had derived from the fact that because the two arguments were run together, it looked as if we had an argument that had the impressive conclusion of the second argument and the innocent premise of the first.

All of these points apply, with very minor adjustments, both to Descartes's ontological argument and to the revised version of his argument (the one that appeals to the notion of necessary existence rather than to simple existence). Let us consider the revised version. When the first premise of the argument is properly disambiguated, we have two arguments:

- Anything that is a perfect being has all perfections.
- Necessary existence is a perfection.
  Hence, Anything that is a perfect being has necessary existence.
- Whatever has necessary existence has existence.
  Hence, Anything that is a perfect being has existence.
- Whatever has existence exists.
  Hence, Anything that is a perfect being exists.

- There is a perfect being that has all perfections.
- Necessary existence is a perfection.
  Hence, There is a perfect being that has necessary existence.
- Whatever has necessary existence has existence.
  Hence, There is a perfect being that has existence.
- Whatever has existence exists.
  Hence, There is a perfect being that exists.

The first of these two arguments proceeds from an obvious premise to a trivial conclusion. The second argument has a non-trivial conclusion, but this conclusion is, essentially, the first premise. Those who grant the first premise of the second argument hardly need the other premises; they can make do with a much simpler argument:

- There is a perfect being that has all perfections.

  Hence, There is a perfect being.

But this argument has—to say the least—little persuasive force. And it should by now be clear that neither Descartes's ontological argument nor our revision of it is any better. Such persuasive force as these arguments have is due simply to the fact that each of them is a jumble of two arguments; in each case, one of the two has an obviously true premise and the other has an interesting conclusion.

It would seem that Descartes's attempt to prove that the non-existence of a perfect being is impossible is a failure and that it therefore cannot be of any help in our inquiry into why there should be anything at all. (Without going into the details of the matter, I will record my conviction that the earlier argument of Saint Anselm is also a failure.) This does not mean, however, that the ontological argument is of no relevance to our inquiry, for it may be that there are other versions of the ontological argument that are not guilty of the fallacy of ambiguity that was the downfall of Descartes's argument. And recent researches in the philosophy of modality (the philosophy of necessity and possibility) do indeed seem to have produced an argument that it is reasonable to call a version of the ontological argument and which does not exploit a hidden ambiguity or commit any other logical fallacy.

This argument, which is usually called the modal ontological argument, is best presented in terms of "possible worlds." This notion may be explained as follows. We have said the "the World" is the totality of everything that there is. But it is obvious that the World might be different—indeed that it might always have been different—from the way it is. There might be fewer cats or more dogs. There might never have been any cats or dogs at all (if, say, evolution had taken a slightly different course). Napoleon might have lost the battle of Austerlitz or won the battle of Waterloo. As we saw in our discussion of the notion of a necessary being, the sun—perhaps even the physical universe— might never have existed. A list of the ways things might have been different (which is the same as a list of the ways the World might have been different) could go on and on without any discernible limit. By a possible world, we mean simply a complete specification of a way the World might have been, a specification that is so precise and definite that it settles every single detail, no matter how minor.[3] If we assume that everything that there is or could be is subject to the flow of time—almost certainly not a wise assumption—we could say that a possible world is a complete history-and-future that the World might have (or might have had), one whose completeness extends to every detail.

In order to make full use of the concept of a possible world, we need the idea of *truth in* a given possible world and we need the idea of *existence* in a given possible world. While various technical accounts of these ideas are available, we shall be content with an intuitive or impressionistic account of them. A few examples should suffice. If in a given world x there are no dogs— if that is how x specifies things: that there are no dogs—then in x dogs do not exist, and it is true in x that there are no dogs, and the proposition (assertion, statement, thesis) that there are no dogs is true in x. If in a given possible world y Napoleon won the battle of Waterloo, then it is true in y that Napoleon won the battle of Waterloo, and the proposition that Napoleon won the battle of Waterloo is true in y. And, of course, Napoleon must *exist* in y, for one cannot win a battle if one does not exist. But there are possible worlds in which Napoleon was never born (or even conceived) and in those possible worlds he does not exist.

Once we have the notion of a proposition's being true in a possible world, we can say what it is for a proposition to be *possibly true* and for a proposition to be *necessarily true*. A proposition is possibly true if it is true in *at least one* possible world, and necessarily true if it is true in *all* possible worlds.

The possible world that specifies the way the World really *is* is called *the actual world*. A more formal definition is this: a possible world w is the actual world just in the case that something is true in w if and only if it is—without qualification—true.[4] It is important not to confuse the actual world with the World. The actual world is a mere specification, a description of a way for things to be. It has only the kind of abstract reality that belongs to a story or a scenario or a computer program. The World, however, is not a description of a way for things to be: it is, so to speak, the things themselves. If it is an individual, it has you and me and every other individual as parts. If it is not an individual but a mere collection, it is at least the collection of all of the individuals. It is the features of the World that make one of the possible worlds the one that is actual, just as it is the geographical features of the earth that make some maps accurate or correct and other maps inaccurate or incorrect. It is the features of the World that make *one* of the ways for things to be the way that things are.

It is not necessary to make use of the concept of a possible world in presenting the "modal ontological argument," but it is advisable, since the English grammatical constructions that are used in formulating modal reasoning are sources of much ambiguity, and this ambiguity can cause arguments that are logically invalid to look as if they were valid.[5] The easiest and most elegant way to avoid these ambiguities is to carry on discussions that involve modal reasoning in terms of possible worlds.

In order to state the modal ontological argument, we need two notions: the notion of a necessary being and the notion of something's having a property (feature, attribute, characteristic) essentially.

We have already met the notion of necessary existence in our discussion of Descartes's ontological argument. A necessary *being* is simply a being that possesses necessary existence. But we may define this concept very simply in terms of the concept of a possible world: a necessary being is a being that exists in all possible worlds (and necessary existence is the property of existing in all possible worlds). Beings that are not necessary are called *contingent*. That is, a contingent being is simply a being that exists in some but not all possible worlds. You and I and every object of our experience are, no doubt, contingent beings. You, for example, do not exist in any possible world in which you were never conceived (and this would certainly seem to be a possible state of affairs).

The concept of the essential possession of a property is this: a thing has a property essentially just in the case that that property is a part of the thing's nature, so inextricably entwined with the thing's being that it could not exist if it did not have that property. We may explain this notion in possible-worlds language as follows: for a thing x to have a given property essentially is for x to have that property in every possible world in which x exists. It should be emphasized that this is a definition, not a recipe. It tells us what the essential possession of a property is, but it does not give us a method for determining whether a particular property is in fact possessed essentially by a particular thing.

Consider you, for example, and the property of humanity, or being human. Obviously you *have* this property—you *are* human—but do you have it *essentially*? Is being human so "inextricably entwined with your being" that you could not exist without being human? Are you a human being in every possible world in which you so much as exist? This is a metaphysical question, and a very controversial one. Philosophers disagree about the answer to this question because they disagree about what *you* are, and, as a consequence, they disagree about what you could have been. But for our present purposes it will not be necessary to have any uncontroversial examples of the essential possession of a property (which is fortunate, for there are few if any examples that are uncontroversial); it is enough that we understand what is meant by the essential possession of a property. It will sometimes be useful to have a term to oppose to 'essentially' in discussions of the possession of a property by a thing. If a thing has a property but does not have it essentially, we say that it has that property *accidentally*.

The ontological argument is, or claims to be, a proof that a perfect being exists. And what is a perfect being? A perfect being, Descartes tells us, is a being that possesses all perfections. But now let us raise a question that is not settled by this formula. When we say that a perfect being possesses all perfections, do we mean that a perfect being possesses all perfections essentially or could a being be a perfect being if, although it indeed had every perfection, it had some or all of its perfections only accidentally? In order to see more clearly what is at stake in this question, let us look at a particular perfection. We may not be sure exactly which properties are perfections, but it seems reasonable to suppose that wisdom is among them. If this is not right, however, it will make no difference to our argument, which—with one exception, as we shall see—does not make any assumptions about which properties are perfections. We choose wisdom only to have something to use as a reasonably plausible example of a perfection.

Let us consider two (equally) wise beings, one of which has its wisdom essentially and the other of which has its wisdom only accidentally. This means that while one of the two beings would have been wise no matter what (as long as it managed to exist at all), the other might have been unwise. The nature of the former being is incompatible with unwisdom, and the nature of the latter is compatible both with wisdom and with unwisdom. Although it is a matter of necessity that the former is wise, given that it exists, it is, speaking metaphysically, an *accident* that the latter is wise. The latter's wisdom is, so to speak, a gift of the circumstances in which that being happens to exist, and that gift would not have been conferred by other sets of circumstances, circumstances in which that being might have found itself. (This is certainly the way most of us look at the wisdom of human beings. If Alice is, as we all agree, wise, we do not suppose that it follows from the undisputed fact of her wisdom that she would have been wise if she had been raised among people who provided her with no examples of wisdom or if she had been raised in grinding poverty that left her with no leisure for reflection. And we should probably agree that she would definitely *not* have been wise if she had, as a small child, suffered brain damage that left her with severely diminished mental capacities.)

Now—we continue to assume for the sake of the illustration that wisdom is a perfection—which of our two beings is a better candidate for the office of perfect being? The example seems to offer fairly strong support for the thesis that the essential possession of a perfection brings a being closer to the status of "perfect" than does the merely accidental possession of that same perfection. Let us therefore say that a perfect being is a being that possesses all perfections and, moreover, possesses those perfections essentially and not merely accidentally—of its own nature, and not merely as a gift of circumstance.

And what properties are perfections? As we said, we shall make only one assumption about this. We shall assume that *necessary existence* is a perfection. And this does not seem to be an implausible assumption. As we said in our discussion of Descartes's ontological argument, a being that has necessary existence is not dependent on the vagaries of chance, for its existence is absolutely inevitable. Is not "just happening to exist" a disqualification for the office of "perfect being"? Must we not, therefore, count necessary existence as a perfection?

That necessary existence is a perfection is one of the premises of the modal ontological argument. The argument has only one other premise: that a perfect being is possible—or, equivalently, that a perfect being is not *impossible*. And such a premise must in some sense be required by any argument for the existence of anything, since an impossible being—a round square, say, or a liquid wine bottle—by definition cannot exist. Here, then, is the modal ontological argument:

- A perfect being (that is, a being that possesses all perfections essentially) is not impossible.
- Necessary existence is a perfection.[6]
  Hence, A perfect being exists.

Our first task will be to show that this argument is logically valid—that is, that its conclusion (that a perfect being exists) follows logically if its two premises are granted. Our next task will be to see whether the two premises *should* be granted. And this will come down to the task of seeing whether the first premise (that a perfect being is not impossible) should be granted, for we have al-

ready said about as much as there is to be said on the question whether
necessary existence is a perfection.

We proceed to show that this argument is valid. It will be easiest to display
the reasoning behind the modal ontological argument diagrammatically. Let
us suppose (just to keep the diagram manageable; our argument in no way depends on how many possible worlds there are) that there are exactly four possible worlds, which we shall call One, Two, Three, and Four. We shall
represent each possible world by a circle. And let us represent the assertion
that, in a given possible world, there exists something that has a given property by placing inside the circle that represents that possible world a symbol
that represents that property. For example, if 'W' represents wisdom, then the
figure

Four   Ⓦ

represents the assertion that in Possible World Four there exists something
that is wise. And let us represent the assertion that a given possible world is
actual by placing the symbol '<' to the right of the circle that represents that
possible world. (We shall call this symbol the 'actuality cursor', since it will be
useful to think of it as a movable "pointer.") Thus, the figure

Two   ◯   <

represents the assertion that Possible World Two is the actual world, and the
figure

One   Ⓦ   <

represents the assertion that Possible World One is actual and contains something wise. By a *world-diagram* we mean a diagram that satisfies two conditions: first, the diagram must contain a circle representing each possible
world, and, secondly, the diagram must contain the actuality cursor (the symbol '<'), placed to the right of exactly one of the circles. (The second condition
corresponds to the fact that exactly one possible world is actual.)

In addition to these two "required" features, a world-diagram may also
have the following "optional" feature: it may contain any number of symbols
representing properties, these symbols being placed inside any or all of the
circles.

Given our assumption that there are just the four possible worlds One,
Two, Three, and Four, the following figure is a world-diagram:

One   Ⓦ
Two   ◯
Three   ◯   <
Four   Ⓦ

A world-diagram tells us which possible worlds there are and which of them is the actual world; it may also tell us whether, in various of those possible worlds, there are things having certain specified properties. The above diagram represents the assertion that there are exactly four possible worlds, One, Two, Three, and Four, that Three is the actual world, and that in worlds One and Four there is something wise.

A world-diagram is said to be "correct in" a given possible world if (and only if) every assertion represented in the diagram is true in that possible world. The above diagram is correct in Possible World Three if it is true in Three that there exist exactly the four possible worlds displayed in the diagram, that Possible World Three is the one that is actual, and that in two of the other worlds, One and Four, there is something that is wise.

Let us now see how world-diagrams can help us with the question whether the conclusion of the modal ontological argument follows from its two premises. Let us assume for the sake of argument that both of the premises of the modal ontological argument are true and see whether we can deduce its conclusion from this assumption. The first premise tells us that a perfect being, a being having all perfections essentially, is possible, and that is the same thing as saying that in at least one possible world there exists a being who has all perfections essentially. Let us arbitrarily assume that such a being exists in Possible World Two—that Two is the possible world, or one of the possible worlds, in which there is a perfect being. Our arbitrary choice of Possible World Two as a "starting point" can do no harm since, according to the premise whose truth we have assumed, a perfect being must exist either in One or in Two or in Three or in Four (or else in more than one of these four possible worlds), and we shall see that the reasoning that we are about to examine would lead to the same conclusion no matter which possible world we took as our starting point.

Let us use the symbol 'P' to stand for the property of being a perfect being (that is, the property of having all perfections essentially), and let us suppose that a certain inhabitant of Possible World Two, William, is set the task of drawing a world-diagram that shows how the property P is, as we might say, distributed among the four possible worlds. William, let us suppose, knows that there is a perfect being in Two, and he therefore begins drawing his diagram as follows:

Two   (P)   <

Why does William place the actuality cursor to the right of the circle representing Possible World Two? Well, we are imagining William's constructing his diagram *in* Possible World Two, and it is true in Possible World Two that Possible World Two is the actual world. (In general, it is true in any given possible world that *that* possible world is the actual world—just as it is true in any story that everything in that story is true.)

Now how is William to fill in the rest of the world-diagram he is constructing? William, we may imagine, reasons as follows. "Let's see ... I know that

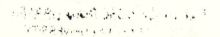

there is a perfect being. Suppose I call that being—or one of them if there is more than one—'X'. X has all perfections, and one perfection is necessary existence. Therefore, X exists in all possible worlds. Moreover, I know that X has all perfections essentially. That is, I know that X has all perfections in every possible world in which X exists. I can infer that there is something in every possible world—namely X—that has the property P. Therefore, the following world-diagram

$$
\begin{array}{ll}
\text{One} & \text{P} \\
 & \text{P} \quad < \\
\text{Three} & \text{P} \\
\text{Four} & \text{P}
\end{array}
$$

correctly represents the distribution of the property P among the various possible worlds."

Let us assume for the moment that the reasoning that we have attributed to William is correct. Then—given the truth of our two premises—it follows that the world-diagram William has drawn is correct in Possible World Two. Can we infer from this anything about which world-diagrams are correct in the other three possible worlds? We certainly cannot infer that *this* world-diagram is correct in any other possible world, for this diagram tells us that Possible World Two is the actual world, and that proposition is, as we have seen, true only in Two. But suppose that we make just one change in William's diagram; suppose that we take the actuality cursor and "slide it down a notch," so that it is placed beside the circle representing Possible World Three:

$$
\begin{array}{ll}
\text{One} & \text{P} \\
\text{Two} & \text{P} \\
\text{Three} & \text{P} \quad < \\
\text{Four} & \text{P}
\end{array}
$$

The revised diagram says that Possible World Three is the actual world. This assertion is true in Possible World Three. Does it follow from the assumption that William's diagram is correct in Two that the revised diagram is correct in Three? The following general principle of modal reasoning would justify this conclusion:

If a world-diagram is correct in the possible world x, then the diagram obtained from it by moving the actuality cursor until it is beside the circle representing the possible world y is correct in the possible world y.

This principle seems intuitively very plausible. All it really says is that the "inner" or intrinsic features of a given possible world are features that world has from the perspective of all the possible worlds. It could be summed up in the following slogan: the only thing that changes from possible world to possible world is which possible world is actual. But this slogan is ambiguous, for there is a sense in which lots of other things "change from possible world to possible world": who won the battle of Waterloo, the population of Russia, whether I exist—in fact, everything that could be different. A more cautious way to put the thought the slogan is intended to convey is this: The only thing about a possible world x that can "change" or "look different" when x is "viewed from" various possible worlds (including x itself) is whether x is actual.

Thus, the only feature of the whole set of possible worlds that two possible worlds "disagree" about is which member of that set is the actual world. (They must, of course, disagree about *at least* this much, since it is true in each possible world that *it* is the actual world. Our principle says that this is *all* they disagree about.) We have, in fact, already assumed this principle, or something very much like it. We assumed it when we were describing William's reasoning. William, we remember, reasoned (in part) as follows: "I can infer that there is something in every possible world—namely X—that has the property P. Therefore, the following world-diagram

One   (P)
Two   (P)   <
Three   (P)
Four   (P)

correctly represents the distribution of the property P among the various possible worlds." But what—a carping critic might ask—allows us to assume that William, having reached the conclusion that something in every possible world had the property P, would go on to draw the world-diagram displayed above? Why shouldn't he go on to draw, say, the following diagram?

One   (P)
Two   (P)   <
Three   (P)

"But we are assuming that there are four possible worlds, and a world-diagram, by definition, contains circles representing *all* of the possible worlds." True, the carping critic replies, but it does not follow from the assumption that there are four possible worlds, Possible World Two among them, that *in Possible World Two* there are four possible worlds. That would only follow if we assumed that Possible World Two was the actual world (in which case what was true would be true in Two) or at least that the possible worlds that exist from the point of view of Two are the same ones that exist from the point of view of the actual world. But suppose that (say) Possible World Four is the actual world and that, according to Possible World Two, there are only the three possible worlds One, Two, and Three. How do we know that the following world-diagram isn't correct in Four?

One   Ⓟ
Two   Ⓟ
Three Ⓟ
Four   ◯   <

If this diagram is indeed correct in Possible World Four, then it might well be that there is no perfect being in Four (which, remember, is the actual world) even though it is true in Two that a perfect being exists in all possible worlds—for it might just be that from the point of view of Possible World Two, there *is* no such possible world as Four. And this shows that the conclusion of the modal ontological argument does not follow from its premises; for all we know we are in just the situation we have imagined: a perfect being is *possible* because it exists in a certain possible world, but it does not *in fact exist* because the possible world that is in fact the actual world does not exist—even as a possibility—from the point of view of the world in which the perfect being exists.

Here ends the carping critic's carping. What the critic is suggesting is, in effect, that what is possible is not fixed and necessary: certain things that are in fact possible might not have been even possible. For example, if Possible World Four does not exist from the point of view of Possible World Two, this means—given that Four is the actual world—that the way things are might not even have been possible. The critic is in fact suggesting that what is possible and impossible might have been different. And this does not seem to be a very plausible notion.

At any rate, it does not seem to be very plausible if by "possible and impossible" we understand those things that are possible and impossible "in themselves," as opposed to those things that are possible and impossible in relation to other things. Perhaps some examples will make the proposed distinction clearer. It is now impossible for anyone to own a passenger pigeon; that is because passenger pigeons are now extinct. It was impossible for anyone to fly to the moon in 1930; that was because the relevant technology had not yet been invented. Such impossibilities as these we might call conditional impossibilities, since their impossibility is conditional on something that might have been different: *if* passenger pigeons had not become extinct (as they might well not have), it *wouldn't* be impossible to own one; *if* the pace of technological development since the beginning of the industrial revolution had been considerably more rapid (as presumably it might have been), it *wouldn't* have been impossible to fly to the moon in 1930. One might even argue that, although it is in fact impossible to travel at 400,000 kilometers per second, it wouldn't have been impossible if the speed of light were twice what it is, and that the speed of light could have been—in some sense of 'could have been'—twice what it is. But the impossibility of a round square or a liquid wine bottle is not conditional on anything; such things are simply, without qualification, impossible. This kind of impossibility we may call *intrinsic* impossibility, and we may say that what is not intrinsically impossible is intrinsically possible.

It seems very plausible to suppose that although what is conditionally impossible may be different in different possible worlds, what is intrinsically impossible (and intrinsically possible) is the same in all possible worlds. A round square is intrinsically impossible, and it would have been intrinsically impossible no matter what: not only is there no possible world in which there are round squares, but there is no possible world in which it is true that there *could be* round squares. A sixty-meter–high marzipan statue of Lassie is intrinsically possible, and it would have been intrinsically possible no matter what: not only is there a possible world in which there is a sixty-meter–high marzipan statue of Lassie, but there is no possible world in which it is true that there *couldn't be* a sixty-meter–high marzipan statue of Lassie.

I said above that our principle rules out the critic's objection. This is not difficult to see. If the above world-diagram were indeed correct in Possible World Four, as suggested, then the "three-world" diagram would not be correct in Two; instead—the principle says—the following diagram would be correct in Two:

$$
\begin{array}{ll}
\text{One} & \text{\textcircled{P}} \\
\text{Two} & \text{\textcircled{P}} \quad < \\
\text{Three} & \text{\textcircled{P}} \\
\text{Four} & \bigcirc \\
\end{array}
$$

Let us assume that our plausible principle is indeed correct. The *actual* existence of a perfect being now follows easily. One of the four possible worlds must be actual, and it does not make any difference (in the matter of the validity of the modal ontological argument) which of them it is, since, in each of them, a world-diagram obtained from the figure

$$
\begin{array}{ll}
\text{One} & \text{\textcircled{P}} \\
\text{Two} & \text{\textcircled{P}} \\
\text{Three} & \text{\textcircled{P}} \\
\text{Four} & \text{\textcircled{P}} \\
\end{array}
$$

by an appropriate placement of the actuality cursor is correct. (The world-diagram obtained by placing the actuality cursor on the top line of the figure is correct in Possible World One, and so on.) Therefore, no matter which of the four worlds the actual world is, a perfect being exists in the actual world. (It should now be evident that our argument did not depend on our simplifying assumption that there were just four possible worlds. And neither did it depend on our arbitrary choice of Possible World Two as our "starting point": if we had begun by assuming that a perfect being existed in One or in Three or in Four, we should have got the same result.)

Have we therefore proved the existence of a perfect being? If we have, then we have answered the question, Why should there be anything at all? If there has to be a perfect being—and the modal ontological argument claims to show not only that there *is* a perfect being, but that there *has to be* one—then it is impossible for there to be nothing at all. But the modal ontological argument rests on two premises and a principle of modal inference. And at least one of these three things is far from evident: that a perfect being is not impossible. Our argument perhaps shows that the concept of a perfect being is in an important way unlike the concept of a lion or a unicorn. It is not impossible for there to be unicorns,[7] but there are none. If there were no lions, it would nevertheless be possible for there to be lions, and lions, despite their possibility, would not exist. A perfect being, however, is not like that: if a perfect being is so much as intrinsically possible—like a unicorn, and unlike a liquid wine bottle—then a perfect being really does exist. But is a perfect being possible?

This is a question that we cannot evade, for there can be no presumption in favor of possibility. It may be that in many areas of thought and inquiry one is entitled to assume that a certain concept is possible—not self-contradictory, not intrinsically impossible—in the absence of a specific argument for its impossibility, rather as, under Common Law, a person is to be presumed innocent of a charge till proved guilty. But this cannot be a presumption in any area of inquiry in which modal reasoning like that which we have been considering is employed. This contention is easily demonstrated by the fact that such a presumption of possibility would lead to contradictory results.

To see that this *is* a fact, consider the concept of a "knowno": the concept of a being who knows that there is no perfect being. There would seem to be no reason, on the face of it, to suppose that there being a knowno is an intrinsically impossible state of affairs, like there being a liquid wine bottle. But consider. If a knowno is not intrinsically impossible, then there is a knowno in some possible world. But then there is a possible world in which there is no perfect being, since, if someone knows something, then what that person knows is true. And, as we have seen, if a perfect being is possible, then there exists a perfect being in every possible world. It follows that if a knowno is possible, then a perfect being is impossible—and it also follows that if a perfect being is possible, then a knowno is impossible.

We have, therefore, a pair of concepts—the concept of a perfect being and the concept of a knowno—that is such that either is possible if and only if the other is impossible. We know, therefore, that one of these concepts is possible and the other impossible. But, at present, we have no grounds for saying of either of the two concepts that it is the one that is the possible one. But if we adopted the general rule "A concept is to be assumed to be possible in the absence of a specific argument for its impossibility," we should have to assume both of these concepts to be possible, and we know that it is false that they are both possible. (It is interesting to note that we cannot consistently adopt the Common Law principle "A person is to be presumed innocent of a charge till proved guilty" if we know that either Alice or Bertram murdered Clara but have no reason to think that Alice murdered her and no reason to think that Bertram murdered her. The best we can do in such a case if we want to be logically consistent is not to assume that Alice is guilty and not to assume that Bertram is guilty.)

If we wish to evaluate the modal ontological argument, therefore, there is no alternative to attempting to find some specific argument for the conclusion that the concept of a perfect being is possible or else some specific argument for the conclusion that a perfect being is impossible.

How shall we do this? Well, how, in general, do we go about finding out whether a concept is possible? The most reliable way of showing that a concept is possible is to show that is has *instances*. That is, the most reliable way of showing that the concept of a dog is possible is to show that there are dogs; the most reliable way of showing that the concept of a unicorn is possible is to show that there are unicorns, and so on. But this method will not help us to find out whether the concept of a perfect being is possible, since we do not know whether there are any perfect beings. (Or, if some among us do know that there is a perfect being, or do know that there is no perfect being, this knowledge is certainly not *common* knowledge, and it is not, therefore, knowledge that we can appeal to in presenting a metaphysical argument that is not addressed to any particular group of people.)

What other methods are there? There is always the method of abstract metaphysical argument. The seventeenth-century metaphysician G. W. Leibniz claimed to have discovered a metaphysical argument demonstrating the possibility of a perfect being. (Leibniz, a very acute modal reasoner, saw that any successful version of the ontological argument must include a proof that a perfect being was not impossible.) His reasoning was as follows. A perfect being is a being who has all perfections and thus is possible if all perfections are consistent with one another. And every perfection is a "simple, positive property." (A simple property is one that is not a complex that includes simpler properties, as *being both red and round* is a complex that includes both *being red* and *being round*. A positive property is a property that is not negative: *being red* and *being round* are positive properties, and *not being red* and *being non-round* are negative properties.) And all simple, positive properties are consistent with one another, since the only way for two properties to be inconsistent is for one to be the negation of the other (example: *not being red* is the negation of *being red*) or for one to be a complex that includes the negation of the other or the negation of a property included in the other (example: *being round and not red* is inconsistent with both *being red* and *being hard and red*).

Leibniz held that most of our everyday adjectives stood for elaborate complexes of simple, positive properties and their negations. This is what makes it possible for, say, 'hard' and 'soft' to denote incompatible properties; a complete analysis of hardness and softness would show that there is some simple, positive property F such that one of them includes F and the other includes the negation of F. It obviously follows from this analysis of inconsistency that no simple, positive properties are inconsistent with one another, and, if every perfection is indeed a simple, positive property, it follows that a being who has all perfections is possible. (It does not, however, follow that a perfect being, in our sense of the term, is possible, for we have defined a perfect being as a being who has all perfections *essentially*. To reach the further conclusion that a perfect being, in our sense, was possible, we should need some further premise, such as 'If a property is a perfection, then the property of having *that* property essentially is also a perfection'. An instance of this general thesis would be: If wisdom is a perfection, then *having wisdom essentially* is also a perfection.)

There are a great many problems with Leibniz's argument. I will mention only one of them. It is by no means clear that the idea of a simple, positive property makes any sense. Let us look just at the idea of a positive property (remarks similar to those that follow apply to the idea of a simple property). Consider the property *not having parts*. This would seem to be a pretty good example of a negative property, being obviously the negation of the property *having parts*. But suppose we call the property of not having parts 'simplicity', as Leibniz himself did. (He in fact regarded it as one of the perfections, and thus as a simple, positive property.) Then we can call the property of having parts 'non-simplicity', and, if we do our thinking in this terminology, it looks as if non-simplicity is the negative property, being the negation of simplicity. This case suggests that properties are not negative or positive *in themselves* and that the belief that they are is a mistaken inference from the fact that properties can have names that have negative or positive forms—sometimes both a negative and a positive name for one and the same property. There is a good deal more to this issue, however, and Leibniz would have a lot to say in reply to what I have said. In this brief passage I have tried only to give a rough idea of why I regard Leibniz's argument for the possibility of a perfect being as unsatisfactory.

If we find it difficult to show that the concept of a perfect being is possible, this could be because that concept is in fact impossible. If this were true, is there any way in which it might be demonstrated? It is sometimes possible to show that a concept is impossible by showing that some sort of impossibility can be deduced from the proposition that that concept applies to something. For example, we can show that the concept of a round square is impossible by pointing out that if there were a round square it would have corners (since it is square) and would also *not* have corners (since it is round).

The Anglo-American philosopher J. N. Findlay once claimed to be able to show that an impossibility could be derived from the concept of a perfect being. His argument was that a perfect being must be a necessary being, and that an impossibility follows from the concept of a necessary being. An impossibility follows from the concept of a necessary being, Findlay argues, because if there were a necessary being, there would have to be at least one necessarily true existential proposition, and necessarily true existential propositions are impossible. (An existential proposition is a proposition that asserts the existence of something, a proposition of the form "There is an *x*" or "There exists an *x*" or "An *x* exists.") And necessarily true existential propositions are impossible because necessary truths are just those truths that owe their status as truths to the meanings of words. (For example, it is necessarily true that all nuns are female; but the necessity of all nuns' being female is due simply to the fact that "female" is a part of the meaning of the word 'nun': we simply don't apply the word 'nun' to males—not even to members of religious orders—for 'nun' simply *means* 'woman belonging to a religious order, membership in which implies vows of poverty, chastity, and obedience'.)

Now it is obviously impossible (the argument continues) for there to be a true existential proposition that owes its truth to the meanings of words. It may be a consequence of the meanings of the word A and the word B that whatever A applies to, B applies to also—as with 'nun' and 'female'. But it can never be a consequence simply of the meaning of the word A that A applies to anything. We may give to 'nun' or 'aardvark' or 'molybdenum' whatever meanings we like, but these meanings will never guarantee that there is anything to which these words apply. But for there to be a necessary existential proposition, there would have to be a word or words whose meaning guaranteed that they applied to something, and this, as we have seen is impossible.

To retrace the steps of the argument: there can be no such thing as a necessary existential proposition, so there can be no such thing as a necessary being, so there can be no such thing as a perfect being. And, therefore, the modal ontological argument has a false premise: that a perfect being is not impossible. And, therefore, the modal ontological argument is a failure, and we are still without an answer to the question, Why should there be anything at all?

The main problem with Findlay's argument lies in the theory of necessary truth that it appeals to. Why should we accept the thesis that all necessary truths are due to the meanings of words and the consequent judgment that there can be no necessary existential propositions? This theory was almost universally accepted by English-speaking philosophers at the time at which Findlay wrote (1948).[8] It was widely, if not universally, regarded as a theory that philosophical investigation had shown to be true. As of the time of this writing, however, it has become merely a part of the history of philosophy. A great many philosophers of logic and language currently working would argue that the proposition 'The atomic number of iron is 26' is necessarily true and that its truth is not due to the meanings of words. They would argue that this proposition is necessarily true because the atomic structure of an element is of its very essence and that no matter how much some possible metal might superficially resemble iron, unless the nuclei of the atoms that composed it contained twenty-six protons, it would simply not *be* iron. And yet, these philosophers would argue, it is not a part of the meaning of the word 'iron' that it apply only to a substance that is a chemical element having the atomic number 26—not, at least if something can be a part of the meaning of a word only if a person who knows the meaning of that word knows that it is (as, for example, someone who knows the meaning of the word 'nun' knows that a nun has to be female).

That this is so is evident from such facts as the following: lots of people who have no idea that there is such a concept as "atomic number" know the meaning of the word 'iron' perfectly well; Queen Elizabeth I meant by the word 'iron' just what you and I mean by it, even though she died long before the advent of modern chemistry (lots of English words have changed their meanings since the sixteenth century, but 'iron' is not one of them); the Latin word 'ferrum' means exactly what the English word 'iron' means, even though

Latin ceased to be a living language a thousand years or more before the advent of modern chemistry.

We should note, however, that even if these philosophers are right, it does not follow that there can be necessary existential propositions, for 'The atomic number of iron is 26' is not an existential proposition: if the currently popular theory I have sketched is right, this proposition states one of the essential characteristics of iron, but it does not say that there *is* any iron. But it does at least follow from this theory that the account of necessary truth on which Findlay bases his conclusion that there can be no necessary existential propositions is mistaken. And there are propositions that many philosophers would say were necessary existential propositions. Mathematics provides many plausible examples of necessary existential propositions, such as 'There exists a number that can be expressed in more than one way as the sum of two cubes'. It is true that the mathematical examples provide only cases of necessary propositions that assert the existence of universals, such as numbers. Still, they tend to undermine Findlay's position, since his argument and its conclusion are very general. His argument proceeds from premises about the nature of language, and its conclusion should hold for any proposition, regardless of its subject-matter. His conclusion would therefore appear to be refuted by examples of necessary existential propositions no matter what their subject-matter. If his argument were sound, it should show that there could not be necessary existential propositions even in mathematics.

If this much is correct, however, it does not show that there could be a necessarily existent *individual thing*. Perhaps it is only universals like numbers that can be necessarily existent. And a perfect being would certainly have to be an individual thing. Findlay's argument may be refuted by the observation that it proves too much (that there could not be necessarily existent universals), but even if this is granted, it has no tendency to show that his stated conclusion—the impossibility of a perfect being—is wrong. I know of no argument that purports to show that there could not be a necessarily existent individual thing, with the exception of Findlay-style arguments for the conclusion that there could not be a necessarily existent *anything*. Such an argument would have to show that the two properties *being necessarily existent* and *being an individual thing* were inconsistent with each other, and I can see no way of constructing even a plausible candidate for such an argument.

It is interesting to note that if these two properties are *not* inconsistent, then there is in fact a necessarily existent individual thing. This can be shown by a simplified version of the reasoning that we used to show the validity of the modal ontological argument:

> If a necessarily existent individual thing is possible, then there is a necessarily existent individual thing in some possible world. Since that individual thing is necessarily existent in that possible world, it is true in that possible world that it, that very individual thing, exists in all possible worlds. It follows that it is true in every possible world that that thing exists in all possible worlds, since "nothing changes from possible world to possible world but which possible world is actual." Moreover, it seems

evident that the property *being an individual thing* is essential to whatever has it; if something is an individual thing, then it could not have been a universal or a mere collection or a stuff or any other kind of non-individual thing. Therefore, this being not only exists in every possible world but is also an individual thing in every possible world. And there is thus a necessarily existent individual thing in every possible world, including, of course, whichever world is the actual world. Therefore, there actually is a necessarily existent individual thing.

This argument, which we may call the minimal modal ontological argument, shows that the reasoning that underlies the modal ontological argument does not really have anything to do with the concept of a perfect being. What this reasoning really shows is that, for any set of properties whatever, if it is possible for there to be a thing that is necessarily existent and has all of these properties essentially, then there actually is something that is necessarily existent and has all of these properties essentially. (A perfect being is a being that has all perfections and has them essentially; a perfect being is thus a being that is necessarily existent—necessary existence being a perfection—and has a certain set of properties essentially.) It is interesting to note that the minimal modal ontological argument will do as well as the modal ontological argument itself for our purposes. (Our question is, Why is there something rather than nothing? and any individual thing is a "something.") It is free from logical error if and only if the modal ontological argument itself is free from logical error, and its controversial premise—a necessarily existent individual thing is possible—is true if the corresponding premise of the modal ontological argument is true. I say 'if' and not 'only if' because the proposition that a perfect being is possible entails that a necessarily existent individual thing is possible, but the reverse entailment does not hold, or at least does not obviously hold. A perfect being has to be a necessarily existent individual thing, but a necessarily existent individual thing does not have to be a perfect being, or does not obviously have to be a perfect being. It looks as if the premise of the minimal modal ontological argument might well be easier to investigate than the premise of the modal ontological argument. And the conclusion of the minimal modal ontological argument suffices for our present purposes, since we are investigating the question, Why should there be anything (i.e., any individual thing) at all?

Let us therefore turn our attention to the minimal modal ontological argument and ask whether its premise is true; that is, whether a necessarily existent individual thing is possible; that is, whether the properties *existing necessarily* and *being an individual thing* are compatible. It does not seem possible to deduce any formal contradiction from the assumption that there is a necessarily existent individual thing.

Nevertheless, these two properties may well be incompatible. It is hard to believe that the two properties *being a solid sheet of iron* and *being as transparent as glass* are compatible, but there is no way of deriving a formal contradiction from the proposition 'There is a solid sheet of iron that is as transparent as glass'. On the other hand, the two properties may well be compatible. How can one know? I am at a loss to answer this question. In general, there are only two "foolproof" ways to discover whether two properties are compatible. One knows that two properties are compatible if one knows that there is in fact something that has both of them. And one knows that two properties are incompatible if one can deduce a formal contradiction from the assumption that something has both of them. As I have said, I know of no way to apply the latter method in the case of necessary existence and individuality. And as to the former method, if I knew how to show that there was a necessarily existent individual thing, I should have no need of the minimal modal ontological argument, since I should know that its conclusion—that there is a necessarily existent individual thing—was true independently of the minimal modal ontological argument.

If we cannot show that a necessarily existent individual thing is possible, then we certainly cannot show that a perfect being is possible, since a perfect being is a being that is a necessarily existent individual thing *and* has various other properties—such as wisdom and goodness and unlimited power (or whatever the perfections other than necessary existence may be). And while there might in theory be a proof that a perfect being was impossible that did not prove that a necessarily existent individual thing was impossible—a proof, say, that wisdom was a perfection, together with a proof that wisdom was incompatible with necessary existence—no one has in fact proposed such a proof and no such proof suggests itself. All the proofs of the thesis that a perfect being is impossible that have ever been proposed are (supposed) proofs of the impossibility of necessary existence. It would seem, therefore, that the long history of the ontological argument, from Saint Anselm to the present day, is at best inconclusive. Every version of the argument either contains some logical error or other or else depends upon a premise whose claim to truth we are unable to adjudicate. And, therefore, we have not found an answer to the question, Why should there be anything at all?

There is, nevertheless, one valuable lesson we have learned from our study of the ontological argument. If we could show that there was a necessary being, a necessarily existing individual thing, we should have an answer to our question. For if there were a necessary being, then it would be impossible for there to be nothing. And if we could show that it was impossible for there to be nothing, that, surely, would count as an answer to our question.

Is there any approach to the question whether there is a necessary being other than *via* the ontological argument? There is indeed. It has often been suggested that if there were no necessary being there could not be any beings at all. If this "if" statement could be shown to be true, we could combine it with the obvious truth that there is something to show that there is a necessary being.

Suggestions for Further Reading

Plantinga's *The Ontological Argument* is an excellent collection. See especially the selections from Anselm, Gaunilo, Aquinas, Descartes (including Descartes's replies to the objections of various philosophers), Leibniz, Kant, Findlay, Malcolm, and Hartshorne. Plantinga's *God, Freedom, and Evil* contains a powerful and sophisticated discussion of the ontological argument in various versions, including the "modal" version (pp. 85–111).

Hume's seminal argument for the conclusion that there can be no necessary existential propositions occurs in *Dialogues Concerning Natural Religion*, Part IX. Current "anti-Humean" views on the nature of necessary truth are contained in Kripke's *Naming and Necessity* and Putnam's "The Meaning of 'Meaning'. " These are difficult works for those without formal philosophical training, but are, at least in large part, accessible to the highly motivated reader. Schwartz's *Naming, Necessity, and Natural Kinds* is a useful collection of essays on the issues raised by Kripke and Putnam. Kripke's important essay "Identity and Necessity" is particularly recommended.

6

Necessary Being: The Cosmological Argument

THE ARGUMENT WE SHALL EXAMINE in this chapter is based on the so-called Principle of Sufficient Reason: for every truth, for everything that is so, there is a sufficient reason for its being true or being so.[1] What the Principle of Sufficient Reason tells us can best be appreciated by looking at the way it applies in the case of a particular fact and then generalizing what we see. Consider the fact that my car wouldn't start last Tuesday. What the Principle of Sufficient Reason tells us is that if someone asked, "*Why* wouldn't van Inwagen's car start last Tuesday?" there is an answer that could be given to that person's question, an answer that is both correct and fully satisfying and informative. And, in general, for anything that is so, there is an answer to the question why that thing is so: this is the Principle of Sufficient Reason.

Before we go on, it may be advisable to clear up a possible confusion. The words 'why' and 'reason' and many related words are used in various senses. Suppose someone were to ask why Adrian, who was hit by a truck whose brakes had failed, died. Here are two answers to this question:

- There was no reason at all for his death; he just happened to be at the wrong place at the wrong time.
- He died of massive trauma, which was due to his having been struck by a large, heavy vehicle moving at a considerable velocity.

The first of these answers presupposes that the question was a request for something that would display the *meaning* or *purpose* of Adrian's death. But the Principle of Sufficient Reason—which I shall mostly call the Principle for the remainder of this discussion—does not tell us that everything that happens has a meaning or a purpose. And that is certainly to the credit of the Principle, for it is as clear as anything could be that it is not true that everything has a meaning or purpose. (If I knock over a bottle of wine while gesturing expansively at dinner, the shape of the resulting stain on the carpet pretty clearly has no meaning or purpose.) What the Principle tells us is that an answer of the *second* kind is available to every "why" question. (An answer of the second kind need not be at all interesting. Shakespeare and Cervantes died on the same day, and if someone asks why they died on the same day, the Principle asserts that that person's question has an answer. But it is consistent with the Principle that the answer be nothing more interesting than an explanation of the fact that Shakespeare died on 23 April 1616, together with a wholly unrelated explanation of the fact that Cervantes died on 23 April 1616.)

The Principle of Sufficient Reason is a principle that has a lot of intuitive appeal. Some might argue that it lies at the basis of all science. The ancient astronomers were content carefully to describe the motions of the planets and the stars. If you had asked them *why* the lights in the sky moved according to the enormously complicated set of rules that they had extracted from their observations, you would not have awakened much interest. A Babylonian astronomer might have said, "Well, they're gods. Obviously, gods move as they like. It would be impious to enquire further." A Greek might have said, "Well, the philosopher Aristotle said that the planets move in circles because circular motion is the most perfect motion. But that's too deep for me. I'm just a simple astronomer. All *I* can do is to tell you the way they actually do move." But modern science takes an entirely different attitude to "why" questions about observed phenomena. According to modern science, for example, the rules that describe the motion of the planets can actually be explained (by, roughly speaking, deducing those rules from Newton's laws of motion and his law of universal gravitation). And—so some would argue—modern science is never content to say that something just *is*, and that's all that there is to say about it. No scientist would be content to say that mountains are just *there*, and that's all there is to say about the existence of mountains. Modern science, therefore, presupposes the Principle, and so do all of us who live in a scientific age and a scientific culture. Whether or not it is right to say that the Principle is a presupposition of modern science, it does seem right to say that there is a good deal of plausibility to it. Let us, for the moment, accept the Principle and see what follows from it.

We can begin by taking a look round us and noting that the World contains things. Whatever features these things may have, it is obvious that there *are* some things. (Even if the Monist is right, there is *one* thing.) All of the things we observe would appear to be contingent things. At any rate, let us assume that all of the things we observe are contingent. (If any of them were necessary, we could conclude our argument at this point.) The following statement may therefore be reasonably appealed to as a premise in an argument for the existence of at least one necessary thing:

There are some contingent things.

Now if the Principle is correct, there is some explanation for the truth of this statement, some answer to the question 'Why are there contingent things?' But what would an explanation of there being contingent things look like? What is a possible candidate for an explanation of the existence of contingent things, even if it is not a correct explanation? One possible explanation is the following:

There is a necessarily existent thing that is in some way responsible for the fact that there are contingent things.

This is, or course, not a very detailed explanation, but it seems to be a perfectly satisfactory explanation as far as it goes. It is conceivable that someone might object to it on the ground that it "merely pushes the problem of the existence of things back a step." The worry here is something like this: "All right, the necessarily existent thing explains the existence of the contingent things, but what explains *its* existence? Why does *it* exist?" But to say this is to neglect the fact that a necessary being is one whose non-existence is impossible. Thus, for any necessary being, there is by definition a sufficient reason for its existence: there could hardly be a more satisfying explanation for the existence of a thing than that its non-existence was impossible.

As to the fact that the explanation is almost wholly lacking in specifics, we should note that there are few if any explanations that could not be given in greater detail. The explanation could be "filled in" in various ways, some of them inconsistent with one another. Here, for example, are two inconsistent explanations of there being contingent things that come from filling in the details of the above explanation in different ways:

- God is necessarily existent and is the source of the existence of all other things; although He was under no compulsion to create anything, of His own free will He made things other than Himself; His purpose in bringing these things into existence surpasses human understanding.[2]
- A formless, necessarily existent Chaos is the source of the existence of all other things; swirls and local condensations occur by chance within the Chaos, and it is these that give rise to contingent things.

We are interested only in the question whether *some* version of the explanation is correct. The details by which such an explanation might be filled in and made more complete, although they are interesting and important, need not detain us. But is some version of this explanation correct? Is there any other way to explain the existence of contingent things than by appealing to the existence of a necessary being that is in some manner responsible for the existence of contingent things? Let us see whether we can conceive of an alternative explanation. An alternative explanation would be one that explained the existence of contingent beings without appealing in any way to a necessary being that was responsible for their existence. There seem to be grave problems with the idea of such an explanation.

Suppose that there were only contingent things. (We are concerned only with individual things, or "individuals," as we shall call them in this chapter. Some or all universals may be necessarily existent, but universals by themselves cannot explain the existence of individuals. Only individuals can explain the existence of individuals. For example, the existence of properties and numbers does not explain the fact that there are individuals to have those properties and to be counted by those numbers. Since the term 'necessary being' is the term that is usual in contexts in which necessary existence is opposed to contingent existence, let us use this term with the understanding that a necessary *being* is a thing that can be responsible for the existence of particular contingent individuals.) Could there then be an explanation of the fact that there were contingent things? Could there be an answer to the question 'Why are there contingent things'?

It is hard to see how there could be. Any statement that was true in a world in which there were only contingent things—and whatever else a correct explanation may involve, the statements made in the course of giving the explanation must all be true—would derive its truth from the way those contingent things were arranged (that is, from the number of them and their individual intrinsic properties and the relations they bore to one another). And all such statements would appear to presuppose the existence of contingent things. It seems wholly implausible to suppose that a series of statements all of which presuppose the existence of contingent things could add up to an explanation of the existence of contingent things. One might as well try to explain the fact that there are human beings by setting out a series of statements about the properties of human beings and the relations they bear to one another.

In general, to explain the existence of the members of any class of contingent things, one must cite facts about the properties and relations of things outside that class. For example, to explain the existence of the human species, one must cite some facts about God or about the evolutionary process or about *something* besides human beings. And doesn't this rule apply to the whole class of contingent things? To explain the fact that there are contingent things at all, one must cite some facts about non-contingent things. And non-contingent things are just necessarily existent things. And since facts wholly about universals will not explain the existence of contingent things, it follows that any explanation of the existence of contingent things must involve facts about one or more necessary beings.

If this reasoning is correct, then, given that there are contingent things, and given the Principle of Sufficient Reason, there is at least one necessary being. (This reasoning is a version of the "cosmological argument." The name comes from the Greek word *kosmos*, which means 'the universe' or 'the totality of contingent things'.) And if there is a necessary being, we have our answer to the question, Why should there be anything at all? (For, if there is a necessary being, then "There being nothing" is an impossible state of affairs.) Indeed, as we have seen, our reasoning does not even require the premise that there are contingent things. The premise that there is *something* would suffice. For everything is either necessary or contingent; therefore, if there is something, there is either something necessary or something contingent (or both); if there is something necessary, there is, of course, something necessary; if there is something contingent, then (as the cosmological argument shows) there is something necessary; hence, there is something necessary. Indeed, we do not even require the premise that there *is* something. The premise that there *could be* something would suffice. For if there could be something, then in some possible world there is something. And the above reasoning, carried out in that possible world, would show that in that possible world there was a necessary being. (The cosmological argument, together with the premise that it is possible for there to be *something*, thus supplies the doubtful premise of the minimal modal ontological argument: that it is possible for there to be a necessary being.) And, as we saw in our discussion of the modal ontological argument, if there is a necessary being in some possible world, there is a necessary being in the actual world. The cosmological argument therefore in effect shows that if there can be something, there has to be something: if it is not impossible for there to be something, then it is impossible for there to be nothing. And we could hardly be asked to do better with the question, Why should there be anything at all? than to deduce the impossibility of there being nothing from the mere possibility of there being something.

Unfortunately we have not deduced this impressive conclusion from the single premise that it is possible for there to be something. Our argument has a second premise: the Principle of Sufficient Reason. It is time to ask how plausible this premise is. It turns out that this premise is not very plausible at all.

In the first place there are scientific difficulties. According to quantum mechanics, nature is filled with events whose occurrence has no explanation whatever. If, for example, the nucleus of a certain radium atom decays at a certain time, there is no explanation whatever for its decaying at that time rather than some other time. Or, at least, this is true according to the standard versions of quantum mechanics. It is possible to construct "hidden variable" versions of quantum mechanics—or alternatives to quantum mechanics; whether one calls them versions of quantum mechanics or alternatives to quantum mechanics depends on how one wants to use the term 'quantum mechanics'—according to which there is an explanation for these events. But hidden-variable theories have various unattractive features, and most physicists do not find them of much interest. Whether or not the standard version of quantum mechanics is correct, these facts at least cast considerable doubt on the Principle.

In the second place, a careful examination of the Principle shows that it has a consequence that most people would have a very hard time accepting: that all true propositions are necessarily true. In broad outline, the argument is this: if there are any contingent propositions (that is, contingently true propositions), then there is a set of all contingent propositions; but an explanation of any set of contingent propositions must appeal to some contingent propositions outside that set; hence, the whole set of contingent propositions can have no explanation; hence, if every set of true propositions is such that there is an explanation for the fact that it contains only truths (as the Principle implies), there can be only necessary truths.

But this "broad outline" is too compressed to be of much use. It is intended only to give the reader some sense of where the following rather lengthy piece of reasoning is going. Here is our plan: we shall assume for the sake of argument that there are contingent propositions, and we shall deduce from this assumption the conclusion that the Principle of Sufficient Reason is false.

Suppose, then, that there are some contingent propositions. It follows that there are propositions that are true in some possible worlds and false in others. But then there is more than one possible world. Our argument will not depend on how many there are, so long as we assume that there is more than one. Let us suppose that there are four—the same four that figured in our discussion of the modal ontological argument. Exactly one of these four possible worlds must be actual. Our argument will not depend on *which*, so let us arbitrarily suppose that it is Possible World Two that is the actual world.

If the Principle of Sufficient Reason is correct, there is a sufficient reason for the fact that Possible World Two is the actual world; alternatively, there is a complete and correct explanation of this fact, or there is a complete and correct answer to the question 'Why is Possible World Two the actual world?' Let us use 'S' to stand for the series of statements that one would make if one were giving this explanation or this answer. We know that S must be true in Possible World Two (that is, we know that each statement in the series of statements S must be true in Possible World Two), for every statement made in the course of giving a correct explanation must be true, and Possible World Two is the actual world, and any statement that is true is true in the actual world.

Could it be that S is also true in one or more of the other possible worlds? Not if S is, as the Principle demands, a *complete* explanation of the fact that Possible World Two is the actual world. Here is an analogy that will help to explain why this is the case. Suppose that the cancer rate in Watkins Grove is much higher than the national average, and the City Council wants to know why. Suppose that it is pointed out that there are many chemical plants in Watkins Grove, and it is suggested that the presence of these plants is the explanation the City Council is looking for. But if it turns out that many communities the size of Watkins Grove contain a comparable number of chemical plants and yet have a cancer rate that is not much different from the national average, this fact by itself will show that the explanation the City Council has been offered cannot be *complete*: if it were, the cancer rate would be as high in those other communities as it is in Watkins Grove. It may well be that the chemical plants are an important *part* of a complete explanation of the high cancer rate in Watkins Grove, but, as the idiom has it, "there must be more to it than that." (The particular chemicals produced in Watkins Grove, or the way in which the plants dispose of their chemical wastes, or some combination of any of literally hundreds of factors must also be a part of the complete explanation of the cancer rate in Watkins Grove.)

A *complete* explanation of the cancer rate in Watkins Grove must be a series of statements that does not leave open any possibility that the cancer rate in Watkins Grove be other than what it is. By analogy, a complete explanation of the actuality of Possible World Two must be a series of statements that does not leave open any possibility that Possible World Two be non-actual. But then if S, which is by stipulation a *complete* explanation of the fact that Possible World Two is the actual world, were true in, say, Possible World Four, then it would be true in Possible World Four that Possible World Two was the actual world. (And this, of course, is impossible, for the only possible world that is actual in Possible World Four is Possible World Four itself.)

In evaluating this reasoning, we must not confuse the notion of a complete explanation with the notion of "all the explanation there is." If the Principle were false, it might be that some facts had only partial explanations. A partial explanation of a fact might be "complete" in the sense that it left nothing out. But it would not be complete in the sense that if all the statements made in the course of giving the explanation were true, then the fact being explained would have to obtain. If it turned out that some chemical plants caused cancer, and that other, exactly similar, chemical plants in exactly similar environments did not cause cancer, then the presence of such plants in Watkins Grove might be a "complete" explanation of the high cancer rate in that community in the former or "weak" sense, but in the latter or "strong" sense (which is the sense of 'complete' in which, according to the Principle, every fact has a complete explanation; a moment's thought will show that it is true by definition that every fact has a complete explanation in the weak sense) it would simply be the case that there *was* no complete explanation of the high cancer rate in Watkins Grove.

So S must be true in Possible World Two and in no other possible world. What propositions have this feature? Only one: the proposition that Possible World Two is the actual world. (For consider any proposition that is true in Possible World Two. The proposition that Stockholm is the capital of Sweden will do as well as any as an example. If this proposition were true in Possible World Two *alone*, then it would follow from the fact that Stockholm was the capital of Sweden that Possible World Two was the actual world. That is, the truth of the proposition that Stockholm was the capital of Sweden would settle or determine everything else: it would follow from the fact that Stockholm was the capital of Sweden that Mars had two moons and that spiders had eight legs and that British forces under the command of Lord Elgin burned the Summer Palace at Pekin in 1860 and that ... well, *everything*—everything true, that is—would follow. It would be absolutely impossible for Stockholm to be the capital of Sweden and for any of these things to be false. And this is absurd. There is only one true proposition whose truth necessitates all other truths, and that is the proposition that Possible World Two is the actual world.[3]) But it is as evident as anything could be that the fact that Possible World Two is the actual world cannot serve as an explanation of the fact that Possible World Two is the actual world. "Because Possible World Two is the actual world" is not a proper answer to the question "Why is Possible World Two the actual world?" To say that it was would be no better than saying that "Because the sky is blue" was a proper answer to the question "Why is the sky blue?"

Our conclusion must be that there can be no answer to the question "Why is Possible World Two the actual world?" Another way to put this point would be to say that there can be no explanation for the whole set of truths—for the actual world is simply that possible world such that whatever is true is true in *it*; what makes a particular possible world the actual one is that it "contains" all the truths and none of the falsehoods. And this conclusion is not implausible. One cannot explain the fact that a given contingent proposition is a truth simply by appealing to necessary truths. Therefore, any explanation of a contingent truth must appeal to other contingent truths, and, as a consequence, the whole set of contingent truths cannot be explained because there are no contingent truths outside this set to appeal to. But then the Principle of Sufficient Reason is false.

We have, therefore, as we promised, deduced the falsity of the Principle from the assumption that there are contingent propositions. It follows that if the Principle is true, then there are no contingent propositions; if the Principle is true, then every truth is a necessary truth. Such propositions as "Stockholm is the capital of Sweden" and "Mars has two moons" and "Spiders have eight legs" and "British forces under the command of Lord Elgin burned the Summer Palace at Pekin in 1860" would be necessary truths in the same sense as that in which "5 + 7 = 12" and "There are no liquid wine bottles" are necessary truths. But this is absurd. We must therefore conclude that the Principle of Sufficient Reason is false.[4] And, therefore, the crucial premise of the cosmological argument is false. (It is worth noting that if we were willing to accept the conclusion that every truth was a necessary truth, we should not need the cosmological argument. The conclusion that we derived from this argument was that if something exists, then it is a necessary truth that something exists. But this obviously follows from the thesis that all truths are necessary truths. Another way to put this point would be to say that it is not very surprising that if a certain proposition entails that all truths are necessary truths, then it is possible to construct an argument, having that proposition as a premise, the conclusion of which is that if something exists, then it is a necessary truth that something exists.) If we suppose that there is real contingency in the world, then we must regard the question, Why is there anything at all? as still unanswered.

Let us make one more attempt to answer this question. There are other versions of the cosmological argument than the one we have been discussing. That is, there are other ways of reasoning from the fact that there are things of the kinds we observe, to the conclusion that there is something of a kind we do not observe, something that has a stronger grip on existence than the things we observe. One way is the so-called First-Cause Argument. The most famous statement of the argument is that of Saint Thomas Aquinas, which is essentially this:

> The chain of causes that has produced the coming-to-be of any given object of the kind we observe in the world about us (Caesar or the sun or the Taj Mahal) cannot "go back forever." Such a chain of causes must, therefore, have a first member, an initiator. (We are to think of the members of the chain of causes as *beings* that are responsible for the comings-to-be of other beings and not as *events* that cause the comings-to-be of beings.) The initiator of a chain cannot itself have come to be, for no being can come to

be unless some being is (or some beings are) responsible for its coming-to-be, and no being can be responsible for its own coming-to-be. Therefore, there exists at least one "First Cause": a being that has never come to be (that is, a being that has always existed or is somehow "outside time") and is an initiator of chains of causes of the kind that have produced the comings-to-be of the objects we observe.

Most of the controversy about this argument has focused on the premise that a chain of causes must have an initiator. We shall not enter into this controversy, for even if the argument proves its conclusion beyond all shadow of doubt, that conclusion is not strong enough for our purposes; its conclusion will not provide us with an answer to the question, Why should there be anything at all? The First-Cause Argument, if it proves anything, proves only this: that there is (or once was) at least one being that did not come into existence and is (or was) capable of initiating causal chains. But even if we knew that there was such a being, we could still raise the question *why* there was such a being. And "Because it has always existed" is no answer to the question "Why is there a being that has always existed?"

There are, however, versions of the cosmological argument that claim to prove the existence of a necessary being and yet do not depend on the Principle of Sufficient Reason. Let us examine one of them.

Let us say that a being is an *independent being* if it depends on no being outside itself for its existence. (That is, it depends on no other beings except its own parts.) If a being is not independent, we call it *dependent*. It is important to realize that if a being depends on other beings for its existence, it does not follow that those beings or any facts about them constitute a sufficient reason (in the sense demanded by the Principle of Sufficient Reason) for its existence. You and I, for example, depend upon our parents and all of our other ancestors for our existence. And, for all anyone knows, there is no complete explanation for the fact that my or your parents met and had offspring. But if there was indeed no such complete explanation, that would not change the fact that we depend upon our parents for our existence and are therefore dependent beings.

All of the beings we are aware of would seem to be dependent beings. What would an independent being be like? What would be a reasonable candidate for the office of independent being? Well, a *necessary* being looks like a pretty good candidate. (It is not, however, easily demonstrable that just any necessary being would be an independent being. Anyone who wanted to demonstrate this conclusion would have somehow to prove the impossibility of cases like the following one. Suppose that A is a necessary being and that A causes the existence of B and that it is necessary that A cause the existence of B. Then B will be a necessary being—B will exist in all possible worlds, since A exists in all possible worlds, and, in every possible world in which it exists, causes B to exist in that possible world—but B will nonetheless depend upon A for its existence.)

Could there be a being that was independent and *contingent?* It is possible to construct cases that argue that there could be. Suppose that a being "popped into existence" in empty space, and that there was no reason whatever for this: it just *did*. And (if this is not implied by what we have already supposed) let us suppose that no other being was in any way causally connected in the slightest, most remote degree with the coming into existence of this being. Since there was no reason whatever for this being's coming into existence, it can be plausibly maintained that it might just as well not have come into existence; it can be plausibly maintained, that is, that it is a contingent being. And, since its existence in no way depends on the existence or properties of any other being, it seems evident that it has to be classified as an independent being.

It can, moreover, be argued that there could be a being that was not only independent and contingent but also never came into existence: there could be an independent and contingent being that has always existed. Suppose, for example, that there is a being, X, that has always existed and has always been made of the parts A, B, and C. Suppose that X is essentially made of just those parts: suppose that X could exist only if A, B, and C existed and were joined in a certain way. And suppose that there is no necessity in the arrangement of A, B, and C; suppose that it is perfectly possible for them to have been arranged in some other way. And suppose, finally, that A, B, and C do not depend for their existence or their arrangement on any other beings. Now either A, B, and C are all necessary beings or else at least one of them is contingent. If one of them is contingent, it is an independent and contingent being that has always existed. But even if all three of them are necessary beings, the being that is made of them, X, is an independent and contingent being that has always existed—for it would not have existed if A, B, and C had not been arranged in just the way that they are, and yet it does not depend on any being outside itself for its own existence.

It may nevertheless be that these cases represent only superficial possibilities and that it is impossible for there to be an independent and contingent being. If we consider the first (alleged) possibility that we examined in the preceding paragraph, the case in which a being simply pops into existence, we may feel a certain metaphysical unease. Isn't there something strange— something positively *weird*, as the contemporary idiom has it—about the idea of something's just popping into existence without *anything's* being even partly responsible for this event? The medieval philosophers had a slogan: *Ex nihil nihil fit:* "Nothing comes from nothing." And this sounds like very good sense. Some may judge it to be self-evident. Others, however, may judge that it rests on the Principle of Sufficient Reason, taken together with the observation that if something really came from nothing, there could be no possible explanation of its existence, since there would be no objects or facts that could be cited in that explanation. And they may contend that if the Principle is discredited the medieval slogan is thereby discredited.

It is important to note, in connection with this slogan, however, that few people have ever denied it. It is not denied by the Judeo-Christian doctrine that God created the universe "from nothing," for that doctrine means only that God did not make the universe out of some pre-existent material that existed independently of His will. After all, the doctrine of Creation implies that the universe depends for its existence on something outside itself and that it does not, therefore, violate the principle (propounded by Christian philosophers) that nothing comes from nothing. It was not denied by the cosmological model called "continuous creation" (popular in the 1950s), for, according to that model, the hydrogen atoms that "popped into existence" in empty space were caused to do so by the local gravitational potential, which was dependent on the distribution of already existent matter. It is not denied by the currently standard cosmological model, the "Big Bang," for this model addresses only questions concerning events subsequent to the initial singularity. (The Big Bang model can be *supplemented* with an attempt to explain the singularity itself. One might, for example, supplement it with the thesis that God is responsible for the existence of the singularity. But all such supplements appeal to the existence of objects that did not themselves evolve out of the singularity. We shall presently examine an apparent exception to this generalization.) It is not denied by the ubiquitous "popping into existence" of so-called virtual particles that is a consequence of quantum field theory, for these particles pop into existence owing to the action of a physical entity called the quantum field (a point to which we shall presently return). The thesis that objects do not simply pop into existence without any help from antecedently existent objects would therefore seem to be at least very plausible.

If it seems strange to suppose that there might be an independent and contingent object that begins to exist at a certain moment, it can seem hardly less strange to suppose that there might be an independent and contingent object that has always existed. Suppose that, one day while strolling through the forest, we were to come upon a mysterious translucent sphere about two meters in diameter.[5] It would not occur to us to doubt that there was some explanation for its existence—even if we were aware of the difficulties that face the Principle of Sufficient Reason. Even if we cannot accept the thesis that everything has a complete explanation, we may be convinced that many kinds of things—the existence of two-meter translucent spheres among them—have at least partial explanations. And such an explanation would not be provided by the assertion that the ball had always existed. "Because it has always existed" is simply not an answer to the question "Why is there such a thing as this mysterious two-meter translucent sphere?" ('It has always existed' is not even a partial answer to this question, although it might conceivably be a part of the answer. That is, it might conceivably be one of the statements one would find it necessary to make in setting out the answer. In a similar vein, one could point out that 'He wasn't feeling well that night' is not even a partial or incomplete answer to the question 'Where was Alfred on the night of the eleventh?' although it might conceivably be one of the statements one would find it necessary to make in setting out the answer. It should be contrasted with 'Well, he wasn't at home', which is a partial or incomplete answer to the question.)

It would seem that it makes sense to ask why a thing exists even if that thing has always existed. It is certainly possible to imagine explanations of the existence of something that has always existed. If, for example, the sun has always existed and has always been a radiating body, then there has always been sunlight. And there will be an explanation for the fact that there has always been sunlight: "Because the sun has always existed and has always been a radiating body."

It seems, therefore, to be at least somewhat plausible to suppose that there are and could be no independent and contingent beings (whether ones that had just popped into existence at some time in the past or ones that had always existed). An equivalent statement of this "at least somewhat plausible" thesis would be this: it is a necessary truth that if there are any beings that in no way or in any degree depend for their existence on things outside themselves, then those beings are necessary beings. We may sum up the "intuition" that underlies the plausibility of this thesis as follows: for every being that exists, there must be at least a partial explanation for the fact of its existence, and if a being was truly *independent,* then there could be only one explanation of any sort for its existence: that its nonexistence was impossible.

This premise allows us to construct a version of the cosmological argument that does not depend upon the Principle of Sufficient Reason and whose conclusion is that there is at least one necessary being:

> Suppose for the sake of argument that there are only contingent beings. Then the World, which is a being, is a contingent being. But the World is an independent being: since, by definition, there exists nothing outside the World, the World cannot in any way depend upon something outside itself for its existence. Hence, if there are only contingent beings, then the World is an independent and contingent being. But (here we appeal to our premise) there are no beings that are both independent and contingent. There are none because there cannot be any: such beings are impossible. It is therefore false that there are only contingent beings. But every being is either necessary or contingent, and there are beings. It follows that there is at least one necessary being. In fact, the World itself must be a necessary being. For if the World were contingent, then, as we have seen, it would be both independent and contingent. (And it can plausibly be argued that there must also be other necessary beings, necessary beings that are *parts* of the World—at least if Monism is false and the World *has* any parts. For it is clear that if the World has parts, then some of them are contingent: you and I and the Taj Mahal, for example. But it is plausible to suppose that a necessary being cannot be composed entirely of contingent parts. This is not self-evident. After all, an infinite being can be composed entirely of finite parts, and an eternal being could be composed entirely of short-lived parts. But it does seem plausible. And if the World indeed cannot be composed entirely of contingent parts, then, in addition to the contingent parts of the World that we observe, the World must have other parts that are non-contingent.)

Is this a proof of the existence of a necessary being? Or is it at least a proof of the existence of a necessary being if the premise is granted that there cannot be an independent and contingent being? It is not, for it depends not only upon the premise that an independent and contingent being is impossible but upon another premise as well, and that second premise is very doubtful. It is this:

that the World is a being, an individual thing. (We said in Chapter 2 that the question whether the World, the sum total of all individuals, was itself an individual thing would later become important.) The alternative to the World's being an individual thing—it is obviously not a stuff or a universal or an event—is the World's being a mere collection of individuals. If the World is a mere collection, then there is not in the strictest sense any such thing (any such *thing*) as "the World." If the World is a mere collection, then any use of the phrase 'the World' is a mere manner of speaking; use of this phrase is no more than a device for speaking collectively about all individuals. If every individual thing was, say, an elementary particle like an electron or a quark, then the words 'the World' would simply be a linguistic device—no doubt one that could be dispensed with in principle—for making general statements about the distributions of all of the elementary particles. (We must keep in mind throughout this discussion that the World is not necessarily the same as the cosmos or physical universe. That the cosmos is the World is a metaphysical theory, one that may or may not be true. If it is not true—because, say, the World contains God or some other individual thing that is not a part of the cosmos—the present discussion will be irrelevant to the question whether the cosmos is an individual thing. I raise this point because Kant said some things about the cosmos that bear some superficial resemblance to the thesis that the World is not an individual thing, and I want to dissociate the present discussion from Kant's views. If I interpret Kant correctly, he held that the cosmos cannot consistently be treated as a unified object with a determinate and discoverable set of properties. I take this position to have been refuted by the modern science of cosmology. Having said this much, I must say one more thing: if the cosmos *can* be consistently treated as a unified object with a determinate and discoverable set of properties, it does not in my view follow that it is an individual thing in the strict and metaphysical sense. A metaphysician might hold that the planet Jupiter was, strictly and metaphysically speaking, a mere collection of particles and also hold that this should not prevent astronomers from treating those particles as if they composed an object that had a certain diameter, a certain mass, and so on.)

If the World is a mere collection, then perhaps it is possible that there are only contingent beings and that none of them is an independent being. Perhaps it is possible that the World is a collection that contains *infinitely many* individuals, and perhaps it is possible that the individual thing A depends for its existence upon the individual thing B, and that B depends upon C, and that C depends upon D, and so on forever (or that A depends upon B and C, and that B depends upon D and E, and that C depends upon D, F, and G, ...) And if these things are possible, then the present version of the cosmological argument fails.

And there is really a great deal to be said against the thesis that the World is an individual thing. Atheists, who tend to identify the World with the cosmos, often put forward a thesis about the mutual dependency of the elements of the cosmos that is more or less the same as the model sketched in the preceding paragraph. And those theists who believe, as almost all theists do, that God did not have to create anything, and who accept the other premise of the present version of the cosmological argument (the impossibility of an independent and contingent being), will want to reject the thesis that the World is an individual thing.

To see this, let us suppose that the World *is* an individual thing, and let us also suppose that there are no independent and contingent beings, and let us see what consequences these suppositions have for theism. We shall call the individual thing that is the World 'W'. If W is a true individual thing and not a mere collection, then it has God as a part, its other parts being the various things that God has created. Now let us consider one of the possible worlds in which God chose not to create anything—Possible World Four, let us say. In Possible World Four, there exist no individuals besides God (and God's parts, if God has or could have parts). Now W is, as we have seen, an independent being. Even though God is a part of W and all of the other parts of W are dependent beings (they depend upon God for their existence), it remains true that W depends upon nothing outside itself for its existence. Since there are no independent and contingent beings, it follows that W is a necessary being, and hence exists in Possible World Four. So both God and W exist in Possible World Four. But there is nothing in Possible World Four but God and the parts (if any) that God would have in Possible World Four. It seems fairly evident that W could not be a part of God in Possible World Four, even if God could have parts. (And all theists I am aware of would deny that God could have parts. For example, the first of the Anglican Articles of Religion begins, "There is but one ... God, without body, parts, or passions. ... ") After all, in actuality God is a part of W. Therefore, in Possible World Four, W and God would be identical; that is, "they" would be one and the same individual thing. But in actuality W and God are two individuals: the Taj Mahal, to take just one example, is a part of W, but it is not a part of God. And it is impossible for *two* individuals to be such that they could have been one and the same individual thing. (Of course, two individuals may be so related that they could have been *parts* of one and the same individual thing. For that matter, two individuals often *are* parts of one and the same individual thing.)

If anyone is doubtful about this, let us look at the matter the other way round. Suppose, once more, that Possible World Two is the actual world. If W and God are the same individual thing in Possible World Four, then it is true of this one individual thing in Possible World Four that it could have been two individuals. God (or W) in Possible World Four could correctly speak as follows: "In Possible World Two, there are two individuals, one of which has created beings as parts and the other of which has no created beings as parts. And if Possible World Two had been the actual world, I should have been both of them. If Possible World Two had been the actual world, it would have been true of Me that I had created beings as parts, and it would *also* have been true of Me that I had *no* created beings as parts." But this is a manifestly impossible speech. It is not a speech that any being could make (correctly) in *any* possible world. The assumptions that have led to this contradiction (other than various theses that are integral to theism) are the two premises of the present version of the cosmological argument. The theist, therefore, will want to reject one or both of these premises. Since, as we have seen, the atheist will also want to reject one or both of these premises, they are hardly premises that we can assume to be true without some very strong arguments in their favor.

We have seen that there may be arguments that lend some plausibility to the premise that there cannot be a being that is both independent and contingent, but I should not want to classify these arguments as "very strong." And I know of no argument at all for the premise that the World is an individual thing and not a mere collection of individual things.

We have therefore not succeeded in showing that there is a necessary being. Could it be that there is no necessary being? If there were no necessary being, it seems to me, there could be no answer to the question, Why is there anything at all? I concede that it may be a necessary truth that there is something, even though there is no necessary being. It may be that there exists something—some individual thing—in every possible world, even though there is nothing, no individual thing, that exists in every possible world. (If it is a merely contingent truth that something exists, then it is very hard to see what could explain this truth or how there could be any answer to the question why anything exists. If it is a merely contingent truth that something exists, then there is at least one perfectly good possible world in which there exist no individual things, and it is very hard to see how there could be any explanation of the contingent truth that that world, or one of those worlds, is not the actual world. Explanations of contingent truths must, as we have seen, cite other contingent truths, and what contingent truth or truths could be cited in an explanation of there being anything at all? If it is a contingent truth that something exists, then it must just happen that something exists, and that must be all there is to say.) Even if there is no necessary being, it could *for all we know* still be a necessary truth that something exists.

Nevertheless, it is not clear that this idea is coherent. Imagine two beings, Alice and Bertram, who are the only individuals that there are in Possible World One. Suppose that in Possible World One Alice knows that there are at least two other possible worlds, in one of which (Two) she alone exists and in the other of which (Three) Bertram alone exists. If these were the only three possible worlds, then it would be a necessary truth that something existed, and yet there would be no necessary being. But wouldn't it be reasonable for Alice, given what she knows in Possible World One, to conclude that there was a fourth world, a world in which neither she nor Bertram nor anything else existed? She knows that she can exist without Bertram and that Bertram's failure to exist need not be "compensated for" by the existence of some third individual thing (Possible World Two) and that she need not exist at all (Possible World Three). And she knows that Bertram can exist without her and that her failure to exist need not be compensated for by the existence of some third individual thing and that Bertram need not exist at all. Where then is the impossibility in the following state of affairs: Neither Alice nor Bertram nor any other individual thing exists? Where is the impossibility in there being nothing at all? It seems reasonable to conclude that if there is no necessary being, then it may well be possible for there to be nothing at all.

We may, finally, conclude that metaphysics can provide us with no answer to the question, Why should there by anything at all? It would seem that the only way to answer this question would be to demonstrate the existence of a necessary being, and we have been unable to do this. Whether we have failed because there is no necessary being or because, although there is a necessary being, there is no way of demonstrating its existence or because there is a demonstration of the existence of a necessary being that we have simply not got the intellectual equipment to discover—this question is left to the readers of this book to answer for themselves.

Before leaving this topic, I wish to examine briefly the suggestion that science can succeed—or has already succeeded—where metaphysics has failed. This suggestion has its origins in current scientific speculations about how one might explain the singularity out of which the cosmos arose. (According to the almost universally accepted cosmological model, underwritten both by astronomical observation and the general theory of relativity, there was less space in the past than there is now, and the further back one goes into the past, the less space there was; if one goes far enough back—ten or fifteen thousand million years—one finds that the totality of space dwindles toward a limit, a mathematical point: the "singularity." The emergence of the cosmos from this point is—because of its violence—known as the "Big Bang.")

One such set of speculations employs the slogan "Nothingness is unstable," the implication being, roughly, that it is impossible for nothingness to remain nothingness: the intrinsic nature of nothingness is such as to give rise, of necessity, to *things*. Many celebrated scientists seem to be impressed by this slogan (which I call a slogan because it is a vague phrase of ordinary English whose use is by no means dictated by the mathematically formulated speculations that it is supposed to summarize). Other equally celebrated scientists are skeptical or even contemptuous. There is a certain amount of party politics here: the strongest advocates of taking these speculations seriously are usually anti-religious and see them as a way of showing that the coming-to-be of the cosmos had nothing to do with a Creator. In contrast, scientists who believe in God (for example, John Polkinghorne, who resigned his position as Professor of Mathematical Physics in Cambridge University to become an Anglican priest, the Harvard astrophysicist Owen Gingerich, or Alan Sandage, who is sometimes called "the father of modern astronomy") deprecate the claims of some scientists to be able to explain why there is anything at all. Sandage, for example, says, "Science cannot answer the deepest questions. As soon as you ask why there is something instead of nothing, you have gone beyond science."[6] (There may well be other motives than religious and purely scientific ones behind such statements. They may be expressions of a fear that some scientists are making grandiose public statements that will bring science into disrepute or even cause it to be held up to ridicule.)

Whatever the scientists themselves may think, there are philosophers who have been impressed by the claim of some scientists to have explained (or to be about to explain) why there is something rather than nothing. Here is a quotation from a recent textbook:

> Many philosophers past and present think that the question of why something exists rather than nothing is unscientific. Some have claimed that the question is

meaningless because it could never, even in principle, be answered. Others have claimed that the question lies in the realm of metaphysics, forever beyond the reach of science.

Science has proven these philosophers wrong. Modern science has not ignored the question of why something exists rather than nothing. For the first time ever, the question has a possible scientific answer based on the idea that because nothingness is necessarily unstable, the universe necessarily exists. Why is there something rather than nothing? Ultimately, because something—the universe—necessarily exists.[7]

But what does it mean to say that "nothingness is unstable"? As we have seen, 'nothingness' is not the name of an object, and one would suppose that the adjective 'unstable' expresses a property, and, of course, only an object can have a property. For there to be instability, something must be *there* to be unstable: there must be an unstable object (an object in a certain state that is liable to slip over into some other state) or a plurality of objects that stand in unstable relations to one another. And if there is an object of any sort—even if you call it 'nothingness'—then there is not nothing. Curiously enough, the authors of the above passage are aware of this point. A moment before, they had said: "*An unstable nothingness?* It sounds as if 'nothingness' is a sort of thing—a mysterious energy-free, space-free, time-free, matter-free object that just happened to be unstable. But nothingness is *not* a thing. Nothingness is just nothing."[8]

Having recognized this difficulty, however, the authors do nothing to resolve it. The wording of this second passage, moreover, raises an additional difficulty. The authors recognize that if there were nothing, then there would be no such thing as the passage of time. But the idea of instability is an inherently temporal idea. To say that a certain state of affairs is unstable is to say that if it obtained at a given time, there would be a tendency for it to cease and be replaced by some other, incompatible state of affairs at some later time. To say that nothingness is unstable, therefore, can only mean that if there were nothing at a particular time, then this state of affairs would have a tendency to cease and to be replaced by the state of affairs "there being something" at some later time. But if there being nothing is incompatible with there being such a thing as the passage of time, then the idea of an unstable nothingness is meaningless for a second reason (a second reason, that is, besides the obvious reason that if there is nothing there is nothing to have the property of instability).

If this way of talking is meaningless, why are there people who engage in it? The answer, I believe, is that its meaninglessness is disguised by some confusions generated by the word 'vacuum'. According to modern quantum field theory, objects can pop into (temporary) existence in what is called the "quantum vacuum." And the word 'vacuum' strongly suggests nothingness. But even in the seventeenth century, a vacuum was not really *nothing*, since it had various properties (spatial extension if no others) and "nothing" cannot have properties. The modern quantum vacuum is *very* far from being nothing. It is simply the lowest energy state of the quantum field (the quantum vacuum is, therefore, a mere modification of the quantum field: the words 'quantum vacuum' are a name that is applied to the quantum field when it is in a certain state, just as 'fist' is a name that is applied to a hand when it is in a certain state), and the quantum field is a physical object with a very complicated structure, a structure that is specified by a set of equations that contain a variety of apparently arbitrary numbers. Now the quantum vacuum is unstable. That is, the equations that describe the structure of the quantum field do not allow it to remain in its lowest energy state continuously and at every point. When the quantum field locally and temporarily departs from its lowest energy state, particles appear (a particle and its anti-particle or a single particle that is its own anti-particle). One *might* describe this consequence of quantum field theory in the words "Nothingness is unstable," but these words can be no more than a figure of speech. They do not describe the sober metaphysical truth of the matter. (I cannot deny the *appropriateness* of the figure, however. The quantum vacuum is not called a "vacuum" without reason, and, like the world of Narnia at its beginning, it is "really very remarkably like Nothing." The quantum field is observable only when and where it departs from its lowest energy state, and so a quantum vacuum *looks* like "nothing"; that is to say, it looks like what used to be called 'empty space'.) The particles do not truly emerge from sheer emptiness, but from the physical object called the quantum field.

The speculations that are summed up in the slogan "Nothingness is unstable" do not contend that the cosmos arose from a local fluctuation in the quantum field. The quantum field, after all, is a part of the cosmos. (Actually, current physical theory is forced to postulate more than one quantum field, but physicists regard this as an unsatisfactory feature of current theories and are working to reduce the number of fields to one. Gravity, moreover, cannot yet be satisfactorily described as a quantum-field phenomenon, but physicists hope to be able to provide a quantum theory of gravity, and to unify the theory that describes the quantum-gravitational field with the theory that describes the others. It will be simplest for our purposes to suppose that all this has been done. It is this supposition that allows us to talk of *the* quantum field.)

These speculations proceed, rather, by attempting to describe the properties of some object that is *analogous* to the familiar quantum field, and they assert that the cosmos arose out of a fluctuation that was due to the inherent instability of that object. Well, good luck to them. The point is that even if they are successful, they will explain the existence of the cosmos only by postulating an object having certain properties and by showing how an object having those properties could give birth to an object like the cosmos. (And this is just how scientific explanation works: one explains a phenomenon in terms of the properties of something that can be described independently of that phenomenon. One explains superconductivity, for example, by appealing to physical laws that would be in operation even if there were no solid matter and showing how the working of those laws generates the phenomenon of superconductivity when matter is arranged the way it is arranged in materials that exhibit superconductivity.) And even if they are successful, one can still ask why there is such an object as *that*.

If the scientists who had managed to explain the genesis of the cosmos in the way we have imagined really had an answer to the question, Why is there anything at all? they would have to be able to show that this object was necessarily existent or at least that it was a necessary truth that there was an object of *some* sort. And how would they show that? They certainly have not yet done anything that looks like showing that. The current speculations about the reasons for the existence of the singularity out of which the cosmos arose come no closer to showing that the existence of something is a necessary truth than current speculations about the explanation of superconductivity do to showing that the existence of superconductivity is a necessary truth. Any appearance to the contrary is due to games played with the words 'nothing' and 'vacuum'.

Science has not, therefore, succeeded where metaphysics has failed. The scientists are unable to help the metaphysicians, and the metaphysicians are unable to help themselves. We have no answer to the question, Why should there be anything at all?

Suggestions for Further Reading

Burrill's *The Cosmological Arguments* is a useful collection. Chapter 11 of Taylor's *Metaphysics* contains a brilliant presentation and defense of a version of the cosmological argument based on the Principle of Sufficient Reason. For discussions of the Principle of Sufficient Reason, see Liebniz, *Principles of Nature and Grace* (particularly §7), Rowe, *Philosophy of Religion,* Chapter 3, and van Inwagen, *An Essay on Free Will,* pp. 202–204.

For an account of the role played by the quantum field in current physics, see Polkinghorne's *The Particle Play.*

PART THREE

The Inhabitants of the World

THE FINAL PART of this book is about *us*, the inhabitants of the World. That is, it is about human beings and any other beings that there may be that are sufficiently similar to us that it would be reasonable to consider them our fellow inhabitants of the World. (While it may be reasonable to use the word 'inhabitants' in a sense in which apes and beavers and elephants—and perhaps even ants—are "our fellow inhabitants of the World," I shall use the word in the sense suggested by the adjective 'inhabited'—as in the question "Is that island inhabited?") The traditional term that is used to describe us and those beings that are "sufficiently similar" to us is 'rational'. Human beings, however irrationally they may behave, and angels and Martians (if there are angels or Martians) are rational in the required sense. Apes and beavers and elephants are not rational in the required sense.[1] (But non-human terrestrial animals—especially apes—may be very *intelligent*. It is for this reason that I avoid using the term 'intelligent' to do any of the work I have assigned to the word 'rational'. The use of 'intelligent' to refer to mental capacities not possessed by even the brightest apes is quite common, as may be seen from such common phrases as 'the search for intelligent life elsewhere in the universe'. In this phrase, 'intelligent' means just exactly what I mean by 'rational': anyone who said that there was intelligent life elsewhere in the universe would be taken to mean that there were beings somewhere that shared with us mental capacities that the most "intelligent" apes do not share with us.[2])

And what is rationality? Let us begin to try to answer this question by considering another question, a question asked by the philosopher Ludwig Wittgenstein: "We say that a dog is afraid that his master will beat him, but not that he is afraid that his master will beat him tomorrow. Why not?" The beginning of the answer to this question is that the idea that is expressed by the word 'tomorrow' is wholly foreign to the mental world of the dog. If the dog can be said to have ideas at all, the ideas that constitute the content of its thought at any moment are ideas of things it is then aware of or of things that might well

119

be immediate consequences of the operations of the things it is then aware of (such as an imminent beating). This point is often put by saying that dogs—and all other non-human terrestrial animals—are "incapable of abstract thought." This idea (applied to a primitive member of our genus) is well expressed in a bit of verse by W. V. Quine:

> The unrefined and sluggish mind
> Of *Homo javanensis*
> Could only treat of things concrete
> And present to the senses.

One might, however, wonder whether dogs and other beasts—other non-human terrestrial animals—are not capable of a *little* abstract thought. After all, "being beaten by one's master" is a sort of abstraction, a universal that has been abstracted from various concrete situations and which could have any number of instances. A dog that fears being beaten by its master would seem to fear that something that has happened before will happen again. And it does not fear the occurrence of an exact duplicate of some earlier event; it fears the occurrence of an event that will be the same as a certain earlier event *in a certain respect*: however the feared event may differ from the earlier event, it will be like the earlier event in being a beating by the dog's master. As to the matter of "present to the senses," it suffices to point out that a feared beating that has not yet happened is *not* present to the senses. (It may of course be that it is simply not true that dogs ever fear being beaten, or not in the same sense as that in which human beings fear being beaten. It may be that we use words like these to describe the mental states of dogs simply because we have no others. Perhaps our use of these words is an example of our tendency to anthropomorphism, like 'The sun is trying to come out' or 'The car doesn't want to start'. But I shall assume that our simple, everyday descriptions of the beliefs, hopes, and fears of dogs and other beasts can be literally correct.)

Rationality, then, does not consist simply in the capacity for abstract thought. It consists in the capacity for a certain *kind* of abstract thought. A rational being is one that can do the following:

> It can represent to itself complex states of affairs, including non-actual states of affairs, that are quite strikingly remote from its present sense-perceptions. (For example: Jane's coming to visit a week from next Thursday; someone's ordering the second-cheapest item on the menu; the government's preventing a recurrence of bubonic plague by finding a new way to dispose of the refuse that feeds the rats that carry the fleas that are infected with the bacterium that causes the plague.) It can believe that certain states of affairs are actual and that others are non-actual. It can desire that certain states of affairs be actual and others non-actual. It can contemplate states of affairs without raising the question whether they are actual or non-actual. ("I'm trying to imagine what our life will be like if we really go ahead and have a child.") It can be aware of logical and causal relations between states of affairs. It can sort states of affairs into the categories "probable" and "improbable." It can assign relative values to

states of affairs. ("I'm sorry I embarrassed you. I didn't *want* to, you know. But I thought that would be preferable to telling an outright lie.") It can devise plans of action that draw on its beliefs about which states of affairs are actual and non-actual and probable and improbable and about the logical and causal relations that hold among both actual and non-actual states of affairs in order to attempt to cause states of affairs it values to become actual. It is capable of recognizing other beings as having all these capacities, and it is capable of communicating to those that do facts and orders and questions related to the states of affairs it represents to itself and to its beliefs and desires and values in respect of those states of affairs. A rational being, therefore, is a being that is capable of making statements and giving orders and asking questions; this implies that, in itself and independently of any such communication, it "has" something to make statements and give orders and ask questions about.

This is rationality. Rationality marks a great divide, a discontinuity between humanity and the beasts. It is wrong to suppose that there is something that apes and elephants and beavers have a little of and we have more of and that, as a consequence, we are rational and they are not.[3]

It is not that we are, say, "more intelligent" than apes and that that is why we are rational and apes are not—as Alice is able to solve word-analogy problems and spatial-relation problems faster than Alfred because she is more intelligent. (Whatever that means. There. That was a relief. Whenever I write the words 'more intelligent' I feel a very strong urge to add the words 'whatever that means'.) We may indeed be more intelligent than apes; indeed I suppose we are. But if so, that is not why we are rational and apes are not. If there is a connection, it goes the other way: we are more intelligent than apes because we are rational and therefore have more use for intelligence—for intelligence, if it is anything, is the ability to manipulate mental representations of states of affairs in various useful ways, and we have a lot more, and a lot more complex, representations to manipulate than apes do. To suppose that we were rational and apes weren't because we were more intelligent than apes would be like supposing that bats could fly and mice couldn't because bats were more "physically agile" than mice. (Bats probably do have greater physical agility than mice, whatever than means. They need greater physical agility because they can fly and mice can't.) Human beings who are of subnormal intelligence owing to injuries or genetic defects do not have minds at all like the minds of apes, any more than apes of subnormal intelligence have minds like the minds of elephants or beavers. Rather, they have human minds that are of diminished capacity in respect of dealing with the demands of life in human society.

We shall consider four questions about rational beings:

- What rational beings are there, and why do they exist?
- What is the place of rational beings in the World?
- What is the nature of rational beings?
- What are the powers of rational beings?

7

What Rational Beings Are There?

THE ONLY RATIONAL BEINGS whose existence is uncontroversial are human beings. The following, if they exist, are rational beings: God, angels, gods, elves and fairies and trolls, rational extra-terrestrial beings; and rational computers or robots. I know of no other candidates, for it is as certain as anything can be that neither chimpanzees nor dolphins nor any other non-human terrestrial creatures are rational.

I suppose that no reader of this book seriously wants to discuss the possible existence of creatures of folklore like trolls, and I suppose that no one seriously wants to discuss the possible existence of Zeus or Odin. There could be no reason for believing in the existence of angels apart from the revelations claimed by particular religions. We shall later discuss (in connection with the question, Why are there rational beings?) the thesis that the physical universe is the product of rational design; this, together with our discussion in Chapters 5 and 6 of the existence of a necessary being, constitutes as much of a discussion of God as lies within the scope of metaphysics. There are at the present time no rational computers or robots (unless they are the work of extra-terrestrial rational beings), and we shall not raise the question—which belongs more properly to the philosophy of mind than to metaphysics—whether rational computers and robots are intrinsically possible. That leaves us with rational extra-terrestrial beings: Martians or Venereans or Arcturans or whatever.

Is there any good reason to believe that such beings exist? A lot of people seem to believe not only that they exist but that the earth has actually been visited by them. Well, a lot of people believe in ghosts and astrology and the Bermuda Triangle as well. There are certainly no Martians or Venereans or other rational inhabitants of the solar planets. As to the Arcturans, travel "in person" over inter-sidereal distances (picture the earth as a grain of sand circling a basketball-sized sun about thirty meters away; the nearest possible extra-solar planet would be another grain separated from "our grain" by the width of the Atlantic) is a feat so difficult that any species that accomplished it would have a technology that stood to ours as ours stands to that of medieval Europe.

One would expect that if extra-terrestrial visitors with literally incredible technological powers wanted us to be aware of them we should be unequivocally aware of them, and no childish hide-and-seek. And if they didn't want us to be aware of them, we should never have noticed any sign of their presence whatever. There are two kinds of scientists who spend a lot of time looking at the sky: meteorologists (who look at it during the day) and astronomers (who look at it during the night). It is significant that no meteorologist or astronomer has ever reported any manifestation of extra-solar visitors—nor has any scrap of material or any artifact allegedly of extra-solar origin ever reached the hands of a scientist.

Nevertheless, the question whether we have actually been visited by extra-solar rational beings does not really have much to do with the question whether there are such beings. And to the latter question, we can answer only that we don't know. We have no reason to think that there are or that there aren't. We know nothing about how common planets are. We know nothing about how life arose on the earth, much less about other ways in which it might possibly arise, and we therefore know nothing about what proportion of such planets as there are might support life.[1] We know only a few facts that are of any relevance to the question whether there are rational extra-terrestrial beings, and those facts do not encourage us to believe that rational beings are at all common in our part of the cosmos.

First, rationality has arisen on the earth only once. There are between two and thirty million species now living, and there may have been as many as a thousand million species that are now extinct. And yet only one of them is or ever has been rational (unless some extinct species of our genus was also rational; if that were so, it would still be true that rationality has arisen on the earth only once). If we compare rationality with vision or the power of flight, we observe a striking contrast: vision has arisen independently over forty times in the history of terrestrial life,[2] and I, who am no biologist, can point to at least four independent occasions on which the power of flight arose. And the development of rationality depends on at least one "accident" that is independent of the "internal" processes of biological evolution: if the planetoid or comet that collided with the earth to cause the mass extinctions of sixty million years ago had had a slightly different trajectory, we should not be here; it is, in fact, overwhelmingly likely that there would be *no* rational terrestrial species.

Secondly, there is the very good question that was asked by the physicist Enrico Fermi: "Where are they?" It may be difficult to travel in person across the distances that separate the stars, but it is not at all that difficult to communicate by radio across those distances. And yet, despite our best efforts, we detect no extra-solar radio signals. Admittedly, a receiver could miss an extra-solar signal if it, the receiver, were not aimed just right, and the enormous task of "checking out" every square arc-second of sky to see whether it is a source of meaningful radio signals has hardly been begun. For all anyone knows, we shall detect a meaningful signal from the stars tomorrow. Nevertheless, thousands of stars have been investigated, including all of them that can be seen with the naked eye, and no signals have been observed. The absence of radio signals is, however, hard to evaluate for many reasons. (To mention just one, there seems to be no very compelling argument for the conclusion that rational beings would be at all likely to have radios. Our ancestors have been rational beings for at least a hundred thousand years and have had radios for less than a thousandth of that span. And—perhaps this statement is reminiscent of our earlier statement about the evolutionary uniqueness of rationality—only one of the tens of thousands of human cultures has been in a position to invent the radio. Perhaps there are many other rational species in our neck of the galactic woods, but the historical development we call "modern science," on which the radio depends, exists only because of some unlikely turn of events that has not happened in the histories of all those other species.) Nevertheless, our failure to detect extra-solar radio signals is hardly encouraging to those who would like to believe in a "Star Trek" version of the local spiral arm, laden with technological civilizations like ripe apples on the limb of an apple tree at harvest time.

When the fact of our failure to detect extra-solar radio signals is combined with what we know about our own evolutionary history, it seems most reasonable to believe that there are no rational beings other than ourselves anywhere in what might be called (from an astronomical point of view) the vicinity. Most of the cosmos, however, is not in the astronomical vicinity, and it may well be that there are other rational beings somewhere. And it may well be that there are not. It may well be that we are absolutely alone in the cosmos. (Alone in time as well as in space; it may well be that there have never been any other rational beings. It may well be that there are never going to be any, although that is less likely, since the cosmos is very young: it will be ten thousand times its present age when the last star goes out.)

In my view, to make any pronouncements on this topic in the present state of our knowledge would be most inadvisable. It should be noted that we have a very strong urge to make such pronouncements, however. History shows that human beings have an apparently irresistible urge to people unknown regions with non-human rational beings. Present-day science-fiction enthusiasts who believe, or half-believe, in a galaxy filled with Vulcans and Klingons (or something like them) are responding to the same urge that led ninth-century peasants to fill the hills and woods with elves and trolls and led the seventeenth century to populate the interior of Africa with giants with eyes in their bellies and led my grandfather's generation to cover Mars with canals. For all that, it may be that this deeply seated urge, having led us astray so many times, has finally brought us to the truth. If you let a bet ride long enough you will eventually win. Every hypochondriac is right once.

Let us now turn to the second part of our question: Why are there rational beings? Since, as we have seen, we are the only rational beings we know about, let us treat this question as a question about beings like ourselves: rational animals. We shall ask why there are such things as rational animals.

There are two main types of answer to this question: one type of answer attaches some sort of meaning or purpose to the existence of rational animals, and the other type denies that the existence of rational animals has any meaning or purpose. We saw examples of answers of each type in Chapter 1 when we looked at two possible sets of answers to our three metaphysical questions.

Each of these two types may be divided into two sub-types. If there is a meaning or purpose to be found in the existence of beings like us, this meaning may derive from the conscious purposes of some non-human being or beings (in most cases, God) or it may derive from an impersonal "force" that somehow strives toward the goal of producing a more complex, ordered universe. If there is no meaning or purpose to be found in the existence of rational animals, this may be because it is a necessary truth that there are rational animals or it may be because it is a mere matter of chance that there are rational animals.

To my mind, the two interesting possibilities are that the existence of beings like us is due to the purposeful action of a non-human being and that their existence is due to chance. There seems to be no reason whatever to believe in such things as the Dialectic of History or, to descend to a somewhat lower intellectual level, a "Force" out of *Star Wars*. Indeed, it is not easy to make out what these things are supposed to be. And the suggestion that the existence of rational animals is a necessary truth is very hard to believe. We saw in Chapter 6 that it was very hard to believe that *all* truths were necessary truths, and, if there are contingent truths, why should the proposition that rational animals exist not be one of them?

In Chapter 6, we quoted from a textbook the authors of which maintained that the existence of a universe like this one was necessary. Even if this were correct, however—and we shall see presently that there are good reasons to doubt that it is, reasons besides those given in Chapter 6—it would not follow that the existence of rational animals was necessary unless it was a necessary truth that a universe like this one must eventually produce or give birth to or generate rational animals. But if our existence depends on the collision of a planetoid or comet with the earth at just the right moment in evolutionary history, then it can hardly be true that the existence of human beings is necessary (unless there is no contingency at all, but *that* is something that can hardly be true). And if rational animals are rare in the universe and the existence of our own type of rational animal is due to an improbable astronomical event, then it is hard to see why anyone should think that the existence of rational animals is necessary.

Let us turn to the two interesting possibilities. Let us begin by examining the thesis that the existence of rational animals is due to chance. Here is one version of this thesis, the third answer in our second set of answers to our three metaphysical questions in Chapter 1 (but I have substituted 'rational animals' for 'human beings' in this answer):

> Rational animals are complex configurations of matter. Since the World has always existed, it is not surprising that there should be such complex configurations of matter, for in an infinite period of time, all possible configurations of matter will come to exist. Rational animals are just one of those things that happen from time to time. There is no purpose that they serve, for their existence and their features are as much accidents as the existence and shape of a puddle of spilt milk. Their lives—*our* lives—have no meaning (beyond the purely subjective meaning that we or other

rational animals choose to find in them), and they come to an end with physical death, since there is no soul. The only thing that can be said about the place of rational animals in the World is that they are—very temporary—parts of it.

This is, as I said, a picture of the World that was at the height of its popularity in the nineteenth century. (But it did not originate in the nineteenth century. It was invented in ancient Greece.) It might be held that this argument had the conclusion that the existence of rational animals was necessary, at least given that the existence of a beginningless cosmos of matter in motion is necessary, since the probability that an eternal cosmos would not produce rational configurations of matter at some time or other is literally infinitesimal. Whether we should look at the argument that way is a merely verbal question. In one sense, the argument attributes something very like necessity to the existence of rational animals (and to the existence of just about everything else). In another sense, the argument implies that the existence of rational animals is a matter of chance: on each occasion on which a species of rational animals came into existence, the coming to exist of that particular species was a matter of chance. But there is no point in taking any pains over this verbal question, since, however the argument is to be described, it has a premise that is held by most experts to be false. Cosmologists today pretty generally agree that the age of the universe is finite. As a consequence, the argument that "in an infinite period of time, all possible configurations of matter will come to exist" is no longer one that can be appealed to.

It may be, however, that it is still possible to believe that the existence of rational animals depends upon chance. Although the age of the cosmos is finite, it is, by human standards, enormous. It is possible to speculate that the age of the cosmos is sufficient for it to be reasonably probable (although not necessary) that, in the period of time that has elapsed since the beginning of the cosmos, the random combination and recombination of atoms would produce rational beings like ourselves. The most plausible story would be something like this: first, the random combination and recombination of atoms produces some very simple organism (perhaps something on the order of complexity of the simplest bacterium that exists today); thereafter, Darwinian evolution takes over, and eventually there are rational beings; the present age of the cosmos is great enough that it is unsurprising that this sequence of events has had time to happen in at least the one case we know of.

Is this plausible? Well, let us ask the following question. What proportion of the possible configurations of matter that are of about the same size and weight as the simplest known bacterium would correspond to a living organism—not necessarily a bacterium, but any sort of living organism, living by any conceivable definition, however liberal? It is impossible to answer this question with anything like a precise number, but there is no doubt that the proportion is very small indeed. It would be something like this: to imagine one of the possible living configurations having been produced by a random mixing of atoms in a universe the age and size of ours would be like imagining a dart thrown at random toward a target as big as the galaxy hitting a bull's-eye smaller than an atom.

That this is so is due to the laws of physics, which dictate that there is only a small number of kinds of particles, that the particles of each kind have very specific properties, and that there is a very specific range of ways in which two particles can interact. It so happens that only a very small proportion of the bacterium-sized configurations of particles that the laws of physics allow have the properties of a living organism—just as only a very small proportion of the ways in which a wristwatch-sized pile of tiny gears and wheels and springs can be arranged in relation to one another will produce a watch or any other functioning mechanism. (The words 'very small proportion' are an understatement, and the statement that they are an understatement is itself an understatement. One might as well say that "only a very small part" of a galaxy-sized target was occupied by a bull's-eye smaller than an atom.)

If this is correct, then there would seem to be only one way in which chance could be responsible for the living organisms we see about us today. (If the cosmos were packed with planets, and atoms were constantly being randomly mixed at every point on their surfaces, the probability of this procedure producing a single bacterium-sized living configuration of matter by the time the cosmos was a million million times its present age would be essentially zero.) First, chance, or the random mixing of atoms, would have to produce some configuration of matter far simpler than a bacterium, a configuration that was capable of reproducing itself, and then some evolutionary mechanisms—whether the Darwinian mechanisms or some other—that automatically come into play when self-reproducing configurations of matter exist[3] would have eventually to bring it about that the "descendants" of that configuration exhibited the complexity of biological organization that we observe today.

There are difficulties with the thesis that this proposal reflects a scenario that has actually occurred on the earth. All known terrestrial organisms depend on a specific sort of interaction between nucleic acids and proteins, and no one can imagine a self-reproducing assemblage of nucleic acids and proteins that is simpler than the simplest bacteria—much less one so simple that there is a significant probability of its having come about by a random mixing of atoms in a few hundred million years on the surface of the newly cooled earth. (But there are interesting speculations about how nucleic-acid/protein life might have evolved out of life that had another sort of chemical basis, and it may well be that the advocates of these speculations are on to something.) Moreover, the only evolutionary mechanisms that have actually been described in a scientifically respectable way—the Darwinian mechanisms—are such that the idea that they are capable of starting with a self-reproducing molecule and eventually producing beavers and dolphins and human beings is pretty much an article of faith. (But the fact that something is held as an article of faith is no reason for thinking that it isn't true, and even if the Darwinian mechanisms turn out not to be adequate to explain the observed facts of evolution, it may be that there are other mechanisms, yet to be discovered, that are adequate.)

Our present purposes are speculative and metaphysical rather than scientific. Let us, therefore, waive all of these difficulties. Let us imagine that we have an excellent scientific account of the origin of life and the mechanisms by which life evolved to its present degree of complexity. And let us suppose that this account makes it plain that, given a cosmos like this one, it is perfectly reasonable to believe that rational animals would come into existence by chance sooner or later—and let us also suppose that this "sooner or later" factor is of a magnitude that makes the present existence of rational animals (that is, their existence when the cosmos is about fifteen thousand million years old and when there has been life on the one planet they are known to have evolved on for about three-and-a-half thousand million years) a matter of no great surprise to us. Have we an account of how rational animals came about by chance?

In the nineteenth century, it would have been assumed that we had. It was possible to assume this because the cosmos of the nineteenth-century scientific imagination was vague and amorphous. The nineteenth-century scientific imagination saw the universe, basically, as composed of various chunks of matter of arbitrary shapes and sizes moving about in space. This imaginative picture was inconsistent with the actual content of nineteenth-century science. Late nineteenth-century science knew that matter did not come only in solid chunks but could also be in a liquid or gaseous state and that a given quantity of matter could be transformed from one state to another with certain of its important properties remaining constant. It knew that quantities of matter interacted not only by contact but at a distance—across empty space—by heat, light, magnetism, electricity, and gravity. It knew about the odd and beautiful connection between heat and light and electricity and magnetism. It knew about the resistance of chunks of matter to being put into motion and the odd and unexplained connection between this feature of matter and gravity. It knew a lot about the laws of chemical combination, and it knew that each material had a certain density and certain definite ways of responding to outside forces (bending, flowing, shattering, or whatever). Nevertheless, despite its inconsistency with actual scientific knowledge, the imaginative picture continued to exist and to represent the cosmos as something vague and amorphous. And the vague and amorphous is not something that nags at one for an explanation. If one believes in a vague and amorphous cosmos, one will not be likely to raise the question why the cosmos has the general, overall features it has rather than some others. One will be likely to think of the cosmos as being so uncomplicated that the fact that there is a cosmos of that sort rather than some other requires no explanation. What would the alternatives be, after all? What other kind of cosmos could there be than a cosmos of chunks of matter of arbitrary sizes and shapes moving about in empty space?

Today we have a picture of the cosmos that is both much more precise and much more unified. Because the picture is precise, we can construct pictures of other ways a cosmos could be simply by making small changes in our actual picture of the cosmos. (We can imagine a cosmos that is almost like ours but not quite. What would be meant by imagining a cosmos that was almost like a cosmos of matter in motion, but not quite?) Because the picture is unified—a vast and superficially unrelated range of phenomena are related at a deep level by the picture—we can ask what the consequences of these small changes would be for a vast range of things. Because the scientific picture is both precise and unified it is not possible for anyone who has much knowledge of the scientific picture to have, for everyday use, so to speak, an imaginative picture of a vague and amorphous cosmos that ignores a lot of phenomena belonging to the scientific picture that do not fit it very well. Any imaginative picture of a vague and amorphous cosmos will not only have to gloss over some phenomena belonging to the scientific picture that are not well understood; it will also have to have features that are clearly and demonstrably inconsistent with those of the scientific picture.

Our present picture of the cosmos has two main components: our picture of the nature of the elementary particles that make up the cosmos and the forces by which they interact (supplied by physics) and our picture of the large-scale structure and the history of the cosmos, from the Big Bang to the present (supplied by cosmology). These two components form a very tightly integrated whole. Each of these components involves a lot of numbers. The description of the particles and the forces, for example, involves a number called the fine-structure constant, which relates to the way in which electrically charged particles interact with the electromagnetic field. Other constants have to do with other kinds of interaction, such as gravity and special interactions that take place at very short range between some kinds of elementary particles. The description of the large-scale structure of the cosmos involves numbers like the number of elementary particles that belong to each "family" of particles allowed by theory. Lots of the numbers that are needed to describe the cosmos cannot be predicted theoretically. They are numbers that, as the physicists say, "have to be filled in by hand." That is, their values have to be established by the laborious process of measurement and experiment. There seems to be no necessity in the values that these numbers actually have. Therefore, it looks as if there are perfectly possible cosmoi (the plural of 'cosmos') in which these numbers are different, and we can ask what those possible cosmoi would be like. And, because our present picture of the world is so precise and unified, we can often answer such questions. There is quite a lot that can be said in answer to a question like, What features would the cosmos have if the fine-structure constant had twice its actual value?

The interesting thing about the answers to these questions is that it appears that if the cosmos were much different at all, there would be no life (and therefore no rational animals). Small changes in various of these numbers would result in a cosmos that lasted only a few seconds or in which there were no atoms or in which there were only hydrogen and helium atoms or in which all matter was violently radioactive or in which there were no stars. In no cosmos of these sorts could there be life, and, as a consequence, in no cosmos of these sorts could there be human beings or any other rational animals. (And there are many, many other ways in which small changes in certain of the numbers that describe the features of the cosmos would produce a cosmos that was inimical to life.)

Suppose we fancifully think for a moment of the cosmos as the product of a machine designed to produce cosmoi. The machine has a largish number of dials on it, perhaps twenty or thirty, and the overall features of the cosmos are the result of the ways the dials were set when the cosmos was produced. If they had been set in other positions, a different type of cosmos would have emerged from the machine. It seems to be the lesson of modern physics and cosmology that *many* statements like the following ones will be true: 'The pointer on dial 18 is set at .0089578346198711. If it had not been set at some value between .0089578346198709 and .0089578346198712, there would be no carbon atoms and hence no life'; 'The pointer on dial 23 is set at 5.113446 and the pointer on dial 5 is set at 5.113449; if the values of the two readings had been exactly equal, there would have been no matter, but only radiation; if the two readings had differed by more than .000006, all stars would be of a type that would burn out before multicellular organisms could evolve on their planets.[4]

The suggestive metaphor of a cosmos-producing machine with lots of dials on it that must be very precisely set if the machine is to produce a cosmos that could contain life (notice, by the way, that we say 'could contain' and not 'will necessarily produce') has led some writers to say that the cosmos is "fine-tuned" in such a way as to enable it to contain life. Only a vanishingly small proportion of the totality of possible cosmoi are suitable abodes for life, and yet the actual cosmos is one of these very few (in fact, not only is it a suitable abode for life, but it actually contains life; in fact, not only does it actually contain life, but it contains life that is rational; these features make it an even rarer specimen among the totality of possible cosmoi than a mere "life-permitting" cosmos; how *much* rarer is hard to say, but our present presuppositions about the emergence of life and the mechanisms of evolution say, in effect, "Not all that much rarer"). Why is the cosmos one of the few possible cosmoi that permit life? Why does the cosmos appear to have been fine-tuned by someone who had life in mind? Why are the numbers right for life?

One answer to these questions is provided by the so-called teleological argument. Late in the thirteenth century, Saint Thomas Aquinas presented the following argument for the existence of God:

> We observe that things that have no knowledge—objects that we find in
> the natural world, for example—sometimes act for an end. (That this is so
> is proved by the fact that they always, or nearly always, behave in the
> same way, and this way is the way that will lead to the best result. It is
> evident from this that their behaving in these ways is due not to chance but
> to design.) But a thing that has no knowledge cannot act for an end unless
> it is directed by a being that has knowledge and intelligence, as an arrow is
> directed by an archer. There is, therefore, some intelligent being who
> directs all of those things in the natural world that act for an end, and we
> call this being God.

This argument has been variously called the teleological argument (from the Greek *telos,* meaning an end or goal), the argument from design ("due not to chance but to design"), and the analogical argument (because it proceeds by drawing an analogy between the apparently goal-directed behavior of things in the natural world—birds flying south for the winter or the leaves of a phototropic plant turning toward the sun—and the behavior of things designed or controlled by human begins: "as an arrow is directed by an archer").

It is commonly held that the teleological argument has been refuted by the Darwinian account of evolution—indeed by the very existence of the Darwinian account, whether or not we know it to be true. And this may very well be so if we take the scope of the argument to be limited to living organisms (that is, to those objects in the natural world whose features the Darwinian theory gives an account of). But what of the cosmos as a whole? If the cosmos is a very special cosmos among all possible cosmoi, and if it has every appearance of being a cosmos that has been designed to be an abode for life, might not the most obvious explanation of this appearance be that the appearance is reality? Might not the most obvious explanation of the fine-tuning of the cosmos be that it has *been* fine-tuned? That its large-scale features (if no others) have been carefully chosen and put into place by a conscious, purposive being who wanted to make an abode for living things? And if a conscious, purposive being designed the cosmos to be an abode for living things, and if, as we know it does, the cosmos also contains rational beings like ourselves—rational animals—is it not reasonable to infer further that the existence of those rational beings is a part of the purposes of the Designer (who is, after all, also a rational being and may therefore be presumed to take a special interest in rational beings)?

Suggestions for Further Reading

For justification of the claims found in the text concerning the origin of terrestrial life and the likelihood of extraterrestrial rational species, see Shapiro, *Origins,* and Mayr, "The Probability of Extraterrestrial Intelligent Life."

Leslie's *Universes* is a brilliant exposition and discussion of physical cosmology and "fine- tuning."

Aquinas's teleological argument can be found in any collection devoted to the philosophy of religion. It is included in Burrill's *The Cosmological Arguments.*

8

The Place of Rational Beings in the World: Design and Purpose

IF THE EXISTENCE of rational animals was intended by the Designer of the cosmos, the rational animals have a purpose. Their purpose is to be found in the intentions of the Designer, and to discover the purpose of rational animals one need only discover what the Designer's intentions were in bringing them into existence.[1] It is important to realize that if this argument shows that rational animals exist for a purpose, it gives us no clue whatever as to what that purpose is. It is plain enough that we may know that something has a purpose without having any idea what that purpose might be. Many artifacts dug up by archaeologists obviously have a purpose, but what their purpose *is* is often a subject of interminable debate.

The Shorter Catechism of the Church of Scotland opens with the following question and answer (an "inclusive language" version of the catechism is no doubt forthcoming):

Q. What is the chief end of Man?

A. The chief end of Man is to glorify God and to enjoy him forever.

This question and answer provide a very clear example of a belief about the end or purpose of humanity; this is an example of what is meant by saying that human beings have a purpose. But the conclusion of the teleological argument in no way suggests that our purpose is anything of this sort. For one thing, it may be that while *some* rational animals have a purpose, human beings do not. But let us simply assume that if any rational animals have a purpose, human beings are among the ones that have a purpose. Here is a much more important point: the conclusion of the teleological argument does not imply that the Designer has very many of the properties that have traditionally been ascribed to God. There is no reason to suppose—at least none that is supplied by the teleological argument—that the Designer would be all-powerful or would know everything or would recognize any moral obligations as regards the welfare of created rational beings. And because the Designer whose existence the teleological argument purports to prove need have few of these properties that have traditionally been ascribed to God, the Designer's purposes might be entirely unlike the purposes that have traditionally been ascribed to God.

It is consistent with the conclusion of the teleological argument that the Designer's purposes be analogous to a scientist's (we are part of a vast experiment) or a dramatist's ("All the world's a stage," in a sense that is uncomfortably close to the literal). Neither of these purposes would be possible for God: He does not need to conduct experiments, since, being omniscient, He knows how they would turn out without having to conduct them; being loving and good, He would not employ self-aware, flesh-and-blood beings for purely aesthetic purposes—all the more so because He would see all possible dramas laid out simultaneously and in their entirety in the infinite theater of His mind and could therefore have no reason for wanting to watch the actual performance of any play.

The teleological argument, therefore, does not claim to prove the existence of a being that is all-powerful or all-knowing or recognizes any moral obligations toward the rational beings whose existence it is responsible for. A moment's reflection will show that it cannot claim to prove the existence of a being that is infinite or necessarily existent or eternal. (As to eternity, it may be, for all the teleological argument can claim to show, that the Designer has been outlasted by its cosmos, just as the pharaohs have been outlasted by their pyramids.) It is consistent with the conclusion of the teleological argument that the creation of the cosmos was a cooperative endeavor involving the labors of many beings, like the construction of a ship by human beings. For all the teleological argument can claim to show, it may not only be that the cosmos is the work of many beings but also that these beings have to learn to build cosmoi by trial and error; it may be that somewhere outside our ken there are lying about a lot of "botched and bungled" cosmoi that represent their earlier and less successful attempts at a working cosmos; it may be that *our* cosmos is an "early draft" and that various of its more unfortunate features like disease and parasitism and natural disasters are due to their not yet having fully mastered the craft of cosmos building.

Let all this be granted, however, and it still seems to be true that the teleological argument does show that we should think of rational animals in a way somewhat like the way in which we should think of a cache of mysterious artifacts unearthed by an archaeologist: We may not know what their purpose is, but it is clear that they do have a purpose; they exist because some designers—known to us only through their productions—made them to fulfill that unknown purpose. (Of course, the above reflections do not show that no one could, or that no one does, know that purpose. There might be any number of ways of finding it out. Perhaps, for example, someone will devise some marvelously clever theory about a purpose that we might serve in the

134	The Place of Rational Beings in the World

eyes of a cosmos-designer, a purpose that, when we consider it carefully, makes so many hitherto mysterious facts "fall into place" that we feel intellectually compelled to believe that this person has guessed the purposes of the Designer. An analogy might be the clever theory that Stonehenge is an astronomical observatory. Or the Designer might be able and willing to communicate with rational animals and might tell certain of them what end their kind serves. But no one *has* devised any compelling theory about the purpose behind our existence, and supposed revelations of the purposes of the Designer are so plentiful and so wildly inconsistent with one another that the metaphysician who does not desire a severely limited audience can make no use of them.)

If we have a purpose, then our existence "has a meaning" in the only sense that can be given to these words. It must be admitted that it is not at all clear what these words do mean. The term 'meaning' has various senses,[2] but none of them lends any sense to the question, What is the meaning of our existence? other than this sense: Explain why we exist in terms of the purposes we serve. (If Alice surprises a trusted employee who has broken into her office and is going through her files, and if Alice says, "What is the meaning of this?" she is requesting an explanation of a certain state of affairs in terms of the purposes of her employee or those whose agent the employee is.) The question and answer from the Shorter Catechism that were quoted above are a statement— whether true or false—of the meaning of our existence, and any statement of the meaning of our existence must be a statement of the same general sort. At any rate, I can think of no other sort of statement that would count as an answer to the question, What is the meaning of our existence? and if anyone maintains that this statement is not of the right sort to count as an answer to the question, then I do not know what that person means by the question.

The conclusion of the teleological argument seems to imply that we serve some purpose and that our existence therefore has a meaning. But does the teleological argument prove its conclusion—that the cosmos is the product of design and not of chance or necessity—or does it at least make that conclusion more reasonable to believe than not? How might those who deny that the cosmos is a product of design reply to the teleological argument?

There are several replies that are of little or no value and one that seems to me to be decisive.

Some philosophers have argued that there is nothing in the fact that the universe is fine-tuned that should be the occasion for any surprise. After all (the objection runs), if a machine has dials, the dials have to be set *some* way, and any particular setting is as unlikely as any other. Since any setting of the dials is as unlikely as any other, there can be nothing more surprising about the actual setting of the dials, whatever it may be, than there would be about any possible setting of the dials if that possible setting were the actual setting. (Here is a parallel argument. If you toss a coin and it comes up "heads" twenty times in a row, you shouldn't be surprised. After all, you wouldn't be surprised if the sequence HHTTHTHTTTHTHHTTHTHT occurred, and that sequence and the sequence HHHHHHHHHHHHHHHHHHHH both have exactly the same probability of occurring: 1 in 1,048,576, or about .000000954.)

This reasoning is sometimes combined with the point that if "our" numbers hadn't been set into the cosmic dials, the equally improbable setting that did occur would have differed from the actual setting mainly in that there would have been no one there to wonder at its improbability.

This must be one of the most annoyingly obtuse arguments in the history of philosophy. Let us press the "parallel" argument a bit. Suppose that you are in a situation in which you must draw a straw from a bundle of 1,048,576 straws of different length and in which it has been decreed that if you don't draw the shortest straw in the bundle you will be instantly and painlessly killed: you will be killed so fast that you won't have time to realize that you didn't draw the shortest straw. Reluctantly—but you have no alternative—you draw a straw and are astonished to find yourself alive and holding the shortest straw. What should you conclude?

In the absence of further information, only one conclusion is reasonable. Contrary to appearances, you did *not* draw the straw at random; the whole situation in which you find yourself is some kind of "set-up"; the bundle was somehow rigged to ensure that the straw that you drew was the shortest one. The following argument to the contrary is simply silly. "Look, you had to draw some straw or other. Drawing the shortest was no more unlikely than drawing the 256,057th-shortest: the probability in either case was .000000954. But your drawing the 256,057th-shortest straw isn't an outcome that would suggest a 'set-up' or would suggest the need for any sort of explanation, and, therefore, drawing the shortest shouldn't suggest the need for an explanation either. The only real difference between the two cases is that you wouldn't have been around to remark on the unlikelihood of drawing the 256,057th-shortest straw."

It is one thing, however, to note that an argument is silly and another thing to say why it is silly. But an explanation is not hard to come by. The argument is silly because it violates the following principle:

Suppose that there is a certain fact that has no known explanation; suppose that one can think of a possible explanation of that fact, an explanation that (if only it were true) would be a very *good* explanation; then it is wrong to say that that event stands in no more need of an explanation than an otherwise similar event for which no such explanation is available.[3]

My drawing the shortest straw out of a bundle of over a million straws in a situation in which my life depends on my drawing just that straw certainly suggests a possible explanation. If an audience were to observe my drawing the shortest straw, they would very justifiably conclude that I had somehow "cheated": they would conclude that I had had some way of knowing which straw was the shortest and that (to save my life) I had deliberately drawn it. (If I know that I *didn't* know which straw was the shortest—if I am just as astounded as anyone in the audience at my drawing the shortest straw—then the situation will not suggest *to me* that particular explanation of my drawing the shortest straw, but it will suggest the one that I have already mentioned, namely that some unknown benefactor has rigged the drawing in my favor.)

But if an audience were to observe my drawing the 256,057th-shortest straw (and my consequent immediate demise), this would not suggest *any* explanation to them: no one would suppose—nor would it be reasonable for anyone to suppose—that I knew which straw was the 256,057th-shortest and that I deliberately drew it; nor would anyone suppose that someone had rigged the drawing to ensure my getting the 256,057th-shortest straw; nor would any other possible explanation come to anyone's mind.

We have seen that the setting of the cosmic dials does suggest an explanation: the dials were so set by a rational being who wanted the cosmos to be a suitable abode for other rational beings. Therefore, those critics of the teleological argument who say that one setting of the cosmic dials is no more remarkable than any other possible setting are certainly mistaken. We should note that our principle does not say that if one can think of a really good explanation for some fact, one should automatically assume that that explanation is correct; the principle says only that in such cases it would be a mistake simply to assume that that fact required no explanation.

Let us turn to a second reply to the teleological argument. It is much more interesting than the first but—or so it seems to me—wholly unpersuasive. The teleological argument supposes that there are many ways the cosmos could be besides the way it actually is, ways not only different but radically different from the way the cosmos actually is. But perhaps there are no such ways. There are some physicists who hope to find a physical theory that will be so simple and compelling and unarbitrary and beautifully coherent that the mind will be forced to regard it as the only possible physical theory, as the only possible description of the way a cosmos could be set up. In such a theory, even those numbers that appear to us at present to be undeniably contingent (the charge on the electron, for example) will turn out to be necessary. The theory, in short, will require no numbers that have to be "filled in by hand," and all of the numbers it generates will agree with experiment. (Among philosophers, the authors of the textbook quoted at the end of Chapter 6 would appear to be rather confident that this is how things will turn out.)

If the discovery of such a marvelous theory were to occur, it would all but refute the idea that the actual cosmos is one among many radically different possible cosmoi and would therefore all but refute the version of the teleological argument that we are considering. At present, however, there seems to be no particular reason to think that this is how things will turn out. (The belief in and search for such a theory is a recurrent tendency in the history of science. Aristotle, Descartes, Kant, and Einstein were involved in earlier manifestations of this tendency. In the past, the search for an "only possible theory of everything" has always been a deceiver, for we now know that no such theory could possibly have been constructed on the basis of the limited knowledge available when the earlier attempts were made. Nevertheless, as we said in connection with the recurrent tendency to people unknown parts of the world with rational animals, a tendency to belief that has always led us astray in the past might now be on the verge of leading us to the truth.)

I have to record my ignorant layman's conviction that it does not seem to be very plausible to suppose that there will be a theory that presents a compelling case for there being only one intrinsically possible "cosmos design," the one that permits the existence of complex life like ourselves. In a way, such a development would not remove the "coincidental" aspect of a cosmos suitable for life but would simply add the mystery of necessity to it. I will try to explain this statement by means of an analogy.

Suppose that we were to divide a square into a million smaller squares by dividing each of its sides into a thousand equal parts. And suppose that we took the first million digits in the decimal part of π and interpreted each as corresponding to one of the million squares by some simple correspondence rule (something like this: the top left square is assigned the first digit, the next square to the right is assigned the second digit, and so on). And suppose that we assigned a color to each of the numbers 0 through 9 and painted each of the small squares with the color corresponding to the number assigned to it.

What would we say if the result turned out to be a meaningful picture—a landscape or a still life or something equally representational—of surpassing beauty? We certainly could *not* say that some rational being had arranged the values of the first million digits of the decimal part of π so that they represented a meaningful and beautiful picture, for those values are a matter of necessity: the first five are '14159' in every possible world, and none of the others is any less necessary. We should have to say that this is how things were and had to be and that nothing else could be said. But no one would *expect* this picture-generating power to be a feature of π or of e or of any other real number that turned up in the natural course of our mathematical investigations. (There are, admittedly, lots of numbers that do have this power. To find one, we need only paint a beautiful picture, divide it into a million small squares, make up two simple correspondence rules, and mechanically calculate the first million digits of the number using the picture and the rules; the remaining digits can be filled in arbitrarily.)

No doubt π could be "made" into a picture-generating number if the correspondence rules were made very complicated and were specially chosen for that purpose. And there is no doubt *some* million-digit sequence somewhere in the decimal part of π that is picture-generating. What would be amazing is if the *first* million digits of some *mathematically fundamental* number like π or e were to turn out to be picture-generating according to some *simple* set of correspondence rules. This is because the three requirements "first," "fundamental," and "simple" seem somehow to be independent, and their combining to produce a picture-generating number would therefore seem to be in some sense a coincidence. To me, in my ignorance, it seems as unlikely that a "cosmos design" that was the only possible cosmos design should turn out to be life-permitting as that π should turn out to be picture-generating. If the only possible cosmos-design did turn out to have this feature, I'd be as amazed as I should be if π turned out to be picture-generating, for the many requirements on a life-permitting cosmos are independent of one another, in the same sense as that in which the requirements "the first million digits," "mathematically fundamental number," and "simple correspondence rule" are independent of one another.

If this did happen, of course, I'd simply have to accept it and admit that there was no explanation for the fact that the only possible cosmos-design was life-permitting—or rather, the only explanation there was would be of the following "double" form: it is a necessary truth that any cosmos has features X, Y, and Z, *and* it is a necessary truth that life can exist only in a cosmos that has features X, Y, and Z. The fact that the only possible cosmos-design was life-permitting would have an explanation only in the sense that the fact that the fourth digit in the decimal part of π denotes the number of Platonic solids has an explanation: it is a necessary truth that the fourth digit in the decimal part of π is '5', and it is a necessary truth that there are five Platonic solids. (Readers who don't know what a Platonic solid is needn't worry. The essential point is that it is mathematically provable that there are exactly five Platonic solids, and the proof has nothing whatever to do with the fact that the fourth digit in the decimal part of π is '5'.)

Since it seems to me to be antecedently highly improbable that the only possible cosmos-design—if there indeed were only one possible cosmos-design—would be life-permitting, it does not seem to me that the second reply to the teleological argument has much force. If there were some good scientific reason, known to physicists, for supposing that only one cosmos-design was possible, this of course would alter matters. But there is no such reason. The motivations of those physicists looking for an "only possible theory of everything" are pretty clearly aesthetic and metaphysical. These are perfectly respectable motivations, and there is no reason in the world why physicists should not act on them. But the existence of such motivations should not be taken to imply that there is any evidence that reality is going to cooperate with them. This should be all the more evident when we remember that the history of science shows that these motivations represent a natural tendency of the human mind, one that existed antecedently to modern physics and cosmology.

Another possible reply to the teleological argument is to protest that even if the universe has been purposely fine-tuned, it does not follow that it was fine-tuned in order that creatures like ourselves should exist. Perhaps the Designer who carefully adjusted the value of the fine-structure constant and the relative strengths of gravity and the strong nuclear force and many other parameters to astonishingly exact values had *something* in mind for its carefully designed cosmos, but the fact that the cosmos is a suitable abode for rational beings was entirely irrelevant to its purposes. Perhaps we are, so to speak, the mice in the walls of the cosmos. If the mice that lived in the walls of a house were capable of contemplating such matters, they might, after a careful examination of the whole structure of the house, conclude—correctly, of course—that the house was designed for a purpose by a rational being. And they might naturally, but incorrectly, proceed to conclude that it had been designed to be an abode for *them*. (The spaces between the walls are just right for mice, there is lots of food lying about that is nourishing for mice, the house is comfortable for mice even in the dead of winter, and so on. But no doubt the theologians among them would be profoundly troubled by the Problem of the Cat.)

Now this objection is not, properly speaking, an objection to the teleological argument as such (the conclusion of which is that the cosmos was designed by a rational being or beings), but to the secondary conclusion that we drew from the existence of a Designer: that among the Designer's purposes in making the cosmos was to provide an abode for rational beings like ourselves. This secondary conclusion, however, seems to me to be very reasonable, given that the cosmos is a product of intelligent design. The analogy of "the mice within the walls" is defective in several important respects. The properties of mice were "settled" by evolution long before there were houses, and houses just happen to be suitable for infestation by creatures having those properties. There are so many species that it would be surprising if there were not a few that were suited for living within the walls of houses. House mice exist independently of the houses they inhabit, and they infest houses because it happens that houses are suited for them. Houses are not infested by sheep (except in one episode of "Monty Python's Flying Circus") or even by rabbits because the interiors of houses are not suited for occupation by sheep and rabbits. (It is no wonder that the spaces between the walls of a house are just right for mice: the mice would not have moved in if they were not.) If mice had evolved inside houses, and if the slightest change in the design of a house would have the consequence of rendering it uninhabitable by living things, and if houses had been designed by enormous rational mice, the analogy between the two cases would be much closer. But, it seems to me, if we knew all of these things to be true, it would be at least very reasonable for us to conclude that the enormous mice *had* designed houses as abodes for common-or-pantry-variety mice.

I will now turn to a reply to the teleological argument that I believe to be decisive. I said earlier that the common belief that the teleological argument had been refuted by the Darwinian account of evolution (or even by the *possible* truth of this account) was mistaken. It was mistaken because evolution is a phenomenon that occurs only within the realm of living things (or at least of self-reproducing things) and the version of the teleological argument we have been examining applies to the cosmos as a whole. And the cosmos is not a living thing or a self-reproducing thing: it is not the product of the operation of natural selection on ancestral cosmoi that reproduced themselves with variations in an environment that contained limited amounts of the resources needed for cosmic survival and reproduction. Nevertheless, the Darwinian account of evolution does have a feature that can be adapted to the needs of the present discussion. Darwin showed how it was possible, in certain circumstances, for chance to produce results that one might be initially inclined to ascribe to the purposive action of rational beings; some of the ideas on which this demonstration rests are so simple and general that they can be lifted out of the biological context in which Darwin applied them and applied to the apparent design exhibited by the cosmos.

An example will illustrate these ideas. Suppose that each of the citizens of Wormsley Glen has a job; and suppose that each of them has an alarm clock; and suppose that each alarm clock goes off at just the right time each day to enable its owner to get up and get to work on time. For example, Alice's clock goes off at 5:36 each morning, and if it went off even a few minutes later she would frequently be late for work; as it is, she breezes into the office just under the wire every day. And Tim's clock goes off at 6:07, which is just right for letting him sleep as late as possible and still get to work on time. (And so on and so on, for every citizen of Wormsley Glen. They all have clocks that enable them to arise at the optimum time, given the time they are expected at work, the amount of time they need to deal with their morning domestic chores, the amount of time they need to travel to work, and whatever other factors in their lives may be relevant to the times at which they have to get up in the morning.)

Here, we might suppose, is an obvious case of purposive design: on the back of each of the alarm clocks there is a little knob or something that regulates the time at which the alarm rings, and all of the citizens have calculated the times at which they have to get up and have set their individual alarms accordingly. But this is not so. The real explanation is different and rather unpleasant. Not so long ago there were hundreds of times as many people in Wormsley Glen as there are today. Each of them was issued an alarm clock that was unchangeably set to go off at some particular time each day, and no returns or trading allowed. The alarm settings were in every case entirely random, and this had just the consequence you would expect: Almost every alarm was set wrong (that is, was set for a time that was not the time at which its owner needed to get up), and these wrong settings, owing to the laissez-faire economic system that prevailed in Wormsley Glen, had disastrous consequences for their owners. Sally's was set for 11:23 A.M., and she was, as a consequence, consistently late for work and lost her job and starved to death. Frank's was set for 4:11 A.M., and, once it had gone off, he could either go back to sleep and be late for work or stay up and try to deal with the demands of his job (he was a brain surgeon) without having had a good night's sleep. He chose the latter course, but his being chronically short of sleep led him to make a few serious mistakes, and he had to be let go; shortly thereafter, he starved to death.

And that is what happened to everyone in Wormsley Glen who was issued a "bad" alarm clock. (Even those whose clocks were set just slightly wrong lost their competitive edge and were forced out of their jobs by more punctual and better-rested rivals.) Wormsley Glen is no welfare state, and they're all dead of starvation now. Knowing this to be the case we can see that there is no conscious purpose behind the setting of Alice's or Tim's alarms. Each of them received an alarm clock that *just happened* to be set at the "right" time, and each of them therefore survived. And this is what happened with all of the other citizens of Wormsley Glen. It was statistically likely that a certain percentage of the original inhabitants would, simply by the luck of the draw, receive clocks that were set at the time that was right for them. And that is what happened: a certain not-at-all-surprising proportion of the original inhabitants got clocks that were set at the right time, and the unforgiving social arrangements of Wormsley Glen removed everyone else from the picture.

This story is a model for the sort of circumstances in which the action of chance can mimic the productions of a rational being. A rational being, as we have said, can be aware of non-actual states of affairs and can act on values that it happens to have in order to single out some of these states of affairs and cause them to become actual. The operations of chance cannot do that because chance is not, so to speak, aware of any non-actual states of affairs and chance has no values. What chance can sometimes do is to generate a large number of actual states of affairs, and it may happen that the world is arranged in such a way that it will proceed to eliminate from actuality all of them that do not satisfy some condition. The "surviving" states of affairs in the second case may very closely resemble the "chosen" states of affairs in the first. (I have talked of the operations of chance, but it might be better to follow Jacques Monod and talk of the "interplay of chance and necessity": chance generates a large set of actual states of affairs, and necessity eliminates all, or at any rate, most, of the ones that do not meet its demands.)

In our story of Wormsley Glen, chance produced a large number of actual "alarm-clock situations," and the grim necessities of Wormsley Glen then proceeded to eliminate from actuality all of them but a few that closely resembled the alarm-clock situations that a rational being would have chosen from among possible alarm-clock situations to be actual. As rationality decides which possibilities are to be actual, so a non-rational cosmos or nature may decide which actualities (which of a set of actualities generated by chance and displaying a range of characteristics almost as broad as the range of characteristics displayed by the set of possibilities that rationality examines) are to remain actual.

According to Darwin, chance and nature have combined in just this way—but there are a few factors peculiar to the evolutionary process that are not represented in the schema laid out in the preceding paragraph—to produce the appearance of conscious design in living organisms. Chance produces random inheritable variations among the offspring of an organism, and nature (which, like Wormsley Glen, is no welfare state) tends to favor the preservation of those variations that contribute to an organism's ability to have descendants. The appearance of design in organisms is due to the accumulation of such useful (useful for having descendants) variations. Organisms are adapted to their environments—to the extent that they *are* adapted to their environments; adaptation is often imperfect—owing to the fact that the better adapted an organism is to its environment, the more likely it is to have descendants. It will be noted that our "alarm clock" story includes only some of the features of the Darwinian account of apparent design in living things: those that do not involve reproduction and inheritability.

The operations of chance can, moreover, produce an appearance of "design" (the appearance of a purposive choice among possibilities by a rational being) without actually eliminating anything from existence. To produce the *appearance* of design, it is necessary only to render those things whose features would count against a design-hypothesis unobservable. It is of course true that one very effective way to render something unobservable is to destroy it. But that is not the only way. I need not destroy any green things (or even change their colors) to prevent you from observing green things. I could also remove all green things from your vicinity, or move you to a region in which there happened to be only non-green things, or render you color-blind. This consideration suggests that chance could produce the appearance of design by generating a large number of actual objects under conditions in which some "observational selection effect" allowed observers to be aware of only a few of those objects, ones that had (more or less) the features that a rational being would have chosen to accomplish some purpose. (The meaning of 'observational selection effect' is best explained by an example. In 1936, *The Literary Digest* predicted on the basis of a poll conducted by telephone that Alf Landon would be elected president. But Roosevelt was elected by a landslide. It turned out that a vast number of Roosevelt supporters did not have telephones, for the poor tended both to support Roosevelt and not to have telephones. An observational selection effect had rendered a large body of voters "invisible" to the editors of *The Literary Digest*.)

It is the possibility of an interplay of chance and an observational selection effect that is the undoing of the teleological argument in the form in which we are considering it. In our initial statement of the teleological argument, we asked the following question: "Might not the most obvious explanation of the fine-tuning of the cosmos be that it has *been* fine-tuned?" If the answer to this question is No, then the teleological argument fails. And the answer to this question is No if there is even one other explanation of the fine-tuning of the cosmos that is at least as good as the explanation that it has been fine-tuned. And another explanation, one at least as good, is available: an explanation that appeals to the interplay of chance and an observational selection effect.

The alternative explanation goes like this. First, the cosmos is only one among a vast number of *actual* cosmoi. (If there are people who insist on using 'the cosmos' as a name for the whole of physical reality, we could accommodate them by saying instead that what appears to us to be the whole of the cosmos is in reality a very small *part* of the cosmos. The difference between the two statements seems to me to be merely verbal. I shall continue to talk of a multitude of cosmoi, and anyone who does not like my way of talking can easily translate it into talk of a multitude of parts of the one cosmos.)

These cosmoi exhibit a vast number of "cosmos-designs." To see what is intended by this statement, think of our cosmos-designing machine as containing a randomizing device. The randomizing device sets the dials on the machine at random. The machine turns out a cosmos. Then the randomizing device resets the dials and the machine turns out another cosmos, and so on through a very large number of resettings. Alternatively, we could suppose that there were an enormous number of cosmos-producing machines on each of which the dials were set at random and that each machine turned out one cosmos. (Compare the alarm clocks issued to the citizens of Wormsley Glen.) Since the dial settings are random, and since the existence of life is allowed by hardly any of the possible combinations of settings, only a very small proportion of these cosmoi will be suitable abodes for life. Most of them will last only a few seconds or will contain no protons or will contain no atoms or will contain only hydrogen and helium atoms or will be composed entirely of violently radioactive matter or will be devoid of stars or will contain only stars of a kind that would burn out before evolution could get started on their planets.

We suppose, however, that there are so *many* actual cosmoi that it is statistically unsurprising that there are a few of them that are possible abodes for life and in fact that it is statistically unsurprising that there are a few that actually contain life. The total number of cosmoi needed to render unsurprising the existence of even a few cosmoi that were suitable abodes for life would be enormous: perhaps comparable to the number of elementary particles in "our" cosmos, perhaps vastly greater than that. (It is hard to think of a reason to suppose that the number of actual cosmoi would have to be finite. If the number of cosmoi were infinite, it would certainly not be surprising that some of them were suitable abodes for life.)

There are various conceivable mechanisms that are more realistic than our imaginary cosmos-producing machine that might generate an appropriate variety of cosmoi. In Chapter 6, we considered the possibility that the cosmos might have arisen as a fluctuation in some pre-cosmic analogue of the quantum field. Let us, following Milton, refer to this analogue as Chaos and Old Night—Chaos for short. Chaos is a sort of arena in which random fluctuations occur. A very few among these fluctuations are impressive enough to be called cosmoi. We suppose that the cosmoi that arise in Chaos do not resemble one another as closely as the bubbles in a pot of boiling porridge resemble one another. The differences among them—which, we must remember, are the products of chance—are, or can be, of the radical kind that we should describe as differences in the laws of physics and large-scale cosmic structure: different values of the fine-structure constant, different ratios of the strength of the strong nuclear force to the strength of gravity, different numbers of electrons, and so on. And, finally, a very few of the cosmoi have just the right properties to be possible abodes for life.

One might raise the question where Chaos came from or why it is "there" at all, but that is a question that relates to the cosmological rather than to the teleological argument. One might also raise the question why Chaos has properties that fit it for being a generator of random cosmoi. (It is, after all, to be understood by analogy to the quantum field, and the quantum field is a physical object with a very specific set of properties, properties defined in many cases by apparently arbitrary numbers.) This is a question that is relevant to the teleological argument. If there were a large number of "possible chaoses" and only a very few of them had the right properties to be random cosmos generators, then we should have made no progress in appealing to Chaos in our attempt to deal with the teleological argument.

Since we know next to nothing that is relevant to this question, let us simply stipulate that the properties of Chaos are determined by "the laws of hyperphysics" and that there is only one possible set of laws of hyperphysics. (In one sense, the laws of hyperphysics would be the real laws of physics. What we normally think of as the laws of physics would not really be laws, since they would not apply to the whole of physical reality. They would be mere descriptions of local regularities.) It is important to remember in this connection that we are not attempting to construct an explanation for the apparent design of the cosmos that is known to be correct, but only an explanation that is at least as good as the hypothesis that the cosmos was designed by a rational being. And an explanation will be at least as good as that explanation if it contains no element that is known on independent grounds to be false or improbable—for that (together with the fact that it does explain the observed phenomenon of the fine-tuning of the cosmos) is really all that can be said in favor of the hypothesis of rational design.

The final part of our alternative explanation of apparent cosmic design takes the form of an appeal to an observational selection effect: we cannot observe the cosmoi that are unsuitable for life. We cannot observe them because something restricts the scope of our observations to our own cosmos—the space-time curvature of our cosmos, or the simple fact that everything that is not a part of our cosmos is just too far away for us to see, or some other factor.[4] And any rational beings that there may be anywhere in the macrocosm (so to call the aggregate of all the cosmoi) will be in the same position as we. The members of every rational species anywhere in the macrocosm will be able to observe only the "insides" of their own cosmos. It will look to them as if they inhabited a cosmos that was both carefully designed to be an abode for life (it will have to be suitable for life, since they are in it) and unique (since they can't see any of the others). But this will be appearance rather than reality. It will be the result of the interplay between chance and an observational selection effect.

We can gain some insight into the way this reply to the teleological argument works if we look again at the case in which you would have been killed if you had not drawn the shortest straw from a bundle of 1,048,576 straws. You were (you remember) astonished to find that, lo and behold, you had drawn the shortest straw and were still there to be astonished. I said that the most reasonable thing for you to conclude would be that some unknown benefactor had rigged the drawing in your favor. And this is true provided that you know that your situation is unique. But suppose that you knew that your situation was not unique. Suppose that you knew that you were only one among many millions of people who had been placed in a situation in which they had to draw the shortest straw from a bundle of 1,048,576 or else be instantly killed. In that case the most reasonable hypothesis would not be that an unknown benefactor had rigged the drawing in your favor. The most reasonable hypothesis would be that you were just lucky.

If someone tosses a coin exactly twenty times, and if there is no other occasion on which someone tosses a coin twenty or more times, it is most improbable that anyone will *ever* toss a coin "heads" twenty times in a row: the chances are 1 in 1,048,576. If millions of people toss a coin twenty times, it is likely that someone will toss "heads" twenty times in a row. If millions of millions of people toss a coin twenty times, it is a virtual certainty that someone will toss "heads" twenty times in a row. The odds are, of course, the same with respect to drawing the shortest straw from a bundle of 1,048,576 straws. If you draw the shortest straw from a bundle of that size, and if you know that millions of millions of other people have been drawing straws from a bundle of that size, you should reason as follows: "It was all but inevitable that a fair number of people would draw the shortest straw. Luckily for me, I happened to be one of that number." But if you draw the shortest straw and know that you were the only one engaged in such a drawing, you cannot reason this way, for you will know that it was *not* all but inevitable that a fair number of people would draw the shortest straw; on the contrary, you will know that it was all but inevitable that *no one* would draw the shortest straw. It is for that reason that you will have to turn to the alternative hypothesis that someone has rigged the drawing in your favor.

Now given our everyday knowledge of the world, it would never be reasonable for one to believe that millions of millions of other people were in circumstances that almost exactly duplicated one's own, and this would be true with a vengeance if one's circumstances were as bizarre as those laid out in the "straw-drawing" story. But suppose that the conditions of human life were very different from what they actually are. Suppose that you were in the circumstances of the hero of the straw-drawing story and that *for all you knew* there were millions of millions of people in the same circumstances. Suppose that, as far as your knowledge went, the following two hypotheses were about equally probable:

- This is the only drawing, and someone has rigged it in my favor.
- This is only one among millions of millions of such drawings, in some of which the short straw is drawn.

What could you say then? Only this: that you didn't know whether you had an unobserved benefactor or whether you were "surrounded" by millions of millions of such drawings.

This, I believe, is exactly analogous to our situation with respect to the fine-tuning of the cosmos. As far as our present knowledge goes (aside from any divine revelation that certain individuals or groups may be privy to) we have to regard the following two hypotheses as equally probable:

- This is the only cosmos, and some rational being has (or rational beings have) fine-tuned it in such a way that it is a suitable abode for life.
- This is only one among a vast number of cosmoi, some few of which are suitable abodes for life.

We do not know whether the apparently purposive fine-tuning of the cosmos is reality or mere appearance, a product of chance and an observational selection effect. The fine-tuning of the cosmos that has been pretty well established by modern physics and cosmology does, however, make one thing clear: the cosmos does not exist on its own. There is something that accounts for the fact that we observe a cosmos that has very specific features (those required for the existence of life) and, presumably, accounts for the existence of that cosmos as well. Let us call this "something" the *Arche*. (This word—which is pronounced ar-KAY—was used by the Greeks for that which is the beginning of all things, or that which is the foundation on which the existence of all things rests.) But we—that is, we metaphysicians, speaking as metaphysicians—can say little about the Arche beyond the bare assertion of its existence.

The most important of all the questions that we cannot answer about the Arche may be phrased as follows: Is the Arche a Chaos or a Logos? We have already met the word 'chaos'. The difficult Greek world 'logos' is usually translated as 'word'—not in the sense of the basic unit of speech but in the sense of 'that which goes forth from a speaker', as 'Word then came to the king that ... '—or 'reason'. (I have chosen to use 'logos' in this context because 'arche' and 'logos' are associated with each other in the opening words of the Gospel according to Saint John, which are themselves a deliberate echo of the opening words of Genesis. John writes: "In the beginning [*arche*] was the Word [*logos*], and the Word was God. ... ") This question is the most important question that can be asked about the Arche because the question whether there is any meaning or purpose in our existence depends upon the answer: if the Arche is a Chaos, our existence has no meaning; if the Arche is a Logos, our existence has a meaning. If the Arche is a Chaos, then we are just one of those things that happen from time to time. If the Arche is a Logos, then we exist for a purpose, and that is the only sense in which the existence of anything can have a "meaning." (It is worth repeating that it does not follow from the assumption that we exist for a purpose that we can discover that purpose or are capable of understanding that purpose or that we should like that purpose if we knew what it was.)

There is perhaps nothing more that the metaphysician can say about this question except to point out that each of these positions is emotionally attractive to certain people. I suppose that no one would deny that there are people who find the idea that our existence has a meaning or a purpose emotionally attractive. But it is equally worthy of remark, and less often noticed, that the thesis that our existence is without meaning or purpose is immensely attractive to certain kinds of persons. If my life has no purpose, if I and everyone else are the results of a series of accidents that are not part of the purpose of anyone or anything, then I am free to live my life according to my own desires—or at any rate the only obstacles to my doing this will be those often inconvenient features of everyday life (people whose plans are incompatible with mine, the laws of physics, death—that sort of thing) with which everyone is familiar. If, however, there is a rational being who has designed the universe for a purpose, who could say whether that being's plans and mine were compatible or what the consequences might be if they were not? Chaos, having brought us into existence, is unlikely to make any demands on our time or attention; who can tell what a Logos might have in mind for us? A special case of this sort of motivation is nicely expressed in a little verse by Arthur Hugh Clough:

"There is no God," the wicked saith,
"And truly it's a blessing,
For what he might have done with us
It's better only guessing."

But this motivation can be generalized beyond the case of a God who has moral concerns and punishes the wicked. If, moreover, "life, the universe, and everything" are the result of mere chance, then one may well be one of the more important and impressive beings in existence; if the Arche is a Logos, this is certainly not the case. This motivation is transparently present in the following quotation from the Nobel Prize–winning physicist Steven Weinberg (it occurs immediately following a passage in which he discusses the emotional difficulties some people face in believing that our existence is meaningless, a position he believes to be supported by modern science):

> The more the universe seems comprehensible, the more it also seems pointless.
>
> But if there is no solace in the fruits of our research, there is at least some consolation in the research itself. Men and women are not content to comfort themselves with tales of gods and giants, or to confine their thoughts to the daily affairs of life; they also build telescopes and satellites and accelerators, and sit at their desks for endless hours working out the meaning of the data they gather. The effort to understand the universe is one of the very few things that lifts human life a little above the level of farce, and gives it some of the grace of tragedy.[5]

It is pretty clear that these are the thoughts of someone who inhabits a mental world in which scientists are just about the most important and impressive human beings there are. And, as we have seen, human beings are no doubt the only rational beings in (at any rate) this part of the cosmos. It is not hard to guess where a Nobel Prize–winning physicist stands in the cosmic pecking order, as it is perceived by Steven Weinberg. But no human being occupies any such impressive place in a cosmos that is the work of a Logos.

Whatever may be the accuracy of these speculations about the reasons underlying the emotional attractiveness of the thesis that our existence is without meaning or purpose, it is clear that this is an emotionally attractive position for many people. There are a great many people who by no means *reluctantly* embrace the thesis that our existence is without meaning or purpose. There are a great many people who would be quite taken aback by an invitation to move to a world in which human beings *had* been created to serve the purposes of a Logos. (That joy is the appropriate reaction to the supposed discovery that human beings inhabit a world without meaning or purpose has been an important theme in the writings of many nineteenth- and twentieth-century thinkers. The works of the nineteenth-century German writer Friedrich Nietzsche are far more worthy of serious attention than anything else written to the same end.)

Suggestions for Further Reading

Burrill's *The Cosmological Arguments* contains (owing to the editor's conviction that the teleological argument is a version of the cosmological argument) a useful set of readings on the teleological argument.

The greatest single work devoted to the teleological argument is Hume's *Dialogues Concerning Natural Religion* (published in 1779, three years after

Hume's death). This is one of the great masterpieces of destructive philosophical criticism. Although the book is largely devoted to the teleological argument (the version of the argument that Hume considers emphasizes the analogical aspect of the argument, the drawing of an analogy between the cosmos and a machine or other human artifact), parts of it are devoted to other topics. The reader interested primarily in the teleological argument is directed to Parts II through VIII, and particularly to Parts II and V. (Many of the points made in Chapter 8 about the weakness of the conclusion of the teleological argument are taken from the *Dialogues*.) For a powerful and sophisticated defense of the argument against Hume's criticisms, see Swinburne's "The Argument from Design." The greatest of the pre-Darwinian expositions of the teleological argument is Paley's *Natural Theology* (1802).

There is a vast literature on Darwinism and "design in nature." My conviction is that the best way to approach a vast literature (if you do not want to devote your life to it) is to look at a selection of works that take the opposite and extreme positions. Here are four: Dawkins, *The Blind Watchmaker*; Monod, *Chance and Necessity*; Denton, *Evolution: A Theory in Crisis*; Johnson, *Darwin on Trial*. The first two are "extreme" in that they not only maintain that Darwin has shown that the teleological argument is invalid, but that he has shown that its conclusion is false, that there is no purposive design in nature. The authors of the latter two books accept the fact of evolution (that present-day organisms are descended from earlier, less differentiated organisms in a line of descent that goes back hundreds or thousands of millions of years), but argue that Darwin's theory cannot account for the observed facts of evolution. Johnson argues that only intelligent design can account for these facts, and Denton implies that some new and as yet unknown scientific theory is needed.

For Nietzsche's best expression of his "joyous" acceptance of atheism (or perhaps it would be better to say, of the obsolescence of the idea of God) see *Thus Spake Zarathustra*.

9

The Nature of Rational Beings: Dualism and Physicalism

SINCE WE KNOW OF no rational beings besides ourselves, we shall be able to discuss the problem of the nature of rational beings only in relation to ourselves. We have already said something about the nature of rational beings in one sense of 'nature': we have set out the defining characteristics of rationality. Our question will be this: What is it about human beings that enables them to be rational? Perhaps we can best understand what is meant by this question by drawing an analogy with a question about an everyday physical concept like liquidity. We may know that a "liquid" is a stuff that changes its shape to fit the shape of the container in which it is placed but retains a particular volume throughout all changes of shape. But this does not tell us what it is about water (that is, the chemical compound whose molecules are formed from two hydrogen atoms and an oxygen atom) that accounts for the fact that it is a liquid at temperatures and pressures at which table salt is a solid and carbon dioxide a gas. Explanations of this fact are available. (They appeal principally to the forces that operate between H_2O molecules and the way in which these forces are determined by the properties of hydrogen and oxygen atoms and their arrangement in the H_2O molecule.) We want to find an analogous explanation of the way in which rationality is "realized" in human beings (analogous, that is, to the way in which liquidity is realized in water): we want to know what "underlying" features of human beings enable them to have the properties that are listed in the abstract definition of rationality.

The short answer to this question is that no one knows. The rationality that is, as far as we know, unique to human beings is a mystery, as is the conscious experience that human beings share with many other animals. The two questions 'How is rationality realized?' and 'How is conscious experience realized?' are generally viewed by philosophers as belonging more to the area of philosophy called "the philosophy of mind" than to metaphysics. Or at least this is true when these questions are considered in their entirety. But there is a question that could be thought of as a part of these questions (an answer to it would be a part of the answers to them) that is pretty clearly within the domain of metaphysics. We shall devote this chapter and the following chapter to this question.

The question we shall be addressing is rather hard to state if we want to state it in a way that does not favor one answer to it over other possible answers. We might try this: What *kind* of thing are we human beings? But this formulation is too abstract to convey much. It often happens in philosophy that philosophers pose a question and suggest various answers to it and that the answers are clearer than the question. The present case is one of them. One way to deal with such a difficulty is to let the answers define the question: it is the question to which those statements are possible answers. Let us try that strategy.

The possible answers to the question we are trying to understand (at least the possible answers that are taken at all seriously today) are all forms of either *dualism* or *physicalism*. The first step in trying to understand our question is to understand these terms.

Suppose that by a "physical" thing we mean an individual thing that is made entirely of those things whose nature physics investigates. If current physics is correct, all of the objects of our sensory experience—pieces of chalk, beetles, stars, and everything else we can touch or see—are made entirely of three kinds of elementary particles: up-quarks, down-quarks, and electrons (plus a few kinds of particles, such as photons, whose exchange by quarks and electrons enables the quarks and electrons to interact). It is an interesting technical question what we mean by 'made entirely of', but let us suppose that we have an adequate intuitive understanding of this phrase. (Here is an example to aid our intuitions: A sand castle is made entirely of grains of sand—provided that the child who built it did not incorporate into its structure a twig or lollipop stick or anything else not made of sand.) Thus, by the terms of our definition, all of the objects of our sensory experience are physical things.

Let us call a "non-physical" thing anything that has no parts that are physical things. The two classifications "physical" and "non-physical" are not exhaustive: an object composed of both physical things and non-physical things would be neither. We could call such an object a "composite." I shall generally ignore the possibility of composites, except in one place where I am explicitly discussing them. Thus, when I talk of things that are "not physical," my remarks are meant to apply only to non-physical things and not to composites, even though composites are, strictly speaking, not physical.

In addition to the concept of a physical thing, it will occasionally be useful to have the concept of a physical *property*: we shall understand a physical property to be a property that can be possessed by and only by a physical thing.

Since we can see and touch human beings, and since we *are* human beings, it might be thought to follow from our definition of a physical thing that we are physical things. But let us make some distinctions. Let us say that a *human organism* is that which a biologist would classify as a member of the species *Homo sapiens*. And let us say that a *human person* is that which we refer to when we use the first-person-singular pronoun ('I', 'me', 'moi', 'ego', 'ich', ...). When I have used the words 'human being' in this and earlier chapters, I have been assuming that human persons and human organisms are one and the same. To call *x* a human being is to call *x* a human person, but with the understanding or implication that *x* is a human organism, a rational animal. (Or this, at least, is what I take 'human being' to mean. Perhaps there are those who would disagree with this definition.) But the thesis that human persons and human organisms are one and the same is controversial.

If human persons and human organisms are one and the same, then, since human organisms are obviously physical things, it follows that human persons are physical things. The thesis that human persons are physical things is called *physicalism*. (This word is also used as a name for the stronger thesis that the only individual things that exist are physical things. And the stronger and weaker senses of the word tend not to be carefully distinguished, owing to the fact that most philosophers who believe that human persons are physical things also believe that the only individual things that exist are physical things. I shall use 'physicalism' only for the thesis that human persons are physical things.[1])

And if human persons are not physical things, what are they? What does it mean to say of a thing that it is not physical? Or, rather, what does it imply? The concept of a thing that is not physical is a purely negative concept. Some philosophers have said that human persons are not physical things, but what, if anything, does this imply about human persons beyond the bare, negative assertion that they are *not* physical, are *not* composed entirely of those things whose natures physics investigates? We shall presently return to this interesting question.

The thesis that human persons are non-physical things is called *dualism*. (More exactly, the thesis that there are both physical and non-physical things and that human persons are among the non-physical things is called dualism. Some idealists perhaps hold that there are only non-physical things, persons among them.) This word comes from the Latin word for 'two'. The dualist believes that human persons have a "dual" nature. The person is, strictly speaking, a non-physical thing, but it is very intimately associated with a certain physical thing, a human organism, which is called the person's *body*. The body, not the person, is the thing that a biologist would classify as a member of the species *Homo sapiens*. The dualist will concede that we frequently make assertions by which we appear to ascribe physical properties to human persons, assertions like, "John weighs 46 kilograms" or "Alice is 165 centimeters tall." But, according to the dualist, it is not strictly true that John weighs 46 kilograms or has any other weight; and it is not strictly true that Alice is 165 centimeters tall or has any other height. John and Alice, rather, possess such properties only vicariously: it is, strictly speaking, not they but their bodies that have weights and heights. This does not mean that there is anything wrong with saying "John weighs 46 kilograms" in ordinary contexts; this statement is to be understood as a kind of shorthand expression of the assertion that John's body weighs 46 kilograms, just as Alice's statement "I'm carrying 1,400 tons of pig iron" is a shorthand expression of the assertion that the ship of which she is the cargo officer is carrying 1,400 tons of pig iron. A "dual-istic" analysis of the ordinary statement "John weighs more than he likes" well illustrates what is meant by saying that, according to the dualist, human persons have a "dual nature." Nothing, according to the dualist, could liter-ally weigh more than it liked. Rather, the dualist holds, it is John, the non-physical person, who does the disliking, and it is his body, the physical organ-ism, that has the weight that is the object of the dislike.

What is the "intimate association" that holds between the person and the person's body? Dualists have answered this question in more than one way. The most obvious answer, and the one that commands the widest allegiance among dualists, is contained in a theory called "dualistic interactionism." In order to set out the content of this theory, let us look at a typical human person and see what dualistic interactionism says about the relations that have to hold between a person and an organism for that organism to be that person's body. Let us consider one Jane Tyler, the author of the well-regarded novel *The Sinews of Thy Heart*, whom we may suppose to be a typical human person. And let us consider the following words and phrases:

- 'Jane Tyler'
- 'the author of *The Sinews of Thy Heart*'
- 'I' (spoken by Jane Tyler)
- 'you' (spoken by someone addressing Jane Tyler)
- 'she' (spoken by someone relating an anecdote about Jane Tyler)
- 'that woman over there' (spoken by someone calling someone's attention to Jane Tyler)
- 'Jane Tyler's mind'
- 'Jane Tyler's soul'

According to the dualist, all of these phrases, when they are spoken in the in-dicated contexts, denote or name or stand for or refer to the same thing, a non-physical thing, a thing that is not composed of elementary particles and is not observable by the senses, a thing that has no weight or mass (since gravity and inertia are concepts that apply only to physical things), and has no position in space—at least it is hard to see how a non-physical thing could have a position in space, although Saint Thomas Aquinas believed that angels were non-physical things that had positions in space. (The dualist will probably also want to say that this thing has no parts: as metaphysicians say, it is a *simple*. But, in principle, one could be a dualist and hold that a human person had parts, provided they were all non-physical parts.)

In addition to Jane Tyler there is Jane Tyler's body, a physical thing, a living human organism. Our question is: What is it that makes one particular human organism *Jane Tyler's* body and not some other person's body—or no one's body at all? Dualistic interactionism tells us that this particular organism is Jane Tyler's body because of a certain two-way causal connection that holds between Jane—let us get on familiar terms with her—and that organism. A certain organism is Jane's body because she affects it and it affects her. But we must be more specific than this, because cause-and-effect relations can hold between any human person and any human organism.

There is, interactionists maintain, a very special way in which Jane can affect the one particular human organism that is her body: she can cause changes in it without causing changes in any other organism (other than its own parts; multicellular organisms have cells, which are themselves organisms, as parts). And there is a very special way in which one particular organism can affect her: it can cause changes in her without causing changes in any organism besides itself (and its own parts). Suppose, for example, that Jane begins to whistle. In doing this she brings about changes in a certain organism (electrical currents flow along very specific neural pathways in the organism, its lips assume a specific configuration, and many other changes occur in it). And it may be that in beginning to whistle, she brings about changes in no organism besides this one and some of the cells that are parts of it. Now *I* can also do things that will bring about changes in that organism; I can, for example, open a window on a freezing day and cause it to begin to shiver. But I can do this only by bringing about changes in another, wholly distinct, organism, *my* body.

Now let us consider the special way in which changes in the organism that is Jane's body can bring about changes in Jane the person. Suppose that Jane steps on a tack. The resulting puncture wound in her foot will cause *her* to be in pain. (Pain would seem clearly to be a property of the person. Pain—the *sensation* we call "pain"—is a property of the organism only if the organism *is* the person.) It is true that changes in other organisms than Jane's body can bring about changes in Jane. If I step on a tack, the resulting puncture wound in my foot may cause *her* to feel concern (and feeling concern is clearly a property of the person). But a change in my body can cause a change in Jane only by causing a change in another organism, *her* body, that is not a part of my body.

This account of the causal relations between Jane and a certain organism that make that organism *her body* (or, more generally, that make a given organism a given person's body) is dualistic interactionism. It is called that because it asserts that a person (which is not a physical thing) and that person's body (which is a physical thing) can act upon each other. The two most important dualists in the history of metaphysics, Plato and Descartes, were both interactionists. Other dualists, however, have rejected interactionism, generally because of the physical or metaphysical difficulties raised by the thesis that a non-physical thing (a thing that has no physical properties like mass or electrical charge) could affect a physical thing. Descartes's follower Nicholas Malebranche, for example, held that when a person "wills" or "tries" or "sets out" to whistle, God effects appropriate changes in a certain human organism. Similarly, he held that when a human organism is punctured by a tack, God causes a certain person to experience appropriate sensations of pain. This theory is called "occasionalism," since it holds that changes in the person are never the *causes* of changes in an organism but are only the "occasions" of changes in an organism; in the same way, changes in an organism are never causes of, but only occasions of, changes in a person.

A second dualistic alternative to interactionism is "epiphenomenalism" (from a Greek word meaning 'by-product'). According to this theory, changes in a person can be caused "directly" by changes in a particular organism, but changes in the person never cause changes in that organism. Each change in the organism is caused by prior changes in the organism or in its immediate physical environment, and these physical events also sometimes cause changes in the person—but there is no "feedback" from the person to the organism: the non-physical events that are changes in the person never have physical effects. Persons are thus related to their bodies as billows of smoke are to the fires from which they issue; persons exist and are non-physical, but they are mere by-products of the physical activity that is going on in certain physical organisms. (Or this is one way to understand epiphenomenalism. Epiphenomenalists have not generally expressed themselves very clearly. It is possible that at least some epiphenomenalists want to say that the person *is* the organism and that it is people's *sensations and thoughts* that are the by-products of the events going on in the organism. Other epiphenomenalists write in such a way as to suggest that persons are not individual things at all but are mere collections of the thoughts and sensations generated by "their" organisms. I can make nothing of either of these ideas.) It is a consequence of this theory that our belief that we can influence the motions of our bodies is an illusion. The illusion is itself, according to epiphenomenalism, a by-product of the physical activity of the body. There are several other dualistic theories of the nature of the person-body relation, but we shall not discuss them. Nor shall we further discuss occasionalism and epiphenomenalism.

There is one other point about dualistic interactionism that we should take note of: it does not obviously follow from dualistic interactionism that the non-physical human person can exist without being in interaction with a human body. Some argument would be required to establish that a dualistic interactionist should believe that a human person could exist without a body. Plato believed that the soul—that is, the person—would "automatically" continue to exist when the body it was associated with died. And he did have an argument for this thesis: that the soul is a metaphysical simple, and that a thing can cease to exist only by "coming apart," by being resolved into its elements; a simple, a thing that has no parts, must therefore be imperishable. This argument, however, is not particularly convincing. For example, the premise that a thing can cease to exist only by coming apart deserves further discussion. One might cite the fact that current physics treats electrons and various other particles as having no parts; yet an electron can be "annihilated" by a collision with a positron. But we shall not pursue this subject. We shall not try to discover whether Plato's argument is ultimately defensible or whether there might be other interesting arguments for the same conclusion.

The physicalist, who holds that the human person just *is* the human organism (or some part of it), does not face the problem of explaining the relation between the person and the organism. Since, for the physicalist, the person and the organism (or a part of the organism) are identical, a change in the person is a change in the organism. And since the organism is a physical thing, and a physical thing is made entirely of quarks and electrons, it would seem that any change in a human person must be a change in the physical properties of the person: a change in the properties of the quarks and electrons that make the person up, or else a change in the way the quarks and electrons that make the person up are related to one another. Such a change—one that involves only a change in the physical properties of a thing—we may call a purely physical change; examples of purely physical changes would be *receiving a puncture wound in the foot* and *undergoing a sudden rise in body temperature* and *having a brain in which electrical currents suddenly begin to flow in such-and-such a way.* If a human person is a physical thing, then any change whatever in a human person must be a purely physical change. If, for example, Tim becomes elated because of some news that was contained in a letter he has just received, this change in Tim, his becoming elated, must be the very same thing (or perhaps we should say the very same event) as some purely physical change.

If it is indeed true that Tim's becoming elated is the very same thing as some purely physical change, then, given what we know about human physiology, it is presumably the same event as some event involving some of the particles that make up Tim's brain—no doubt a change in the way in which electrical currents flow in Tim's brain. Thus, if physicalism is correct about the nature of persons, all of those changes in a person that we should unreflectively call "mental" or "psychological"—whatever, exactly, these terms may mean—are physical changes in the person (and presumably changes in the person's cerebral cortex, that part of the brain that is associated with conscious mental activity). The thesis that mental changes (in human persons at least) just *are* certain physical changes is called the "identity theory." The identity theory is not quite the same thing as physicalism. Physicalism (the theory that human persons are physical things) entails the identity theory (that mental changes in human persons are identical with certain purely physical changes) only on the assumption that mental changes in human persons really exist. And there are philosophers and psychologists who deny the existence of the mental (mental changes and mental states) altogether. We shall not discuss the views of these philosophers and psychologists, who subscribe to theories with names like "behaviorism" and "eliminative physicalism." We shall take the reality of the mental for granted, as do most philosophers and psychologists and, indeed, most physicalists. (Because most physicalists take the reality of the mental for granted, it is safe to say that most physicalists subscribe to the identity theory.)

The two most important theories about the nature of the only rational beings whose existence is uncontroversial (ourselves) are, therefore, dualistic interactionism and physicalism. What can be said for and against each of these theories? Can either be shown to be superior to the other?[2]

We shall begin our attempt to answer these questions by examining some arguments for dualism. (We shall not concern ourselves with defending dualistic *interactionism*; we shall take it for granted that interactionism is the most plausible form of dualism and shall investigate the question, What can be said in defense of dualism?) Arguments for dualism have this general form: you and I and other human persons are not human organisms or any other physical things because we have properties that could not belong to a physical thing. (It is obviously a valid general principle of reasoning that a thing *x* and a thing *y* cannot be identical, cannot be one and the same thing, if *x* has a property or feature or characteristic that *y* lacks.) There are many such arguments. We shall consider five of them. The first argument that we shall examine is from Descartes's *Meditations on First Philosophy.*

Descartes argues that I can conceive of my body's not existing—indeed, I can conceive of there being no physical world at all—but I cannot conceive of *my* not existing.[3] When Descartes says that I can conceive of my body's not existing, he is not advancing the thesis that I can form a conception of the way things would have been if my body had not existed (no doubt I can, but that I can is not his thesis); he is advancing the stronger thesis that it is possible for me to conceive of the following: things being *just as they seem to me to be* and yet there being no such thing as my body. To conceive of this, I could imagine that there exists some powerful spirit (the "evil genius" we met in Chapter 3) who has decided to deceive me about the existence of a world of physical objects: there are no physical objects, but the spirit deceitfully "feeds" me a series of sense impressions that is like the series of sense impressions that I should be experiencing if I were perceiving a world of physical objects.

And when Descartes says that I cannot conceive of *my* not existing, he is not saying that I cannot form a conception of the way things would have been if I had not existed (that would be false; I *can* conceive of that); he is saying rather that I cannot conceive of the following: things being *just as they seem to me to be* and yet there being no such thing as myself. In other words, Descartes holds that, however absurd it may seem, the hypothesis that I exist and do not have a body is a hypothesis that it is *possible* for me to entertain. But the hypothesis that I do not exist is not simply a hypothesis that I find absurd; it is a hypothesis that it is literally impossible for me to entertain. It is remotely possible that my conviction that there are physical things, including my own body, is an illusion. It is not even *remotely* possible that it is an illusion of mine that *I* exist. Not an illusion of *mine*: if I am "there" to have the illusion, then I must exist.

The argument, then, is that my body has the following property:

can be conceived by me not to exist,

as does every other physical thing. But *I* do not have that property. Therefore, I am identical neither with my body nor with any other physical thing.

The trouble with this argument is that it proves too much. There are obviously *some* statements of the form "I am (identical with) ... " (where the blank is to be filled by something other than 'I' or 'me' or 'myself') that I can make and thereby say something true, but Descartes's argument can be used to refute them all. Let us look at an example. The statement

I am the author of *An Essay on Free Will*

is true; that is, if I were to speak these words, I should say something true, for there is a book of that title, and I am its sole author. But suppose I were to reason as follows:

I can conceive of there being no such thing as the author of *An Essay on Free Will*. That is, I can conceive of things being just as they seem to me to be and there being no such thing as the author of *An Essay on Free Will*. The easiest way would be for me to suppose that there is no such book: my apparent memories of having written and published such a book are fantasies. But I cannot conceive of there being no such thing as myself. Therefore, while the author of *An Essay on Free Will* has the property "can be conceived by me not to exist," I do not have that property. Therefore, I am not the author of *An Essay on Free Will*.

Since this argument starts from true premises and yet has a false conclusion, it must contain some error of logic. Most philosophers would agree that the error is this: the words 'can be conceived by me not to exist' do not name or express a property, but the argument treats them as if they did. If these words did name or express a property, then we ought to be able to take a sentence like 'The author of *An Essay on Free Will* can be conceived by me not to exist' and substitute for 'the author of *An Essay on Free Will*' any word or phrase that denotes (designates, refers to, is a name for) the same thing and get a sentence that is true if the original sentence is true.

But this is not what in fact happens. The word 'I' denotes (at least when *I* use it) the same thing as 'the author of *An Essay on Free Will*'; but 'The author of *An Essay on Free Will* can be conceived by me not to exist' is true, and 'I can be conceived by me not to exist' is false. Let us compare 'can be conceived by me not to exist' with some phrase that really does name a property—say, 'was born during the Second World War'. The author of *An Essay on Free Will* was born during the Second World War (take my word for it). The word 'I', when I speak it, and the words 'the author of *An Essay on Free Will*' are two names for the same thing. The appropriate substitution produces the sentence 'I was born during the Second World War'. Is it true that I was born during the Second World War? Well, of course it is. It has to be, given that the author of *An Essay on Free Will* was born during the Second World War and that I *am* the author of *An Essay on Free Will*.

If a phrase that looks as if it named a property (like 'can be conceived by me not to exist') does not obey this simple substitution rule, then, contrary to appearance, it does not name a property. Therefore, 'can be conceived by me not to exist' does not name a property. And, therefore, Descartes's attempt to prove that persons are not physical things contains an error. There is nothing wrong with the principle of reasoning 'If x has a property that y lacks, then x is not identical with y', but Descartes misapplied this valid principle as a result of his treating 'can be conceived by me not to exist' as a name of a property.

We now turn to our second argument for dualism, a very popular one:

Physical things are incapable of thought and sensation. Only mental things are capable of thought and sensation, and mental things are not physical things. But human persons are capable of thought and sensation. Therefore, human persons are not physical things.

This argument raises two questions:

- Why should we believe that physical things are incapable of thought and sensation?
- What is a "mental thing"?

Let us consider the first question. I am willing to grant that if we try seriously and in detail to imagine a physical thing having thoughts and sensations, we can find this notion—the notion of a physical thing having thoughts and sensations—very puzzling. There is a famous passage in Leibniz's *Monadology* that very clearly brings out the puzzling aspects of this notion:

> Furthermore, we must admit that *perception,* and whatever depends on it, *cannot be explained on mechanical principles,* i.e. by shapes and movements. If we pretend that there is a machine whose structure makes it think, sense and have perception, then we can conceive it enlarged, but keeping to the same proportions, so that we might go inside it as into a mill. Suppose that we do: then if we inspect the interior we shall find there nothing but parts which push one another, and never anything which could explain a perception. Thus, perception must be sought in simple substance, not in what is composite or in machines.[4]

To take a more modern example, suppose that someone were to claim to have programmed a computer so that it could think (in a sense that implies conscious experience and self-awareness) or to have constructed a thinking robot. If the computer or robot were enlarged so that people could walk about inside it, a party of tourists being led through the vast machine would see nothing but physical objects interacting physically. And this would be no illusion. It's not as if the thought and conscious experience were hidden away in some part of the machine that was off limits to visitors.

But then where *are* the thoughts and the experience? Where *could* they be? How could the mere physical interaction of bits of metal and plastic and silicon "add up to" thoughts and experience? It is important to realize that this point has nothing to do with the specific kinds of physical material that a computer or robot would be likely to be made of. The point has to do only with the fact that the materials are *physical.* The point would be unchanged if we imagined a party of tourists being conducted through *ourselves* (or our bodies), as in Isaac Asimov's interesting science-fiction novel *Fantastic Voyage* (or the unspeakably silly movie of the same title). If we could be greatly reduced in size and go inside a functioning human brain and have a look round, we should see no thoughts or experience, not even if we saw everything there was to see. If God looks inside a human brain, even He sees nothing but unthinking physical things like neurons and Nissl granules and amino-acid molecules and electrons in continuous mutual physical interaction. Where then, are the thoughts? Where are the sudden feelings of elation or despair? Where are the sensations of heat and pain and pressure and color? The answer is, obviously, that they are elsewhere. And that "elsewhere" must be a place that is receptive to the presence of such things, a place where they *could* exist. They must exist in a mind: a mental thing.

Various physicalists—who must of course believe that physical things are capable of thought and sensation—will reply to this argument in various ways. What follows is my own reply. Some physicalists would reject some parts of it.

Let us begin with the question, *Where* are the thoughts and sensations? The answer is that since these things are changes in the cerebral cortex, they are all around you (you who have in imagination been reduced in size and are physically inside someone's brain). It does not follow from this that you *see* them, since they may involve the whole cerebral cortex or the whole brain or widely scattered parts of the brain: it may be that you cannot see them for the same reason that you cannot see the event called 'the election' on election day. But let us suppose for the sake of argument that these events are sufficiently localized that you can see them. (Or some aspects of them: a human being cannot see every aspect of any event. You can see the street lamps come on in your neighborhood, but you cannot see the flow of electrons that is an indispensable component of this event.) Of course, these events do not *look* to you like mental events, but then what would you expect a mental event to look like? ("Well, something like the way mental changes in *myself* look to *me*, as when I experience a sharp pain in my left shoulder or a thrill of fear or an intellectual insight." But that's what it's like to experience *having* or *being the subject of* a mental change. That's what a *mental change in you* "looks like" to you. What would you expect mental changes in someone *else* to look like to you?) And, anyway, a change may be of a certain type without its being evident that it is of that type. Suppose that a computer has been programmed to compute the orbit of a certain satellite. Suppose that the computer were greatly enlarged and that you went inside it, "as into a mill." You would not see any orbital computations going on—or at least you would not see anything that "looked like" orbital computation. (What would you expect orbital computation to look like?) The Leibnizian thought-experiment, therefore, should cause the physicalist no unease. Things inside the brain look just the way they would look if physicalism were correct.

Many physicalists would think that this was a sufficient reply to the charge that the notion of a physical thing that thinks is mysterious. I cannot agree with them. I do not deny that everything said in the preceding paragraph is correct, as far as it goes. Nevertheless, it seems to me that the notion of a physical thing that thinks is a mysterious notion and that Leibniz's thought-experiment brings out this mystery very effectively. We must remember, however, that our present question is not whether the physicalist is faced with a mystery; our question is whether dualism is to be preferred to physicalism. If thinking is a mystery for the physicalist, this fact will be relevant to our question only if it can be shown that the dualist is not confronted with the same mystery or with some corresponding mystery.

And, I believe, the dualist is. For it is thinking itself that is the source of the mystery of a thinking physical thing. The notion of a non-physical thing that thinks is, I would argue, equally mysterious. How any sort of thing could think is a mystery. It is just that it is a bit easier to see that thinking is a mystery when we suppose that the thing that does the thinking is physical, for we can form mental images of the operations of a physical thing and we can see that the physical interactions that are represented in these images—that are the only interactions that *can* be represented in these images—have no connection with thought or sensation, or none that we are able to imagine, conceive, or articulate. The only reason that we do not readily find the notion of a non-physical thing that thinks equally mysterious is that we have no clear procedure for forming mental images of non-physical things. Still, we are not wholly without resources for constructing mental images of non-physical things. (No doubt most of us associate some sort of mental image with the doctrine of dualistic interactionism: perhaps a human body with a vague "something" inside or above its head.)

Leibniz, in the passage that we have quoted, argues that a thinking thing must be a simple, a thing that has no parts. Well, let us represent, in our thought, a simple non-physical thing by a dot, and a composite non-physical thing by a bunch of dots, perhaps a bunch that is in constant internal motion like a swarm of bees. But if the simples that make up a composite non-physical thing do not think individually, then where is the thinking in our picture? How can a bunch of things that do not individually think or feel or exhibit self-awareness add up to something that does think or feel or exhibit self-awareness? How could their causal interaction produce such properties? Note that this seems to be essentially the same difficulty whether the individual, non-thinking simples are physical or non-physical: the only real difference between the two cases is that the mental images in the case of the composite physical thing have reasonably "sharp" constituents drawn from our experience of actual physical things (images of gears and wheels, say), whereas the mental images in the case of the composite non-physical thing are vague and arbitrary (arbitrary because non-physical things necessarily lack visual characteristics; we chose dots because dots come as close to having no characteristics as anything can). Leibniz would no doubt agree with this. After all, his position is that a thinking thing has to be a simple.[5]

But let us look at our mental picture of the simple. It is just a dot. How can we cause it to change in our imagination, so that this change will represent the successive thoughts and sensations of a non-physical simple? Change of position (relative to other imagined dots) will be of no help, because that is a relational change, and thought and sensation are supposed to be intrinsic features of thinking, sensing things. Even a dot must have a shape, but when we use dots to represent non-physical simples we do our best not to attend to their shapes, for insofar as we think of a dot as having a shape, we think of it as being composed of smaller regions, and thus as composite.

We might think of the dot as changing color, I suppose. Let's try that. Imagine a dot continuously changing its color in some very complex way. Are you imagining something thinking or having sensation? Where are the thought and the sensation in the picture that your imagination has created? My point in asking these unanswerable rhetorical questions is not to argue that a non-physical simple cannot think. (Although I believe that human persons are physical things made of smaller physical things, I believe that God is a non-physical simple, so I should hardly want to argue for the conclusion that a non-physical simple cannot think.) My point is that nothing could possibly count as a mental image of a thing that is thinking. Or, at least, nothing could count as a mental image that *shows* or *displays* a thing as thinking (except by convention, as, for example, "thought-balloons" in comic strips do; or via the familiar outward and visible signs of human thought, like those displayed by Rodin's *The Thinker*). And, I am suggesting, the persuasive force of Leibniz's thought-experiment is due entirely to this fact. It is only the difficulty of conducting a similar thought-experiment for non-physical things that keeps us from seeing that his thought-experiment does not favor dualism over physicalism. To argue that the difficulty of imagining how a physical thing could think favors dualism over physicalism is like arguing that the difficulty of imagining how Jean (who was seen in New York when he was supposedly locked up in a French maximum-security prison) could have crossed the Atlantic by air favors the hypothesis that he crossed the Atlantic by ship.

These points about mental images can be generalized so as to apply to any type of representation. Mental images are representations of how things are or might be, but there are representations of many other kinds, such as schematic diagrams on paper, three-dimensional cardboard models, computer models, and scientific theories. In general, to attempt to explain how an underlying reality generates some phenomenon is to construct a representation of the working of that underlying reality, a representation that in some sense "shows how" the underlying reality generates the phenomenon. (The best scientists seem to be able to "translate" their verbally and mathematically formulated representations of the workings of things into images, which they are able to manipulate mentally in fruitful ways.) Essentially the same considerations as those that show that we are unable to form a mental image that displays the generation of thought and sensation by the workings of some underlying reality (whether the underlying reality involves one thing or many, and whether the things it involves are physical or non-physical) show that we are unable to form *any* sort of representation that displays the generation of thought and sensation by the workings of an underlying reality. Thought and sensation are therefore a mystery—although not necessarily an insoluble one. But since the mystery, soluble or insoluble, is entirely independent of whether the elements in the representation are supposed to represent physical or non-physical things, the mystery of thought and sensation does not favor dualism over physicalism.

Has the dualist any way to respond to this counter-argument? The answer to this question depends, I believe, on what the dualist can tell us about the positive nature of non-physical thinking things. If the dualist can say no more about them than that they are non-physical, then dualism gains no advantage over physicalism and perhaps gains the disadvantages of postulating the existence of more kinds of things than physicalism does and of having to account for the interaction between these things and physical things. Let us consider an analogy. Suppose that Sir Aaron Oldham, the well-known imaginary seventeenth-century scientist, set out to explain the observed phenomenon of magnetism. Sir Aaron believed that all physical interaction was transmitted by contact between physical objects, by "pushes and bumps," and he was therefore unable to believe that magnetism was a wholly physical phenomenon, since it could act across empty space and could act "through" a physical object like a sheet of glass or paper without affecting the intermediate object in any way. He therefore postulated that associated with each lump of lodestone (the only magnets he knew about) there was a non-physical thing that had the power to cause nearby iron objects to move toward the lodestone. "Should a Lodestone be enlarged," he wrote, "to such a degree that a Man were enabled to pass among the corpuscules composing it, as an Earthworm might pass among the particles of Soil comprised in my Garden, he would observe naught but corpuscules, whether at rest or in motion, a certain quantity of Motion being on frequent occasion translated from one to another of the same corpuscules by Collision. He would see therein no Action by which the motion of a distant Pin or Nail toward those corpuscules might be effected."

We may imagine—let us shift to the historical present—that one of Sir Aaron's scientific rivals puts forward an alternative theory of magnetism: that there are unknown physical interactions, interactions other than pushes and bumps, that cause pins and nails to move toward lumps of lodestone. It would seem that unless Sir Aaron can say something about the positive nature of the non-physical entities he has postulated—unless he can say something more about them than that they are non-physical—his theory enjoys no advantage over that of his rival. (Unless Sir Aaron and his rival tell us more than they have so far, this is how things stand: each theory ascribes an observed phenomenon to an unknown cause and tells us nothing about that cause that explains how it produces the phenomenon.) And it is arguable that Sir Aaron's theory is burdened by a disadvantage that his rival's is free of: it postulates the existence of non-physical things in addition to physical things, and it faces the problem of explaining how the non-physical can interact with the physical.

Can the dualist tell us anything about the positive nature of human persons? Can the dualist say anything more about human persons than that they are not physical things? Many dualists think that they can. In this they follow Descartes, who held that the essence of a human person is thinking. This would appear to mean that the *only* intrinsic properties that a human person has or could have are "mental" properties, that is, properties that relate to thought and sensation (and that the human person is essentially such: no human person could possibly have any intrinsic properties but mental properties). Thus, if Descartes is right, human persons have such properties as *being in pain* and *feeling depressed* and *wondering how to spend Saturday afternoon*; human persons do not and could not have such properties as *being 165 centimeters tall* and *weighing 46 kilograms*. But that is not all. If Descartes is right, mental properties are the *only* properties that a human person has.[6]

A typical physicalist believes that human persons have both mental and non-mental properties. A dualist might believe this also, although the dualist, unlike the typical physicalist, would have to say that the non-mental properties of the human person were also non-physical—perhaps the members of some utterly unknowable class of properties. A dualist of this sort might even hold that our mental properties were related to these "other" non-physical properties in the way in which the typical physicalist holds that our mental properties are related to our physical properties: as the typical physicalist thinks that physical properties underlie and determine our mental properties, so the dualist might hold that the "other" non-physical properties underlie and determine our mental properties. A dualist *could* hold this, but few if any dualists do, and Descartes certainly does not. Descartes's position is that we are mental "all the way through"; with the exception of certain very abstract properties like being an individual thing and enduring through time and being capable of entering into causal relations, we have *no* intrinsic properties but mental properties. (It is important to remember that a mental property is not *by definition* a non-physical property. Typical dualists believe that mental properties—properties that imply thought or feeling—are non-physical properties because they believe that these properties could be possessed by and only by non-physical things. But physicalists believe that mental properties are not non-physical properties because they believe that these properties could be, and in fact are, possessed by physical things.)

Dualists therefore have available to them an account of the positive nature of the non-physical human person: the human person is a mental thing—loosely speaking, a thing that has only mental properties. And most if not all dualists accept this account of the positive nature of human persons. They have, therefore, an answer to our second question concerning the argument for dualism that we are considering (What is a "mental thing"?) and they are not open to the charge that they have accounted for the phenomenon of thought and sensation simply by postulating a cause for this phenomenon whose positive nature is entirely unknown.

Does their ability to offer this positive account of the nature of human persons provide a reason for preferring dualism to physicalism? It is, I think, plausible to argue that in offering this positive account they have done essentially what Sir Aaron Oldham would have done if he had attempted to give an account of the positive nature of the non-physical things associated with lumps of lodestone by saying that these things had "magnetic" properties and no others. That would not really be an "account" at all, because the words 'magnetic property' could mean nothing but 'power to produce the observed phenomenon of magnetism'. We should have no "hold" on what a magnetic property was except through its observed effects, the very things we want to explain. The dualist who holds that we are things that have only mental properties is simply asserting the existence of things that manifest the phenomenon to be explained (thought and feeling) and which have no properties besides that of manifesting the phenomenon. It is important to stress that this argument does not have the least tendency to show that dualism is wrong. For all we have said so far, there might well be things that had only mental properties. The argument is not designed to show that dualism is wrong, but only that dualism enjoys no advantage over physicalism as regards the mystery of thought and sensation.

The dualist who asserts that thoughts and sensations occur as changes in a thing whose only properties are mental has done no more to address the mystery of thought and sensation than has the physicalist who asserts that thoughts and sensations occur as changes in a thing all of whose properties are physical. It is true that no one has any account of how thoughts and sensations could be features of physical organisms. In fact, no one can say what an account of this would look like, even in broadest outline. But then no one has any account of how there could be a thing that had only mental properties, and no one can say what an account of this would look like, even in broadest outline.

We now turn to a third argument for the conclusion that one is not the same thing as one's body. (That is, for the conclusion that one is not the same thing as the human organism that one can bring about changes in without bringing about changes in any "intermediate" multicellular organism.) This argument proceeds from the observation that we do not seem to ourselves to occupy the same regions of space as our respective bodies. The twentieth-century English philosopher G. E. Moore formulated this observation in a strikingly simple phrase: "I am closer to my hands than I am to my feet." (Think about it. Look at your hands and your feet at the same time. Your feet are farther away, aren't they?) But my body is obviously not closer to my hands than to my feet—to say that would be like saying that Europe was closer to Sweden than to Italy.

The first thing to note about this argument is that, unlike the two arguments we have so far examined, it does not even claim to prove (in my case) that I am not a physical thing. It claims to prove only that I am not a *certain* physical thing: my body. Even if the argument were completely cogent and unobjectionable, it might be true that I was my brain or my left cerebral hemisphere or my cerebral cortex, and all of those things are physical things that are closer to my hands than to my feet. And, of course, the argument has the same limitation when it is applied to you or to any other human person. One might in fact argue that it is not consistent with dualism to suppose that I am closer to my hands than to my feet. I can be closer to my hands than to my feet only if I have a position in space, and as we have remarked it is hard to see how a non-physical thing could have a position in space.

The argument is, however, doubtful even as an argument for the conclusion that one is not one's body. There may be a sense in which it seems to me that I am closer to my hands than to my feet, but this appearance might be mere appearance and not reality. Our sense organs—leaving aside the skin, our organ of touch—cluster around the brain. Is it not plausible to suppose that one might seem to oneself to be located at or near the place where one's sense-organs cluster? We seem to ourselves to be at the center of the environment that our senses reveal to us, and if our sense-organs cluster around some small region, that region will seem to be at the center of our "subjective world." In fact, it is plausible to suppose that sighted persons would seem to themselves to be approximately where their eyes were, even if their ears and other sense-organs were moved to their elbows and ankles, for sighted people construct their internal model of their immediate environment mainly on the basis of visual data. (Consider Helen Keller, who was blind and deaf from very shortly after her birth. Her model of her immediate surroundings was based almost entirely on tactile data, the data of touch. Would she have felt it natural to say that she was closer to her hands than to her feet? Well, perhaps she would have, given the central role her hands played in her knowledge of her immediate environment. But perhaps she would also have felt it natural to say that she was closer to her arms than to her head. One can imagine her touching her arms and saying, "My arms are right here … , " and then reaching up to touch her head and saying, " … but my head is way up here.")

Our fourth argument for the conclusion that we are not physical things proceeds from the premise that whether or not there are other rational beings in the cosmos, there certainly could be: there is nothing intrinsically impossible in the notion. And there is nothing intrinsically impossible in the notion that such beings might be physically very different from us. Therefore, it is intrinsically possible for there to be beings that have thoughts and feelings very much like ours, even though they are *radically* different from us in their anatomy and physiology. Imagine a science-fiction story in which there are beings, the Scorpians, with whom we can carry on intelligent conversations about politics and philosophy and even art and who—it never even *occurs* to us to doubt this—experience pain when they are injured and pleasure when they relax at the end of a hard day in their sulfuric-acid baths. But there is, inside their chitinous shells, nothing that resembles a human brain: there is only purple goo that bears no resemblance whatever, even on the chemical level, to any human tissue. Now suppose that physicalism is correct. If that is so, and if we really do think and feel, then our thoughts and feelings are identical with certain physical processes that go on within our brains. But, obviously, none of the physical processes that go on in the grey matter inside our heads goes on in the purple Scorpian goo.

Suppose, for example, that when one feels pain this event is identical with the firing of C-fibers in one's brain; pain (according to physicalism) has turned out to be the firing of C-fibers, just as bolts of lightning turned out to be massive electrical discharges and water turned out to be H_2O. But there are no C-fibers, or anything remotely resembling them, inside the Scorpians. And, therefore, it must be that if physicalism is true, the Scorpians do not experience pain—just as, if there is no H_2O on their planet, there is no water on their planet. It would therefore seem that if physicalism is true, neither the Scorpians nor any other beings that are radically unlike us in their physical nature can think and feel. Only a being that was either human or very similar to a human being could think and feel. But this conclusion can only be regarded as human (or mammalian or carbon) chauvinism. In any case, it is absurd.

To this argument, the physicalist might well respond with a question: What makes you so sure that it is possible for there to be creatures that are both radically different from us in their physical structure and capable of thought and sensation? And it might not be easy to answer this question unless bluster about chauvinism counts as an answer. But there are two replies available to the physicalist that are consistent with the assumption that the possibility of beings like the Scorpians is a real one.

Each of these replies depends upon a distinction between *types* of events and *tokens* (that is, particular instances) of those types. This distinction is best introduced by example. *War* is a type of event (or an event-type, as philosophers sometimes say), and the First World War and the Seven Years' War and the War of the Austrian Succession are three "tokens" of this one type; Lincoln's death and Caesar's death and the death of Catherine the Great are three tokens of the event-type *death*. A particular, concrete event may be—in fact, all particular, concrete events *must* be—a token of more than one type. Thus, Lincoln's death and Caesar's death are tokens not only of the type *death* but also of the type *assassination*. But, fortunately, not all tokens of the former are tokens of the latter: not all deaths are deaths by assassination. If every event is a token of various types, then every mental event is a token of various types, and every physical event is a token of various types.

Making use of the type-token distinction, we may distinguish two forms of physicalism (or two forms of the identity theory): type-type physicalism and token-token physicalism. Let us first examine type-type physicalism. Consider the physical event-type *a firing of C-fibers* and the mental event-type *feeling pain*. Suppose that someone says that these event-types are identical, are one and the same event-type. This person's thesis could also be put this way, if we neglect some niceties about language that some philosophers will not want to neglect: the phrase 'a firing of C-fibers' and the phrase 'feeling pain' are two different names for the same event-type, just as 'water' and 'the liquid that consists of H_2O molecules' are two names for the same liquid—or just as 'the Morning Star' and 'the planet Venus' are two names for the same celestial object. Type-type physicalism is a generalization of this thesis; according to type-type physicalism, *every* mental event-type is identical with some physical event-type. (But, of course, only an idealist would suppose that the converse holds. Idealists aside, no one would suppose that, for example, the physical event-type *volcanic eruption* was identical with some mental event-type.)

Type-type physicalism is a very strong thesis, so strong that most physicalists decline to accept it; it is either known to be false (some physicalists will say) or at least it goes far beyond the available evidence. How (the enemies of type-type physicalism ask) can we even be sure that when identical twins experience pains that feel exactly the same there are physical events in the brains of each that are exactly alike, or even very much alike? How can we be sure that there is any such pair of physical events to be found? Shouldn't it be left up to the neurophysiologists to determine whether two such events exist? Should this question be settled by metaphysicians, by philosophers who have never made any neurophysiological investigations whatever? Fortunately (most physicalists believe) there is a weaker form of physicalism available, a form of physicalism adherence to which does not require philosophers to become armchair neurophysiologists: *token-token* physicalism.

According to token-token physicalism, each concrete mental event (such as my suddenly experiencing a sharp pain in my left arm at noon yesterday or Tim's gradual realization that Alice has been lying to him) is identical with a concrete physical event: a particular change in the physical state of someone's brain (at least in the case of human beings). But it may well be, the token-token physicalist holds, that no mental event-type is identical with any physical event-type. Perhaps, the token-token physicalist says, when Tim gradually re-

alizes that Alice has been lying to him and his identical twin Tom gradually re-
alizes that Alice has been lying to *him*, each of these two events is identical
with a physical change in the respective brains of Tim and Tom, but these two
physical changes bear little resemblance to each other (for example, it may be
that they take place in different regions in the cerebral cortex). Token-token
physicalism does not go so far as positively to deny that there are mental
event-types that are identical with physical event-types; this thesis simply re-
frains from asserting that such identities exist. If there are such identities, the
token-token physicalist tells us, it is the business of observational sciences like
psychology and neurophysiology to establish them; they are no more to be
embraced on purely metaphysical grounds than are the chemical and astronomical identities mentioned above.

If token-token physicalism is correct, then there is no problem in principle
in saying, for example, that a Scorpian experiences a sensation that is very like
the pain that Jane experiences when she has a migraine. Jane's sensation of
pain is, or let us suppose it is, identical with a certain pattern of C-fiber firings
in her brain; the Scorpian's sensation is identical with some physical process
that takes place in a reservoir of purple goo in the Scorpian's metathorax, a
process that in none of its physical characteristics resembles the firing of C-
fibers in a human brain.

This is the picture provided by token-token physicalism. There are many
analogies that token-token physicalists have employed to make this picture a
plausible one. The following analogy is typical of these. Suppose that three radios are simultaneously receiving the same broadcast. One is an antique crys-
tal set, one a vacuum-tube (valve) radio from the 1950s, and the third is the
latest thing in solid-state technology. We may list three "reception events": radio A's receiving the ABC broadcast of the State of the Union Message, radio
B's receiving this same broadcast, and, finally, radio C's receiving it. Each of
these reception events is identical with a physical process going on inside one
of the three radios, but the three physical processes are very different from one
another. The thesis of "reception physicalism" may be defined as the thesis
that reception events are physical events that go on inside radios. The thesis of
type-type reception physicalism is the thesis that each reception event-type
(like *receiving the ABC broadcast of the State of the Union Message*) is identical
with some physical event-type. The thesis of token-token reception physicalism is the thesis that each reception event-token, or concrete event (like *radio
B's receiving the ABC broadcast of the State of the Union Message yesterday*), is identical with some concrete physical event. No doubt everyone will accept token-
token reception physicalism. But the fact that the physical events that go on inside a vacuum tube are quite different from the physical events that go on inside whatever the latest solid-state devices are called renders type-type
reception physicalism at best doubtful.

Doubtful, perhaps, but not wholly indefensible. I said above that there
were two replies available to the physicalist that were consistent with the assumption that the possibility of thinking, feeling beings like the Scorpians is a
real one. The first was to distinguish type-type and token-token physicalism,
and to maintain that, whatever the problems faced by type-type physicalism,

token-token physicalism is consistent with this possibility. The second reply is an argument for the conclusion that even type-type physicalism is consistent with the possibility of thinking, feeling beings that are radically different from us in anatomy and physiology—or at least that this may be so, that it is true for all we know.

We may note that event-types may be more or less abstract. The more abstract an event-type is, the weaker the conditions are that an event has to satisfy to be a token of that type, and the less abstract an event-type is, the stronger the conditions are that an event has to satisfy to be a token of that type. Here are five event-types arranged in order of decreasing abstraction: *death, killing* (an untimely death caused by an external agency), *murder* (a deliberate and wrongful killing of one human being by another), *assassination* (the murder of a public figure from a political motive), and *terrorist assassination* (an assassination undertaken to create a politically useful climate of fear within some group). A defender of type-type physicalism could argue that the most that the example of the Scorpians shows is that if each mental event-type is identical with some physical event-type, then the physical event-types that figure in the identities must be much more abstract than, say, *a firing of C-fibers.*

Let us return to our "radio" analogy to illustrate this idea. If we think about it, we can see that it is possible to think of a highly abstract physical event-type that has a token in each of the three radios and can plausibly be identified with the reception event-type *receiving broadcast X.* Something like this: *containing some component or components that vibrate in a way determined by the information contained in the radio waves that carry broadcast X, this vibration being amplified to the point at which it generates sound waves that are audible to the human ear.* And it seems at least somewhat plausible to suppose that something similar could be said for the case of our thoughts and feelings and those of the Scorpians. Perhaps there is some very abstract physical event-type that is identical with, for example, the event-type *feeling pain* and which—being so very abstract—is capable of being "tokened" both in human grey matter and in Scorpian purple goo. Perhaps, indeed, every mental event-type is identical with some very abstract physical event-type. Whether or not this defense of (the possibility of) type-type physicalism is correct, it seems fairly clear that physicalism cannot be refuted by an appeal to the possibility of there being creatures that are radically different from us physically and yet have thoughts and feelings much like ours.

Suggestions for Further Reading

Chapters 2, 3, and 4, of Taylor's *Metaphysics* provide a very readable introduction to the "mind- body problem."

The two great classics of dualism are Plato's *Phaedo* and Descartes's *Meditations on First Philosophy* (see particularly Meditations II and VI). The argument ascribed to Descartes in the text is based on a passage in Meditation VI.

10

The Nature of Rational Beings:
Dualism and Personal Identity

OUR FIFTH AND FINAL ARGUMENT for the superiority of dualism over physical-ism is that dualism can account for the so-called identity of the person across time and physicalism cannot. It would seem that we normally suppose that the same person can exist at two different times. You, for example, no doubt believe that you existed ten years ago—not to mention last Tuesday. You ex-hibit this belief every time you say something like, "Ten years ago, I'd never have believed that I'd be doing this today," or "Last Tuesday I finally decided it was time to buy a new car." And, of course, we rarely if ever believe that the present moment is the final moment of our existence. We therefore normally believe that we are going to exist at various times in the future, for the state-ment that one is *not* going to exist at various times in the future is equivalent to the statement that the present moment is the final moment of one's existence.

Some opponents of physicalism argue that physicalism must be false be-cause it contradicts these facts (at least we all suppose them to be facts) about our identity across time. It may be, they argue, that a "static" physical thing like a diamond or a fly in amber can exist on each of two dates that are, say, ten years apart, but this could hardly be possible for a living organism or a part of a living organism. The Koh-i-Noor Diamond is, perhaps, composed of exactly the same matter (exactly the same carbon atoms) that composed it ten years ago, but I am not. If I am, as the physicalists say, a living organism or a part of one, then I have "lost" almost all of the atoms that composed me ten years ago and I am now made almost entirely of atoms that existed ten years ago but were then parts of other things or parts of nothing at all. It is true that I have the same brain-cells I had ten years ago (minus those that have died in the in-terval), but each of those brain-cells is now made of atoms that were not parts of it ten years ago.

If I am a physical thing, therefore, I am made of different matter from the matter that composed the physical thing that bore the name 'Peter van

Inwagen' ten years ago. The physicalist is forced to say that all of our statements that imply that I existed ten years ago must be, strictly speaking, false. Of course—the physicalists could say this much—they may be useful statements even if they are false. After all, there are useful statements that imply that the apparent motion of the sun across the sky is real, as when we say, "It was cooler in the garden after the sun had moved behind the elms." We know that the sun did not really move behind the elms, but we talk as if it did because it is usually too complicated to describe the actual state of affairs that accounts for the apparent motion of the sun. And (the physicalist must say) when Alice says to Jack, "It's hard to believe that ten years have passed since you and I last saw each other," this statement must be understood in a similar way: it is useful—because a metaphysically accurate description of the actual state of affairs would be too complicated—but, strictly speaking, false.

And why is the physicalist committed to this conclusion? Let us consider the famous story (famous among metaphysicians, anyway) of the Ship of Theseus. The hero Theseus has a ship, which is entirely composed of wooden planks. Very gradually, over the course of years, the planks are removed from the ship and replaced. The replacement is so gradual that Theseus and his crew are able to be almost continuously at sea, engaged the while in a long series of adventures with a nautical setting. The planks that have been removed from the ship are not destroyed but are rather stacked in a certain field. When all of the original planks have been replaced, Stilpo the shipwright notices that the field contains all of the components needed to build a ship. Stilpo puts the planks together and puts them together in such a way that they are arranged exactly as they were when they composed Theseus's ship on the day he first took command of it. Stilpo takes his new ship to sea for a shakedown cruise, and his ship and Theseus's ship pass each other at sea.

Call "Theseus's ship on the day he first took command of it" the *Original Ship*. Call the ship Stilpo is sailing now the *Reconstructed Ship*. Call the ship that Theseus is sailing now the *Continuous Ship* (because on any given day after Theseus took command of the Original Ship, the ship he was sailing on that day was made of the same or *almost the same* planks as the ship he was sailing the day before).[1] Is it the Reconstructed Ship or the Continuous Ship that is the Original Ship? The Continuous Ship has the name *Ariadne* painted on its bow, and Theseus swears that he has been sailing one ship, the *Ariadne*, these many years. And the Athenian Office of Marine Registry agrees with him. But isn't it evident that Theseus and the Registry Office bureaucrats are wrong? (Wrong strictly speaking, that is. The statement that Theseus has been sailing one ship, the *Ariadne*, for many years may be a very useful statement for legal and other practical purposes. The statement might be considered a "legal fiction," like the statement that a corporation is a person.) What is a ship but a certain "hunk of matter," a certain assemblage of planks or of atoms or of elementary particles? And the hunk of matter, the assemblage of planks, atoms, and elementary particles that Theseus is standing on now is not the same hunk of matter, the same assemblage of planks, atoms, and elementary particles, that he stood on on the day he took command. But the hunk of matter, the assemblage of planks, atoms, and elementary particles, that *Stilpo* is standing on now *is* the same hunk of matter, the same assemblage of planks, atoms, and elementary particles, that Theseus stood on on the day he took command. It is, therefore, the Reconstructed Ship and not the Continuous ship that is the Original Ship.

Now let us make one change in the story we have told. Suppose that Stilpo had never assembled the planks he found in that field into a ship. Suppose, in fact, that each of the planks that had been a part of the Original Ship was burned to ashes the moment it was removed. Then, of course, it would not be true that the Reconstructed Ship was the Original Ship, since the Reconstructed Ship would not be there at all. But it would still be true that the Continuous Ship was *not* the Original Ship, since it would not be the same hunk of matter as the Original Ship, and a ship is nothing but a hunk of matter arranged in a certain form. It would also seem to follow that there is no such ship as the *Ariadne*, that is, no one ship that has been under Theseus's feet every day since the day he first took command of the Original Ship. For every time a plank was replaced, a different "shipshape" (so to speak) hunk of matter was under Theseus's feet—*almost* the same shipshape hunk of matter as before the replacement, to be sure, but when it comes to identity, a miss is as good as a mile. A miss is as good as a mile because identity is, as logicians say, *transitive.* This means that if A is identical with B (if A and B are one and the same thing), and B is identical with C, then it follows that A is identical with C. Therefore, if the "before" and "after" ships for each individual replacement of a plank are one and the same ship, it follows that the Original Ship and the Continuous Ship are one and the same ship.

Let us now return to the question of physicalism and the identity of the person across time. If physicalism is true, then each of us is a hunk of matter, a certain assemblage of atoms or elementary particles. But you are not, strictly speaking, the same hunk of matter as the one that bore your name ten years ago: the atoms that composed *that* hunk of matter are now pretty well scattered throughout the terrestrial biosphere. It follows that physicalism is incompatible with the reality of personal identity across time; physicalism is therefore absurd. And it cannot be argued that dualism is in the same boat—or ship. It cannot be argued that the identity of persons across time is a mystery that confronts both the physicalist and the dualist in the same way and to the same degree. This reply might conceivably be effective against a dualist who held that each human person was a composite of a large number of "smaller" nonphysical things. But, while this position is, in theory, compatible with dualism, no actual dualist holds it. According to all actual dualists, a human person is not only a non-physical thing but a metaphysical simple, a thing without parts. The problem that faces the physicalist is that if a human person can really exist at two times that are, say, ten years apart, then that person must be made of entirely different parts at those two times. The physicalist must be able to explain how a thing can persist (can continue to exist and retain its identity) through a complete change of parts. And this problem is not one that confronts Plato or Descartes or any other actual dualist: if a thing has no parts, then, obviously, there is no problem of how it can persist through a change of parts. Therefore, the dualist concludes, dualism is to be preferred to physicalism.

What can the physicalists say in response to this? In the above argument, it was suggested that the only course open to them is to accept the incompatibility of physicalism and the reality of personal identity across time and to try to live with it—to treat personal identity across time as some sort of useful fiction. And this is a course that some physicalists have taken. (One philosopher has recently gone so far as to agree with the Buddhists that the idea of personal identity across time is not so much a useful fiction as a pernicious fiction and that realizing that this idea is a fiction is a kind of liberation.) I myself am unable to take this proposal seriously. But that is only a fact about my psychology and it proves nothing. Nevertheless, the idea of personal identity across time—the idea that it is a fact that one and the same human person can strictly and literally exist at different times and that, moreover, this fact is a feature of reality and not of mere appearance—is so central to a vast array of ways of thinking that have served us and our ancestors for millennia that we should abandon it only in the face of an unanswerable argument. And it is clear that we have no such unanswerable argument, for, even if physicalism is inconsistent with the reality of the identity of the human person across time, one could always be a dualist. And if that were the price that had to be paid for a belief in personal identity, the belief would be cheap at the price. That the price is reasonable is a premise of the above argument against physicalism, and that premise I accept. But does this reasonable (but very high) price have to be paid? That is, is there any way—or is there more than one way—for a physicalist consistently to believe in the identity of the human person across time?

A great many of the physicalists now writing, I am sorry to say, believe *inconsistently* in the identity of the human person across time, although they are no doubt unaware that they are being inconsistent. Many physicalists accept what they call a "psychological criterion of personal identity." By this they mean that a hunk of matter that existed ten years ago and a hunk of matter that exists today can both be the same person (you, say) provided only that the memories and other mental properties of the latter have "grown out of" the mental properties of the former by the right sort of causal process, and they believe that the main task that faces the philosopher who thinks about the identity of the person across time is to give a philosophically adequate description of what counts as the right sort of causal process. But in fact no causal process can be adequate to this task. No causal process can accomplish the feat of turning one hunk of matter into another. If, therefore, the hunk of matter that bore your name ten years ago and the hunk of matter that bears your name today are two different hunks of matter, and if a human person is, as physicalism maintains, a hunk of matter, we are dealing with two persons, not one, no matter what causal relations may connect the two hunks of matter. The thing just can't be done.

It can't be done, that is, without a strange assumption about identity or a strange assumption about the way in which things in general—and not only human persons—persist through time. The apparent inconsistency involved in "psychological continuity theories of personal identity" can be resolved by one who is willing to make one or the other of these two assumptions. I accuse "psychological continuity" theorists of contradiction only if they are not willing to make one or the other of the two assumptions. But in fact most of them are not willing to make either assumption. At any rate, most of them have said nothing that indicates an awareness that they must make one of them or of which one it is that they would choose. And since these assumptions are, as I have said, strange, this is a question that the psychological continuity theorist has to face. ("Strange assumption," however, is not the same as "absurd assumption." Current physics is full of assumptions that are strange indeed.)

The first of these assumptions, the one having to do with identity, is that there is really no such thing as identity. There is really no one relation of identity that figures in all of our identity-statements. There are, rather, many different identity-relations, such as *is the same horse as, is the same collection of atoms as, is the same public official as*, and so on. And there is a certain degree of independence among these relations, so that, for example, *x* might be the same horse as *y*, but not the same collection of atoms as *y*. We might, if this assumption is right, compare identity-statements with statements of relative goodness. Is Tom better than Tim? The question is absurd. Better in what respect? one would have to ask in reply. It may well be that Tom is a better tennis player than Tim, but not a better linguist. If this theory of the "relativity of identity," as it is called (relativity, that is, to a specified class, like "horse" or "public official"), is correct, then psychological continuity theorists can say without demonstrable contradiction that *x* is the same person as *y*, but not the same hunk of matter as *y*—even though *x* and *y* are both persons and both hunks of matter. And, once the psychological continuity theorists have been granted the right to say this without facing a charge of formal contradiction, they can go on to say that the relation *is the same person as* holds between *x* and *y* owing to certain facts about the way in which the mental properties of *y* evolved causally out of the mental properties of *x*.

The second assumption, the alternative to the relativity of identity, is that we are not three-dimensional things that *persist through* time but are rather *four*-dimensional things that are *extended in* time. We all grant that through a given point we can draw three lines at right angles to one another: if one of these lines runs north-south, and another east-west, then the third will run up-down. But, according to many philosophers, through the same point there also passes a line, at right angles to the other three, that runs past-future. We are thus inhabitants not only of three-dimensional space but of four-dimensional space-time, and each of us occupies a four-dimensional region of this space-time; I, for example, occupy a region of space-time that extends along the past-future line from the first moment of my existence, through the present, to the last moment of my existence—if there is a last moment of my existence; if there is not, then the region goes on forever. What fills up a three-dimensional region of space at a given moment of time cannot be me, this theory asserts, but is at best only a *part*, a three-dimensional cross section, of me. And this holds not only for me but for all other objects that exist at more than one time.

If "four-dimensionalism" is correct, there *can* be such a ship as the *Ariadne*, a ship that was under Theseus's feet at every moment from the moment of his assuming command to the moment at which his ship passed Stilpo's ship at sea. This ship is a four-dimensional object: it extends in time between these two moments (and presumably "sticks out" a bit beyond these two moments, in both the past and the future directions). And so is Stilpo's ship a four-dimensional object. And each of the planks that was at any time associated with any of the ships in the story of the Ship of Theseus is also a four-dimensional object. But—and this is the crucial point—*none of the planks is, or ever was, a part of any of the ships.* What is rather true is that some *part* of each of the planks was a part of one or more of the ships. Suppose that a certain plank, Plank Sixteen, was, as we should say in the language of everyday life, added to the *Ariadne* on Monday and then removed from the *Ariadne* on Wednesday. Plank Sixteen was not, strictly speaking, a part of the *Ariadne,* says the four-dimensionalist. What is strictly true is that the Monday-Wednesday part of Plank Sixteen, the part of Plank Sixteen that extends along the past-future line from Monday to Wednesday, is, or was, a part of the *Ariadne.* And it may well be that other parts of Plank Sixteen, ones that do not "overlap" the Monday-Wednesday part of Plank Sixteen, are, or have been, parts of other ships, perhaps of Stilpo's ship.

To say that a given plank has been a part of six ships is, from the four-dimensionalist point of view, to say that six separate (non-overlapping) parts of the plank are parts of six ships. And what we have said about planks and ships we can say about atoms and human organisms. Since both I and any atom are four-dimensional objects, and since (to employ the language of everyday life) no atom is a part of me throughout my entire existence, no atom is a part of me at all—not strictly speaking. What *is* true is that certain parts of certain atoms are parts of me. It may, for example, be that the Monday-Wednesday part of a certain atom is a part of me, but that no larger part of that atom—which probably extends for millions of years along the past-future line—is a part of me. Nevertheless, the physicalists can say, as they wish to say, that I am entirely composed of atoms. But by this they must mean, if they are four-dimensionalists, that each momentary three-dimensional cross section of me is composed entirely of momentary three-dimensional cross sections of atoms or, more simply, that I am entirely composed of parts of atoms.

Do the four-dimensionalist physicalists face any problem arising from the assertion that you are a hunk of matter and that different hunks of matter have borne your name at various times? No: what bears your name, they will say, is one four-dimensional hunk of matter that extends, temporally speaking, from the first moment of your existence into the indefinite future. Your name designates this same four-dimensional thing whenever it is spoken, and so does the word 'I' whenever you use it. It is of course true that most of your three-dimensional cross sections are composed of three-dimensional cross sections of different atoms, but this creates no problem concerning the reality of your identity across time.

Moreover, the psychological continuity theory of personal identity can be happily married to four-dimensionalist physicalism. The combined theory simply says that what binds some sequence of three-dimensional "personal cross sections" together to make them the cross sections of a *single* person is some relation of causal and psychological continuity. All of your cross sections make up a single person: you; all of my cross sections make up a single person: me. But my cross sections from the 1950s and those of Nikita Khrushchev from before and after the 1950s do not make up a single person. Mine do, because the right relations of causal and psychological continuity hold among the members of this set of cross sections. The "mixture" of Khrushchev's and mine do not, because the right causal and psychological relations do not hold among the members of that set. (For example, if we were to try to suppose that the members of the latter set composed a person, we should have to suppose that this "person" flashed instantaneously from the Soviet Union to the United States at the end of the 1940s and changed instantaneously from a middle-aged man to a small boy and that "he" instantaneously lost all of "his" memories and acquired a wholly new set of memories, and false ones at that.)

The physicalist can therefore believe in the identity across time of the human person, if only by accepting the relativity of identity or the four-dimensionalist account of objects and their parts. But are there any other alternatives open to the physicalist? Many philosophers will find this a compelling question, because, like me, they will find both the relativity of identity and four-dimensionalism "strange." Very few philosophers have any sympathy with the theory of the relativity of identity. And, while four-dimensionalism has highly respected champions, there are quite a number of philosophers who would agree with the American philosopher Judith Jarvis Thomson's description of four-dimensionalism: "a crazy metaphysic." These two alternatives are certainly ones that *I* should like to avoid if it were at all possible. (But if it could be demonstrated that they were two of exactly four alternatives, the others being dualism and the thesis that the identity of the human person across time was a fiction, I should have to begin to think about which of them I considered the lesser evil.)

Suppose that one wants to be a physicalist, to believe that there is one all-comprehending identity-relation (so that, for example, 'x is the same horse as y' is equivalent to 'x and y are horses, and they stand in the single, all-comprehending identity-relation'), and to believe that people and the other objects of our experience are three-dimensional things that persist through time. Is this combination of beliefs consistent? In my view, it is. To believe all of these things, it is necessary to believe that a thing can change its parts with the passage of time. And to say that it is possible for a thing to change its parts with the passage of time is to say that situations like the following are possible: Where A, B, C, and D are four distinct things (things that have no parts in common) it is possible for something—Alice, for example—to be made of A, B, and C on Monday and of B, C, and D on Wednesday. The "Ship of Theseus" argument involved a strand of reasoning that, if it is correct, shows that this is impossible. If we adapt it to the present case, we get something like this: "Look, suppose that A still exists on Wednesday, as it very well might. Then all three of A, B, and C still exist on Wednesday. Let us use 'A+B+C' to abbreviate 'the thing made up of A, B, and C' and similarly for 'B+C+D'. You are saying that Alice was A+B+C on Monday and B+C+D on Wednesday. But if A, B, and C exist on Wednesday, then A+B+C exits on Wednesday. And if Alice was A+B+C on Monday and was *not* A+B+C on Wednesday, then A+B+C was a different thing on Monday from the thing it was on Wednesday. But that is just impossible. Whenever there is something that is made of A, B, and C, it is the same thing."

This argument has at least two doubtful premises:

- If A, B, and C exist on Wednesday, then something made up of A, B, and C exists on Wednesday.
- Whenever there is something that is made up of A, B, and C, it is the same thing.

As to the former, why should we suppose that if there are three particular things, then there is necessarily something that has them as parts? As to the latter, why should we suppose that the same three parts could not "add up to" different wholes at different times? The idea that A, B, and C must always compose the same whole does not in fact correspond to the ways in which we ordinarily think about parts and wholes. This fact is particularly evident when we consider living organisms.

Let us consider my cat, Taffy—alas, now deceased. Let us call the atoms that Taffy was composed of at noon on the first day of 1985 "the New Year's atoms." (There are, of course, a lot more than three New Year's atoms, but the point we are considering does not depend on numbers.) The New Year's atoms are now presumably scattered throughout the biosphere. If, therefore, there is something that is made of just exactly those atoms right now, it is a sort of rarefied spherical shell about thirteen thousand kilometers across and a few hundreds or thousands of meters thick. We do not normally suppose that there is any such thing. And why should we? Now imagine that, by some fantastic chance, the New Year's atoms were all and only the atoms that at some moment composed a certain fish—it, of course, weighed the same as Taffy did in 1985—that lived in the Indian Ocean some four million years ago. When I stroked Taffy on New Year's Day, 1985, was the physical thing I was touching identical with a physical thing that swam in the Indian Ocean four million years ago? We should not normally say that these two things were identical. We should normally say that one was a prehistoric fish, a thing that no longer existed in 1985, and that the other was a cat that was alive and well in 1985. And why shouldn't we say these things?

Now consider the conclusion of the argument, namely, that a thing must always be composed of the same parts. This conclusion does not fare any better than the two premises when we look at it in the light of the things we are normally inclined to believe about living organisms. Here is an interesting statement about living organisms from a book by the great physiologist J. Z. Young:

> The essence of a living thing is that it consists of atoms of the ordinary chemical elements we have listed, caught up into the living system and made part of it for a while. The living activity takes them up and organizes them in its characteristic way. The life of a man consists essentially in the activity he imposes upon that stuff.[2]

Professor Young goes on to describe the imaginary but typical biochemical adventures of a carbon atom that is taken up into the "living system" that is a particular human being and then expelled from that system. When this series of adventures begins, the atom is a part of a sugar molecule that is ingested by the human being. The adventures end when the atom, now a part of a carbon dioxide molecule, leaves that human being in an exhaled breath of air. These adventures—being carried to different parts of the body and participating in an elaborate sequence of chemical reactions—are of great complexity and yet last only a few minutes.

After telling the story of the atom's brief association with a human body, Young asks, "Can we say that [the carbon atom] has ever formed a part of the living tissue of the body?" and goes on to observe, "Many people when asked this question quickly answer 'No'." But this quick reaction seems to me—as it does to Young—to be wrong. The story of the carbon atom is a story that describes just what it *is* for an atom to come to be and then cease to be a part of a living animal. The life of an animal is a kind of storm of atoms that is constantly, and very rapidly, changing its "membership." Whatever may be true of other physical objects, a living organism would seem not only to be a thing that changes its parts with the passage of time, but to be a thing whose very nature demands that it change its parts with the passage of time.

I conclude that physicalists may consistently believe in the identity of the human person across time even if they do not believe in the relativity of identity or in four-dimensionalism. They need only assert that the human person is identical with the human organism and subscribe to the thesis that an organism can change its parts with the passage of time. It is less clear whether a physicalist can, in the end, consistently hold that a human person is some *part* of a human organism, such as a human brain. But we do not really need to investigate this question. We have done enough to show that the "personal-identity" argument against physicalism does not refute physicalism.

Before leaving the topic of the identity of the person across time, let us address a question that may have been troubling some readers. Does not the thesis of physicalism imply that there is no such thing as "life after death"—that it is impossible for the human person to survive biological death? Isn't it clear that if the human person is a physical thing, then its death is the end of it? Isn't it obvious that whatever physical thing a human person may be (the human organism, the cerebral cortex, or whatever) that physical thing comes to an end with the person's death? It is certainly true that physicalism is incompatible with certain beliefs about life after death. It is incompatible with the belief that we are going to be "reincarnated" after our deaths as human beings or as beasts, and it is incompatible with the belief that each of us is a soul that "goes" to heaven or hell after death. And it is true that many beliefs about life after death resemble these two beliefs in some way that renders them incompatible with physicalism.

There is, however, one belief about life after death that is, or at least may be, compatible with physicalism, and that is the Judeo-Christian doctrine of the resurrection of the dead.[3] Unlike other doctrines of life after death, the doctrine of the resurrection of the dead implies that our future life is not something that happens in the natural course of events but is possible only as the result of a miracle in the strictest and most literal sense of the word. It must be pointed out, however, that the doctrine of the resurrection of the dead, if it is not combined with a belief in a non-physical soul, faces grave metaphysical problems in the area of the identity of the person. If, for example, someone is burned to ashes in a cremation oven, how can any living organism that exists at any time in the future be *that* person? Wouldn't the future organism (if it is a human person) have to be someone else, some new person? If I am to be burned to ashes, and if I do not have a non-physical soul that is unaffected by fires and "carries" my identity with it, how can any organism that will exist thereafter be *me*? How could even an all-powerful being bring about the identity of myself and something that exists subsequently to my total destruction? This is not the place to discuss these questions, for this is not a book about the philosophy of religion. The thesis of this brief digression is that if the physicalist accepts *any* doctrine of life after death, it must be the doctrine of the resurrection of the dead. It may be that further investigation would show that the physicalist cannot accept even that doctrine and must instead conclude that death is the end of the human person.

This completes our examination of arguments against physicalism. We now turn to arguments for physicalism. There are, I believe, four good arguments for physicalism. Like all philosophical arguments, these arguments are not decisive. To my mind, however, they tip the scale in favor of physicalism. (I do not distinguish between arguments for physicalism and arguments against dualism, since, to my mind, physicalism and dualism are the two most plausible theories about our nature, and an argument against dualism— unless it also tells against physicalism—is therefore an argument for physicalism.)

First, there is the *interaction argument*. We have already seen some of the difficulties in supposing that a non-physical thing could interact causally with a physical thing. The interaction argument comprises these difficulties, together with the observation that by far the most plausible form of dualism is dualistic interactionism.

Secondly, there is the *argument from common speech*. We usually talk and act as if we were visible and tangible. We say things like, "I didn't like the way he was looking at me," or "She reached for the seat belt, and buckled herself in." We don't say, "She caused her body's hands to reach for the seat belt and buckle her body in." And, while someone might say, "I didn't like the way he was looking at my body," this would mean something rather special (perhaps, 'I thought he was exhibiting undue sexual interest in me') and it couldn't always be substituted for 'I didn't like the way he was looking at me'. This suggests that our concept of a human person (or our concept of ourselves) is the concept of a thing possessing certain physical characteristics: we normally conceive of ourselves as things made of flesh and blood and shaped roughly like statues of human beings.

Thirdly, there is an argument that I like to call the *remote-control argument*. If dualism is true, our relation to our bodies is analogous to the relation of the operator of a remotely controlled device (such as a radio-controlled model airplane) to that device. Now consider Alfred, who is operating a model airplane by remote control. Suppose that something—an unwary bird or a large hailstone—strikes a heavy blow to the model in midair. If the blow does significant damage to the model, we can expect that both the performance of the model and Alfred's ability to control the model will be impaired. But the blow will have no effect at all on *Alfred*, or no effect beyond his becoming aware of the blow or of some of its effects on the performance of the model and his ability to control it. But if Alfred's *body* were struck a heavy blow, and particularly if it were a blow to the head, this might have an effect on *him*, an effect that goes beyond his becoming aware of the blow and its damaging effects on his body and his ability to control his body: Alfred might well become unconscious.

This is just the sort of effect that we should expect if Alfred were a certain human organism, for if the processes of consciousness are certain physical processes within the organism, a damaging blow might well cause those processes to cease, at least temporarily. But what effects should *dualism* lead us to expect from a blow to the body? I submit that if we are non-physical things and if the processes of consciousness are non-physical processes that do not occur within the body, the most natural thing to expect is that (at the worst) we should lose control of our bodies while continuing to be conscious. The blow to the base of Alfred's skull that in fact produces unconsciousness should, according to dualism, produce the following effects on Alfred: he experiences a sharp pain at the base of his skull; he then notes that his body is falling to the floor and that it no longer responds to his will; his visual sensations and the pain at the base of his skull and all of the other sensations he has been experiencing fade away; and he is left, as it were, floating in darkness, isolated, but fully conscious and able to contemplate his isolated situation and to speculate about its probable causes and its duration. But this is not what happens when one receives a blow at the base of the skull. One never finds oneself conscious but isolated from one's body.

Dualism, therefore, makes the wrong predictions about what the human person will experience in a certain situation. Here is another wrong prediction: if dualism were correct, we should expect that the ingestion of large quantities of alcohol would result in a partial or complete loss of motor control but leave the mind clear. Physicalism, however, would predict the former effect and it would also strongly suggest that the drinker's mental processes would be impaired. Because dualism makes these wrong predictions, it is doubtful. I say 'doubtful' rather than 'false', because the defender of dualism will not have too much difficulty in contriving a hypothesis to explain away the fact that a blow to the base of the skull causes one to lose consciousness or the fact that the ingestion of alcohol impairs one's mental processes. For example, the dualist might suggest that a temporary interruption of the normal causal interaction between the person and the body has a traumatic effect on the person, a salient feature of which is loss of consciousness. But this does not change the fact that the typical effects of a blow to the base of the skull are something that has to be *explained away* by dualists and are therefore an embarrassment to them. I say 'is doubtful' rather than 'faces a difficulty' because it is my hope that the reader will find all of the hypotheses by which the dualist explains away the observed effects of a blow to the base of the skull (or the ingestion of alcohol) to be implausible and *ad hoc*. I find them so; if I am wrong about the typical reaction of the disinterested reader to these hypotheses, then I have claimed too much by using the word 'doubtful'.

Finally, there is the *duplication argument*. This is the single argument for physicalism that I find the most powerful and persuasive. Recall the "duplicating machine" that we imagined in Chapter 2, in connection with our discussion of the concept of an intrinsic property. Let us imagine this machine and its operations in a little more detail. The duplicating machine consists of two chambers connected by an impressive mass of science-fictional gadgetry. If you place any physical object inside one of the chambers and press the big red button, a perfect physical duplicate of the object appears in the other chamber. The notion of a perfect physical duplicate may be explained as follows. A physical thing is composed entirely of quarks and electrons. A perfect physical duplicate of the physical thing x is a thing composed entirely of quarks and electrons arranged in the same way in relation to one another as the quarks and electrons composing x are, and each of the quarks and electrons composing a perfect physical duplicate of x will be in the same physical state as the corresponding particle in x. If, for example, you place the Koh-i-Noor diamond in one of the chambers and press the button, a thing *absolutely indistinguishable from* the Koh-i-Noor (since it is a perfect physical duplicate of the Koh-i-Noor) will appear in the other. If the two objects are placed side by side and then moved in a rapid and confusing way, so that everyone loses track of which was the original and which the duplicate, no one, no jeweler, mineralogist, or physicist, will ever be able to tell, by any test whatever, which of the two played an important role in the history of the British Raj in the nineteenth century and which was created a moment ago in the duplicating machine.

Now let us consider a second case of duplication. A marble is slowly rolling across the floor of one of the chambers. The button is pressed. There appears on the floor of the other chamber a marble of the same shape and size and weight and color that is rolling in the same direction and at the same speed: our machine reproduces not only the "static" properties of a thing, but also its "dynamic" properties.

Now let us place a living mouse in the chamber and press the button. What will appear in the other chamber? Another living mouse, surely? And wouldn't it be a mouse that was in every respect interchangeable with the original? If, for example, the original mouse had been taught to get cheese from a cheese dispenser by pressing a lever when a light flashed, wouldn't the new mouse know this trick too? Knowledge of how and when to press the lever to get cheese must somehow be stored in the mouse's little brain, and since the duplicate mouse's brain is a *perfect* duplicate of the original's brain, right down to the sub-atomic level, the same knowledge must be stored in the duplicate brain. (If you put a computer disk containing your novel into the machine, you wouldn't get a blank disk in the other chamber; you'd get another disk containing your novel: in duplicating *every* physical characteristic of the original disk, the machine automatically duplicates those characteristics of the disk that encode a record of the sequence of keystrokes that form your novel.)

And now, finally, let us put *Alfred* into one of the chambers of the duplicating machine and press the button. What do we find in the other chamber? A very intelligent Muslim student of mine once assured me that what one would find would be a dead human body—since the duplicating machine would not reproduce Alfred's soul, which was the principle of life. This dead body, at the instant of its appearance, would be standing just as Alfred stood, and on its face would be an expression just like the expression on Alfred's face. Even in that first instant, however, the body would not be alive, and, having appeared, it would immediately collapse and lie unmoving, its face the blank mask of a corpse. (As a testimony to the general intellectual capacity of my student, I will mention that he was the salutatorian of his graduating class and went on to earn a Ph.D. in nuclear engineering.) I think that Plato would have agreed with my student. Descartes, however, would not have agreed. Descartes would have contended that a *living* human body would have appeared in the other chamber. But, Descartes would have said, this body would immediately crumple to the floor. It would then lie there breathing and perhaps drooling, and, if you force-fed it, it would digest the food and in time produce excreta. But it would not *do* anything much. It would just lie there breathing and drooling and digesting and excreting. And this, of course, would be because there was no mind or soul or person in interaction with it. As a consequence, no thought or sensation would be in any way associated with the duplicate body. Life, in the strict, biological sense, was for Descartes (as it was not for Plato or for my student) a purely physical phenomenon; thought and sensation were not. Modern biology, I think, has shown that Descartes was right about life—or has at least rendered the thesis that life is a complex physical process vastly more probable than its denial. But what about thought and sensation?

That is the question. It is essentially the question whether physicalism is true. The story of the duplicating machine is a device to focus our thoughts as we consider this question. Dualists must say that since thought and sensation are not physical processes that occur within a living human organism, the human body that the duplicating machine creates will crumple mindlessly, just as Descartes would have predicted. (I doubt whether many people raised and educated in a European or "European-descended" culture would agree with my Muslim student that the duplicating machine would produce a corpse.) But is this really what any of us believes? Aren't we strongly inclined to believe—at least when we are not considering the consequences of what we believe for the metaphysics of the human person—that the duplicate would "have" thoughts and feelings and beliefs and memories (or what felt like memories; they would not, of course, be connected with past events in the way that a real memory is) and desires and emotions? Aren't we strongly inclined to believe that the duplicate would have a conscious mental life like our own and would display the content of this conscious mental life in his observable behavior?

Those who do believe this will concede, after a moment's reflection, that, just as most of the duplicate's memories will not be real memories, so most of his beliefs about himself and his history will be false. The duplicate will, for example, believe that he is Alfred, and he is not. That is, he is not a man who has existed for such-and-such a number of years (he is only a few minutes old) and is married to Winifred (he has never even met her), and so on. The duplicate is in no sense Alfred. He is someone else, for if you stick a pin into Alfred, the duplicate feels no pain. Nevertheless, it *seems* to the duplicate that he is Alfred. What it is *like* to be the duplicate is just exactly what it is like to be Alfred. If the two men were "scrambled" (like the two diamonds in our earlier example), no one, including Alfred and the duplicate, could ever again know which was Alfred and which was the duplicate. Alfred himself would have to say—at least if he were fully, and perhaps inhumanly, reasonable—"For all I know, *I* am the duplicate." And if by some chance it were the duplicate that went home to Winifred, she would never suspect that he was not her husband. And just as Winifred would never suspect that anything was amiss, neither would Alfred's children or his mother or his closest friend or his confessor or his psychiatrist.

If this were indeed the outcome of running Alfred through the duplicating machine, dualism would be effectively refuted. The dualist *could*—this sort of thing is almost always possible—contrive some hypothesis that would explain away this outcome. The dualist might, for example, propose that whenever a human body is perfectly duplicated, God creates a perfect duplicate of the non-physical person who had been interacting with the original body and so arranges matters that the duplicate person is in interaction with the duplicate body. But this would be a desperate move. It would be far more reasonable to conclude that the observed result of our "experiment" should be explained as follows: the thoughts and feelings of a human person are physical processes within a human organism, and, in making a perfect physical duplicate of a human organism, we produce a human organism with the same thoughts and feelings. (The same, that is, at the first moment of the new organism's existence. The thoughts and feelings of the two organisms would probably diverge almost immediately, since the two organisms would probably find themselves almost immediately in different situations.) It would be reasonable to conclude that the mental properties of a human person are related to the physical properties of that person in a way somewhat analogous with the way in which the software associated with a particular computer is related to the physical properties of that computer.

The fact that certain software is associated with (is present in, has been programmed into, is embodied by) a particular computer is as much a physical fact about that computer as are any facts about the hardware that constitutes the "architecture" of that computer. The only real difference between the two kinds of fact is that "software" facts about a computer are, by definition, easily changeable at the keyboard, whereas "hardware" facts about a computer can be changed, if at all, only by technicians and engineers operating on the computer's central components. If I were to take the computer with which I am writing these words and place it (complete with a power source and turned on) in the duplicating machine, the computer the machine produced would not be simply another computer of the same make and model; immediately after the duplication, the same words would be visible on its screen, and, like the original, it would be programmed with WordPerfect 1.0.2, and it would respond in exactly the same way as the original to anything done at the keyboard.

And we have—don't we?—a strong tendency to believe that duplicating a living human organism would have the analogous result as regards the mental life of the human person whose body that organism is: just as, in making a perfect physical duplicate of a working computer, we duplicate all of the software programmed into that computer, so, in making a perfect physical duplicate of a living human organism, we duplicate the entire psychology associated with that organism—everything from a neurotic fear of snakes to a hardly noticeable pain in the left elbow.

Anyone who can honestly reply to this question by saying something along the lines of, "Well, *I* don't observe any such tendency in myself. In fact, I think the duplicate would crumple and fall to the floor and drool, just as Descartes would have predicted," will not be moved by the duplication argument. Anyone who, on reflection, decides that the duplicate would exhibit behavior indistinguishable from Alfred's (in the same situations) should conclude that the duplicate has a mental life like Alfred's and that physicalism is therefore true and dualism false.

This concludes our discussion of the nature of rational beings—or at any rate, of human beings, the only rational beings whose existence is uncontroversial. This discussion has been highly tentative. We should remember that even if we have succeeded in showing that physicalism is the most reasonable theory about the nature of human beings, we have not done anything to dispel the mystery of that nature. Thought and feeling remain as we found them: impenetrable mysteries.

Suggestions for Further Reading

There are two excellent collections of essays devoted to the problem of personal identity: Perry's *Personal Identity* and Rorty's *The Identities of Persons*. For Judith Jarvis Thompson's reasons for thinking that an explanation of identity across time in terms of four-dimensional objects constitutes "a crazy metaphysic," see her "Parthood and Identity across Time" (a very difficult essay for those who are not formally trained in philosophy).

The idea that there is a close analogy between computer hardware and software, on the one hand, and the physical and mental aspects of human beings, on the other, has been extremely influential in philosophy since about the middle of the 1960s. Parts II, III, and IV of Hofstadter and Dennett's *The Mind's I* provide an excellent introduction to the use philosophers have made of this fascinating idea.

11

The Powers of Rational Beings: Freedom of the Will

WE NOW TURN TO another mystery, a mystery about the *powers* of rational beings; that is, a mystery about what human beings are able to do. This mystery is the mystery of free will and determinism. The best way to get an intuitive grip on the problem of free will and determinism is to think of time as a "garden of forking paths." That is, to think of the alternatives that one considers when one is deciding what to do as being parts of various "alternative futures" and to think of these alternative futures diagrammatically, in the way suggested by a path or a river or a road that literally forks:

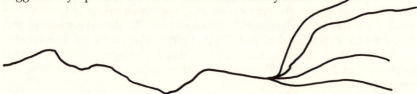

If Jane is trying to decide whether to tell all or to continue her life of deception, she is in a situation strongly analogous to that of someone who is hesitating between forks in a road. That is why this sort of diagram is so suggestive. Let us apply this idea to the problem of free will and determinism.

To say that one has free will is to say that when one decides among forks in the road of time (or, more prosaically, when one decides what to do), one is at least sometimes able to take more than one of the forks. Thus, Jane, who is deciding between a fork that leads to telling all and a fork that leads to a life of continued deception, has free will (on this particular occasion) if she is able to tell all and is also able to continue living a life of deception. One has free will if sometimes more than one of the forks in the road of time is "open" to one. One lacks free will if on every occasion on which one must make a decision only one of the forks before one—of course it will be the fork one in fact takes—is open to one. If John is locked in a room and doesn't know that he is locked in, and if he is in the process of deliberating about whether to leave, one of the alternative futures he is contemplating—leaving—is, in point of fact, not open to him, and he thus lacks free will in the matter of staying or leaving.[1]

It is a common opinion that free will is required by morality. Let us examine this common opinion from the perspective that is provided by looking at time as a garden of forking paths. While it is obviously false—for about six independent reasons—that the whole of morality consists in making judgments of the form 'You should not have done X', we can at least illustrate certain important features of the relation between free will and morality by examining the relation between the concept of free will and the content of such judgments. The judgment that you shouldn't have done X implies that you should have done something else instead; that you should have done something else instead implies that there was something else for you to do; that there was something else for you to do implies that you *could* have done something else; that you could have done something else implies that you have free will. To make a moral judgment about one of your acts is to evaluate your taking one of the forks in the road of time, to characterize it as better or worse than various of the other forks that were open to you. (Note that if you have made a choice by taking one of the forks in what is literally a road, no one could blame you for taking the fork you did if all of the other forks were blocked.) A moral evaluation of what someone has done requires two or more alternative possibilities of action for that person just as surely as a contest requires two or more contestants.

Let us now see what help the conception of time as a garden of forking paths gives us in understanding what is meant by determinism. Determinism is the thesis that it is true at every moment that the way things then are determines a unique future, that only *one* of the alternative futures that may exist relative to a given moment is a physically possible continuation of the state of things at that moment. Or, if you like, we may say that determinism is the thesis that only one continuation of the state of things at a given moment is consistent with the laws of nature. (For it is the laws of nature that determine what is physically possible. It is, for example, now physically possible for you to be in Chicago at noon tomorrow if and only if your being in Chicago at noon tomorrow is consistent with both the present state of things and the laws of nature.) Thus, according to determinism, although it may often seem to us that we confront a sheaf of possible futures (like this)

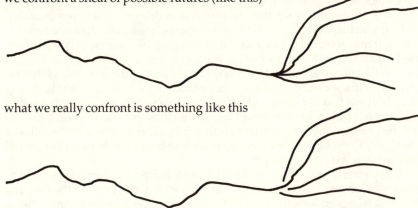

what we really confront is something like this

This figure is almost shaped like a road that splits into four roads, but not quite: three of the four "branches" that lead away from the "fork" are not connected with the original road, although they come very close to it. (Thus they are not really branches in the road, and the place at which they almost touch the road is not really a fork.) If we were to view this figure from a distance—across the room, say—it would seem to us to have the shape of a road that forks. We have to look at it closely to see that what appeared from a distance to be three "branches" are not connected with the long line or with one another. In the figure, the point at which the three unconnected lines *almost* touch the long line represents the present. The unconnected lines represent futures that are not physically possible continuations of the present, and the part of the long line to the right of the "present" represents a future that is a physically possible continuation of the present. The gaps between the long line and the unconnected lines represent causal discontinuities, violations of the laws of nature—in a word, miracles. The reason these futures are not physically possible continuations of the present is that "getting into" any of them from the present would require a miracle. The fact that the part of the long line that lies to the right of the "present" actually proceeds from that point represents the fact that this line-segment corresponds to a physically possible future.

This figure, then, represents four futures, three of which are physically impossible and exactly one of which is physically possible. If these four futures are the only futures that "follow" the present, then this figure represents the way in which each moment of time must be if the universe is deterministic: each moment must be followed by exactly one physically possible future.

The earlier diagram, however, represents an indeterministic situation. The road really does fork. The present is followed by four possible futures. Any one of them could, consistently with the laws of nature, evolve out of the present. Any one of them could, consistently with the laws of nature, turn out to be the actual future. Therefore, it is only if the universe is indeterministic that time *really is* a "garden of forking paths." But even in a deterministic universe, time could *look like* a garden of forking paths. Remember that our figure, when viewed from across the room, *looked* as if it had the shape of a road that forked. We cannot see all, or even very many, of the causes that operate in any situation. It could be, therefore, that the universe is deterministic, even though it looks to our limited vision as if there were sometimes more than one possible future. It may look to Jane as if she faces two possible futures, in one of which she tells all and in the other of which she continues her life of deception. But it may well be that the possibility of one or the other of these contemplated futures is mere appearance—an illusion, in fact. It may be that, in reality, causes already at work in her brain and central nervous system and immediate environment have already "ruled out" one or the other of these futures: it may be that one or the other of them is such that it could not come to pass unless a physically impossible event, a miracle, were to happen in her brain or central nervous system or environment.

Ask yourself this question. What would happen if some supernatural agency—God, say—were to "roll history back" to some point in the past and then "let things go forward again"? Suppose the agency were to cause things to be once more just as they were at high noon, Greenwich time, on 11 March 1893 and were thereafter to let things go on of their own accord. Would history literally repeat itself? Would there be two world wars, each the same in every detail as the wars that occurred the "first time around"? Would a president of the United States called 'John F. Kennedy' be assassinated in Dallas on the date that on the new reckoning is called '22 November 1963'? Would you, or at least someone exactly like you, exist? If the answer to these questions is No, then determinism is false. Equivalently, if determinism is true, the answer to these questions is Yes. If determinism is true, then, if the universe were rolled back to a previous state by a miracle, and if there were no further miracles, the history of the world would repeat itself. And if the universe were rolled back to a previous state thousands of times, this exact duplication would happen every time. If there are no forks in the road of time—if all of the apparent forks are merely apparent, illusions due to our limited knowledge of the causes of things—then restoring the universe to some earlier condition is like moving a traveler on a road without forks back to an earlier point on that road. If there are no forks in the road, then, obviously enough, the traveler must traverse the same path a second time.

It has seemed obvious to most people who have not been exposed (perhaps 'subjected' would be a better word) to philosophy that free will and determinism are incompatible. It is almost impossible to get beginning students of philosophy to take seriously the idea that there could be such a thing as free will in a deterministic universe. Indeed, people who have not been exposed to philosophy usually understand the word 'determinism' (if they know the word at all) to stand for the thesis that there is no free will. And you might think that the incompatibility of free will and determinism deserves to seem obvious— because it is obvious. To say that we have free will is to say that more than one future is sometimes open to us. To affirm determinism is to say that every future that confronts us but one is physically impossible. And, surely, a physically impossible future can't be open to anyone, can it? If we know that a "Star Trek" sort of future is physically impossible (because, say, the "warp drives" and "transporter beams" that figure essentially in such futures are physically impossible), then we know that a "Star Trek" future is not open to us or to our descendants.

People who are convinced by this sort of reasoning are called *incompatibilists*: they hold that free will and determinism are incompatible. As I have hinted, however, many philosophers are *compatibilists*: they hold that free will and determinism are compatible. Compatibilism has an illustrious history among English-speaking philosophers, a history that embraces such figures as the seventeenth-century English philosopher Thomas Hobbes, the eighteenth-century Scottish philosopher David Hume, and the nineteenth-century English philosopher John Stuart Mill. And the majority of twentieth-century English-speaking philosophers have been compatibilists. (But compatibilism has not had many adherents on the continent of Europe. Kant, for example, called it a "wretched subterfuge.")

A modern compatibilist can be expected to reply to the line of reasoning I have just presented in some such way as follows:

Yes, a future, in order to be open to one, does need to be physically possible. It can't, for example, contain faster-than-light travel if faster-than-light travel is physically impossible. But we must distinguish between a future's being physically possible and its having a physically possible connection with the present. A future is physically possible if everything that happens in it is permitted by the laws of nature. A future has a physically possible connection with the present if it could be 'joined' to the present without any violation of the laws of nature. A physically possible future that does not have a physically possible connection with the present is one that, given the present state of things, would have to be 'inaugurated' by a miracle, an event that violated the laws of nature, but in which, thereafter, events proceeded in accordance with the laws. Determinism indeed says that of all the physically possible futures, one and only one has a physically possible connection with the present—one and only one could be joined to the present without a violation of the laws of nature. My position is that some futures that could not be joined to the present without a violation of the laws of nature are, nevertheless, open to us.

Two philosophical problems face the defenders of compatibilism. The easier is to provide a clear statement of *which* futures that do not have a physically possible connection with the present are "open" to us. The more difficult is to make it seem at least plausible that futures that are in this sense open to an agent really deserve to be so described.

An example of a solution to these problems may make the nature of the problems clearer. The solution I shall briefly describe would almost certainly be regarded by all present-day compatibilists as defective, although it has a respectable history. I choose it not to suggest that compatibilists can't do better but simply because it can be described in fairly simple terms.

According to this solution, a future is open to an agent, if, given that the agent chose that future (chose that path leading away from a fork in the road of time), it would come to pass. Thus it is open to me to stop writing this book and do a little dance because, if I so chose, that's what I'd do. But if Alice is locked in a prison cell, it is not open to her to leave: if she chose to leave, her choice would be ineffective because she would come up against a locked prison door. Now consider the future I said was open to me—to stop writing and do a little dance—and suppose that determinism is true. Although a choice on my part to behave in that remarkable fashion would (no doubt) be effective if it occurred, it is as a matter of fact *not* going to occur, and, therefore, given determinism, it is determined by the present state of things and the laws of nature that such a choice is not going to occur. It is in fact determined that *nothing* is going to occur that would have the consequence that I stop writing and do a little dance. Therefore, none of the futures in which I act in that bizarre way is a future that has a physically possible connection with the present: such a future could come to pass only if it were inaugurated by an event of a sort that is ruled out by the present state of things and the laws of nature.

And yet, as we have seen, many of these futures are "open" to me in the sense of 'open' that the compatibilist has proposed.

Is this a reasonable sense to give to this word? (We now take up the second problem that confronts the compatibilist.) This is a very large question. The core of the compatibilist's answer is an attempt to show that the reason we are interested in open or accessible futures is that we are interested in modifying the way people behave. One important way in which we modify behavior is by rewarding behavior that we like and punishing behavior that we dislike. We tell people that we will put them in jail if they steal and that they will get a tax break if they invest their money in such-and-such a way. But there is no point in trying to get people to act in a certain way if that way is not in some sense open to them. There is no point in telling Alfred that he will go to jail if he steals unless it is somehow open to him not to steal.

And what is the relevant sense of "open"? Just the one I have proposed, says the compatibilist. One modifies behavior by modifying the choices people make. That procedure is effective just insofar as choices are effective in producing behavior. If Alfred chooses not to steal (and remains constant in that choice), then he won't steal. But if Alfred chooses not to be subject to the force of gravity, he will nevertheless be subject to the force of gravity. Although it would no doubt be socially useful if there were some people who were not subject to the force of gravity, there is no point in threatening people with grave consequences if they do not break the bonds of gravity, for even if you managed to induce some people to choose not to be subject to the force of gravity, their choice would not be effective. Therefore (the compatibilist concludes), it is entirely appropriate to speak of a future as "open" if it is a future that would be brought about by a choice—even if it were a choice that was determined not to occur. And if Alfred protests when you punish him for not choosing a future that was in this sense open to him, on the ground that it was determined by events that occurred before his birth that he not make the choice that would have inaugurated that future—if he protests that only a *miracle* could have inaugurated such a future—you can tell him that his punishment will not be less effective in modifying his behavior (and the behavior of those who witness his punishment) on *that* account.

When things are put that way, compatibilism can look like nothing more than robust common sense. Why, then, do people have so much trouble believing it? Why does it arouse so much resistance? I think that the reason is that compatibilists can make their doctrine seem like robust common sense only by sweeping a mystery under the carpet and that, despite their best efforts, the bulge shows. People are aware that something is amiss with compatibilism even when they are unable to articulate their misgivings. I believe that it is possible to lift the carpet and display the hidden mystery. The notion of "not having a choice" has a certain logic to it. One of the principles of this logic is, or so it seems, embodied in the following thesis, which I shall refer to as the No Choice Principle:

Suppose that *p* and that no one has (or ever had) any choice about whether *p*. And suppose also that the following conditional (if-then) statement is true and that no one has (or ever had) any choice about whether it is true: if *p*, then *q*. It follows from these two suppositions that *q* and that no one has (or ever had) any choice about whether *q*.

In this statement of the No Choice Principle, any declarative sentences can replace the symbols '*p*' and '*q*'. (But the same sentence must replace '*p*' at each place it occurs, and the same goes for '*q*'.) We might, for example, replace '*p*' with 'Plato died long before I was born' and '*q*' with 'I have never met Plato':

Suppose that Plato died long before I was born and that no one has (or ever had) any choice about whether Plato died long before I was born. And suppose also that the following conditional statement is true and that no one has (or ever had) any choice about whether it is true: if Plato died long before I was born, then I have never met Plato. It follows from these two suppositions that I have never met Plato and that no one has (or ever had) any choice about whether I have never met Plato.

The No Choice Principle seems undeniably correct. How could I have a choice about anything that is an inevitable consequence of something I have no choice about? And yet, as we shall see, the compatibilist must deny the No Choice Principle. To see why this is so, let us suppose that determinism is true and that the No Choice Principle is correct. Now let us consider some state of affairs that we should normally suppose someone had a choice about. Consider, say, the fact that I am writing this book. Most people—at least most people who knew I was writing a book—would assume that I had a choice about whether I was engaged in this project. They would assume that it was open to me to have undertaken some other project or no project at all. But we are supposing that determinism is true, and that means that ten million years ago (say) there was only one physically possible future, a future that included my being engaged in writing this book at the present date (since that is what I am in fact doing): given the way things were ten million years ago and given the laws of nature, it had to be true that I was now engaged in writing this book. But consider the two statements

- Things were thus-and-so ten million years ago.
- If things were thus-and-so ten million years ago, then I am working on this book now.

(Here 'thus-and-so' is a sort of gesture at a complete description or specification of the way things were ten million years ago.) Each of these statements is true. And it is obvious that no one has or ever had any choice about the truth of either. It is obvious that no one—no human being, certainly—has or ever had any choice about whether things *were* thus-and-so ten million years ago, since at that time the first human beings were still millions of years in the future.

And no one has any choice about whether the second statement, the if-then statement, is true because this statement is a consequence of the laws of nature, and no one—no human being, certainly—has any choice about what the laws of nature are. If we imagine a possible world in which, as in the actual world, things were thus-and-so ten million years ago, and in which, unlike in the actual world, I decided to learn to sail instead of writing this book, we are imagining a world in which the laws of nature are different; for the *actual* laws dictate that if at some point in time things are thus-and-so, then, ten million years later I (or at any rate someone just like me) shall be writing and not sailing.

But if both of the above statements are true, then it follows, by the No Choice Principle, that neither I nor anyone else has or ever had any choice about whether I write this book. And, obviously, the content of the particular example—my writing a book—played no role in the derivation of this conclusion. It follows that, given the No Choice Principle, determinism implies that there is no free will. That is why the compatibilist must reject the No Choice Principle. This is the hidden mystery that, I contend, lies behind the façade of bluff common sense that compatibilism presents to the world: the compatibilist must reject the No Choice Principle, and the No Choice Principle seems to be true beyond all possibility of dispute. (Either that or the compatibilist must hold that one can have a choice about what went on in the world before there were any human beings or that one can have a choice about what the laws of nature are. But these alternatives look even more implausible than a rejection of the No Choice Principle.) If the No Choice Principle were false, that would be a great mystery indeed.

We must not forget, however, that mysteries really do exist. There are principles that are commonly held, and with good reason, to be false and whose falsity seems to be just as great a mystery as the falsity of the No Choice Principle would be. Consider, for example the principle that is usually called "the Galilean Law of the Addition of Velocities." This principle is a generalization of cases like the following. Suppose that an airplane is flying at a speed of 800 kilometers per hour relative to the ground; suppose that inside the aircraft a housefly is buzzing along at a speed of 30 kilometers per hour relative to the airplane in the direction of the airplane's travel; then the fly's speed relative to the ground is the sum of these two speeds: 830 kilometers per hour. According to the Special Theory of Relativity, an immensely useful and well-confirmed theory, the Galilean Law of the Addition of Velocities does not hold (although it comes very, very close to holding when it is applied to velocities of the magnitude that we usually consider in everyday life). And yet when one considers this principle in the abstract—in isolation from the considerations that guided Einstein in his development of Special Relativity—it seems to force itself upon the mind as true, to be true beyond all possibility of doubt. It seems, therefore, that the kind of "inner conviction" that sometimes moves one to say things like, "I can just *see* that that proposition *has* to be true" is not infallible.

Nevertheless, a mystery is a mystery. If compatibilism hides a mystery, should we therefore be incompatibilists? Unfortunately, incompatibilism also hides a mystery. Behold, I will show you a mystery.

If we are incompatibilists, we must reject either free will or determinism. What happens if we reject determinism? It is a bit easier now to reject determinism than it was in the nineteenth century, when it was commonly believed, and with reason, that determinism was underwritten by physics. But the quantum-mechanical world of current physics seems to be irreversibly indeterministic, and physics has therefore got out of the business of underwriting determinism. Nevertheless, the physical world is filled with objects and systems that seem to be deterministic "for all practical purposes"—digital computers, for example—and many philosophers and scientists believe that a human organism is deterministic for all practical purposes. But let us not debate this question. Let us suppose for the sake of argument that human organisms display a considerable degree of indeterminism. Let us suppose in fact that each human organism is such that when the human person associated with that organism (we leave aside the question whether the person and the organism are identical) is trying to decide whether to do A or to do B, there is a physically possible future in which the organism behaves in a way appropriate to a decision to do A and that there is also a physically possible future in which the organism behaves in a way appropriate to a decision to do B. We shall see that this supposition leads to a mystery. We shall see that the indeterminism that seems to be required by free will seems also to destroy free will.

Let us look carefully at the consequences of supposing that human behavior is undetermined. Suppose that Jane is in an agony of indecision; if her deliberations go one way, she will in a moment speak the words, "John, I lied to you about Alice," and if her deliberations go the other way, she will bite her lip and remain silent. We have supposed that there is a physically possible future in which each of these things happens. Given the whole state of the physical world at the present moment, and given the laws of nature, both of these things are possible; either might equally well happen.

Each contemplated action will, of course, have antecedents in Jane's cerebral cortex, for it is in that part of Jane (or of her body) that control over her vocal apparatus resides. Let us make a fanciful assumption about these antecedents, since it will make no real difference to our argument what they are. (It will help us to focus our thoughts if we have some sort of mental picture of what goes on inside Jane at the moment of decision.) Let us suppose that there is a certain current-pulse that is proceeding along one of the neural pathways in Jane's brain and that it is about to come to a fork. And let us suppose that if it goes to the left, she will make her confession, and that if it goes to the right, she will remain silent. And let us suppose that it is undetermined which way the pulse will go when it comes to the fork: even an omniscient being with a complete knowledge of the state of Jane's brain and a complete knowledge of the laws of physics and unlimited powers of calculation could say no more than, "The laws and the present state of her brain would allow the pulse to go either way; consequently, no prediction of what the pulse will do when it comes to the fork is possible; it might go to the left, and it might go to the right, and that's all there is to be said."

Now let us ask: Does Jane have any choice about whether the pulse goes to the left or to the right? If we think about this question for a moment, we shall see that it is very hard to see how she could have any choice about that. Nothing in the way things are at the instant before the pulse makes its "decision" to go one way or the other makes it happen that the pulse goes one way or goes the other. If it goes to the left, that *just happens.* If it goes to the right, *that* just happens. There is no way for Jane to *influence* the pulse. There is no way for her to *make* it go one way rather than the other. Or, at least, there is no way for her to make it go one way rather than the other and leave the "choice" it makes an undetermined event. If Jane did something to make the pulse go to the left, then, obviously, its going to the left would *not* be an undetermined event. It is a plausible idea that the only way to have a choice about the outcome of a process is to be able to arrange things in ways that will make it inevitable that this or that outcome occur. If this plausible idea is right, then it would seem that there is no way in which anyone could have any choice about the outcome of an indeterministic process. And it seems to follow that if, when one is trying to decide what to do, it is truly undetermined what the outcome of one's deliberations will be, then one could have no choice about that outcome. It is, therefore, far from clear that incompatibilism is a tenable position. The incompatibilist who believes in free will must say this: it is possible, despite the above argument, for one to have a choice about the outcome of an indeterministic process. But how is the argument to be met?

Some incompatibilists attempt to meet this argument by means of an appeal to a special sort of causation. Metaphysicians have disagreed about what kinds of things stand in the cause-and-effect relation. The orthodox, or Humean position, is that—although our idioms may sometimes suggest otherwise—causes and effects are always events. We may *say* that "Stalin caused" the deaths of millions of people, but when we talk in this way, we are not, in the strictest sense, saying that an *individual* was the cause of certain events. It was, strictly speaking, certain *events* (certain actions of Stalin) that were the cause of certain other events (the millions of deaths). It has been suggested, however, that, although events do indeed cause other events, it is sometimes true that individuals, *persons* or *agents,* cause events. According to this suggestion, it might very well be that an event in Jane's brain—a current-pulse taking the left-hand branch of a neural fork, say—had Jane as its cause. And not some event or change that occurred within Jane, not something Jane *did,* but Jane herself, the person Jane, the agent Jane, the individual thing Jane.

This "type" of causation is usually labeled 'agent-causation', and it is contrasted with 'event- causation', the other "type" of causation, the kind of causation that occurs when one event causes another event. An event is a change in the intrinsic properties of an individual or a change in the way in which certain individuals are related to one another. Event-causation occurs when a change that occurs at a certain time is due to a change that occurred at some earlier time. If there is such a thing as agent-causation, however, some changes are not due to earlier changes but simply to agents.

Let us now return to the question that confronts the incompatibilist who believes in free will: How is it possible for one to have a choice about the outcome of an indeterministic process? Those incompatibilists who appeal to agent-causation answer this question as follows: "A process's having one outcome rather than one of the other outcomes it might have had is an event. For an agent to have a choice about the outcome of a process is for the agent to be able to cause each of the outcomes that process might have. Suppose, for example, that Jane's deciding what to do was an indeterministic process and that this process terminated in her deciding to speak, although, since it was indeterministic, the laws of nature and the way things were when the process was initiated were consistent with its terminating in her remaining silent. But suppose that Jane caused the process to terminate in her speaking and that she had been able to cause it to terminate in her being silent. Then she had a choice about the outcome. That is what it *is* to have had a choice about whether a process terminated in A or B: to have caused it to terminate in one of these two ways, and to have been *able* to cause it to terminate in the other."

There are two "standard" objections to this sort of answer. They take the form of questions. The first question is, "But what does one add to the assertion that Jane decided to speak when one says that she was the agent-cause of her decision to speak?" The second is, "But what about the event *Jane's becoming the agent-cause of her decision to speak?* According to your position, this event occurred and it was undetermined—for if it were determined by some earlier state of things and the laws of nature, then her decision to speak would have been determined by these same factors. Even if there is such a thing as agent-causation and this event occurred, how could Jane have had any choice about whether it occurred? And if Jane was the agent-cause of her decision to speak and had no choice about whether she was the agent-cause of her decision to speak, then she had no choice about whether to speak or be silent."

These two standard objections have standard replies. The first reply is, "I don't know how to answer that question. But that is because causation is a mystery, and not because there is any *special* mystery about *agent*-causation. How would *you* answer the corresponding question about event-causation: What does one add to the assertion that two events occurred in succession when one says that the earlier was the *cause* of the later?" The second reply is, "But Jane did have a choice about which of the two events, *Jane's becoming the agent-cause of her decision to speak* and *Jane's becoming the agent-cause of her decision to remain silent,* would occur. This is because she was the agent-cause of the former and was able to have been the agent-cause of the latter. In any case in which Jane is the agent-cause of an event, she is also the agent-cause of her being the agent-cause of that event, and the agent-cause of her being the agent-cause of her being the agent-cause of that event, and so on 'forever.' Of course, she is not *aware* of being the agent-cause of all these events, but the doctrine of agent-causation does not entail that agents are aware of all of the events of which they are agent-causes."

Perhaps these replies are effective and perhaps not. I reproduce them because they are, as I have said, standard replies to standard objections. I have no clear sense of what is going on in this debate because I do not understand agent-causation. At least I don't think I understand it. To me, the suggestion that an individual thing, as opposed to a *change* in an individual thing, could be the cause of a change is a mystery. I do not intend this as an argument against the *existence* of agent-causation—of some relation between individual things and events that, when it is finally comprehended, will be seen to satisfy the descriptions of "agent-causation" that have been advanced by those who claim to grasp this concept. The world is full of mysteries and of verbal descriptions that seem to some to be nonsense and which later turn out to have been appropriate. ("Curved space! What nonsense! Space is what things that are curved are curved *in*. Space itself can't be curved." And no doubt the phrase 'curved space' *wouldn't* mean anything in particular if it had been made up by, say, a science-fiction writer and had no actual use in science. But the general theory of relativity does imply that it is possible for space to have a feature for which, as it turns out, those who understand the theory all regard 'curved' as an appropriate label.) I am saying only that agent-causation is a mystery and that to explain how it can be that someone can have a choice about the outcome of an indeterministic process by an appeal to agent-causation is to explain a mystery by a mystery.

But now a disquieting possibility suggests itself. Perhaps the explanation of the fact that both compatibilism and incompatibilism seem to lead to mysteries is simply that the concept of free will is self-contradictory. Perhaps free will is, as the incompatibilists say, incompatible with determinism. But perhaps it is also incompatible with *in*determinism, owing to the impossibility of anyone's having a choice about the outcome of an indeterministic process. If free will is incompatible with both determinism and indeterminism, then, since either determinism or indeterminism has to be true, free will is impossible. And, of course, what is impossible does not exist. Can we avoid mystery by accepting the non-existence of free will? If we simply say that no one ever has any choice about anything, then we need not reject the No Choice Principle, and we need not suppose that it is possible for a person to have a choice about the outcome of an indeterministic process.

But consider. Suppose that you are trying to decide what to do. And let us suppose that the choice that confronts you is not a trivial one. Let us not suppose that you are trying to decide which of two movies to see or which flavor of ice cream to order. Let us suppose that the matter is one of great importance—great importance to *you*, at any rate. You are, perhaps, trying to decide whether to marry a certain person or whether to risk losing your job by reporting unethical conduct on the part of a superior or whether to sign a "do not resuscitate" order on behalf of a beloved relative who is critically ill. Pick one of these situations and imagine that you are in it. (If you are in fact faced with a non-trivial choice, then you have no need to imagine anything. Think of your own situation.) Consider the two contemplated courses of action. Hold them before your mind's eye, and let your attention pass back and forth between them. Do you really think that you have no choice about which of these courses of action will become actual? Can you really believe that?

Many philosophers have said that although the choice between contemplated future courses of action always seems "open" to them, when they look back on their past decisions, the particular decision that they have made always or almost always seems inevitable once it has been made. I must say that I do not experience this myself, and, even if I did, I should regard it as an open question whether "foresight" or "hindsight" was more to be trusted. (Why should we suppose that hindsight is trustworthy? Maybe there is within us some psychological mechanism that produces the illusion that our past decisions were inevitable in order to enable us more effectively to put these decisions behind us and to spare us endless retrospective agonizing over them. Maybe we have a natural tendency to reinterpret our past decisions in a way that presents them in the best possible light. One can think of lots of not implausible hypotheses that would have the consequence that our present impression that our past decisions were the only possible ones—if we indeed have this impression—is untrustworthy.)

When I myself look at contemplated future courses of action in the way I have described above, I find an irresistible tendency to believe that I have a real choice as to which one will become actual. It may be, of course, that this tendency is the vehicle of illusion. If the concept of free choice were self-contradictory, it might still be the case that a belief in this self-contradictory thing was indispensable to human action. What would it be like to believe, really to *believe*, that in every circumstance only one course of action was open to one?

It can plausibly be argued that it would be impossible under such circumstances ever to try to decide what to do. Suppose, for example, that you are in a certain room that has a single door and that this door is the only possible exit from the room. Suppose that, as you are thinking about whether to leave the room, you hear a click that may or may not have been the sound of the door being locked. You are now in a state of uncertainty about whether the door is locked and are therefore in a state of uncertainty about whether it is possible for you to leave the room. Can you continue to try to decide whether to leave the room? It would seem that you cannot. (Try the experiment of imagining yourself in this situation and seeing whether you can imagine yourself continuing to try to decide whether to leave.) You cannot because you no longer believe that it is possible for you to leave the room. It's not that you believe that it is *im*possible for you to leave the room. You don't believe that either, for you are in a state of uncertainty about whether it is possible for you to leave. You can, of course, try to decide whether to get up and try the door. But that is something—or at least you probably believe this—that *is* possible for you. And you can try to decide, conditionally, as it were, whether to leave the room *if* the door should prove to be unlocked. But that is not the same thing as trying to decide whether to leave the room.

This thought-experiment convinces me that I cannot try to decide whether to do A or B unless I believe that doing A and doing B are both possible for me. And, therefore, I am convinced that I could not try to decide what to do unless I believed that sometimes more than one course of action was open to me. And if I never decided what to do, I should not be a very effective human being. In the state of nature, I should no doubt starve. In a civilized society, I should probably have to be institutionalized. Belief in one's own free will is therefore something that we can hardly do without. It would seem therefore that it would be an evolutionary necessity—at least for rational beings like ourselves—that we believe in free will. And evolutionary necessity has scant respect for such niceties as logical consistency. It is arguable, therefore, that we cannot trust our conviction that we have free will (if, indeed, we do have this conviction). If evolution would force a certain belief on us—by brutally culling out all those of our ancestors who lacked this belief—then the fact that we hold this belief is no evidence whatever that the belief is true or even logically consistent. (But *aren't* there people who believe that no one has free will, including themselves? Well, there are certainly people who *say* that they believe this, but I suspect that they are not describing their own beliefs correctly. But even if there are people who believe that no one has free will, it does not follow that these people do not believe in free will, for people do have contradictory beliefs. It may be that "on one level"—the abstract and theoretical—certain people believe that no one has free will, although on another level—the concrete and everyday—they believe that people have free will.)

Nevertheless, when all is said and done, I find myself with the belief that sometimes more than one course of action is open to me, and I cannot give it up. (As Dr. Johnson said, "Sir, we know our will is free, and there's an end on't.") And I don't find the least plausibility in the hypothesis that this belief is an illusion. It can sometimes seem attractive to hold the view that free will is an illusion. To think this—or to toy with the idea in a theoretical sort of way—can be attractive to someone who has betrayed a friend or achieved success by spreading vicious rumors. If you had done something of that sort, wouldn't you want to believe that you had no choice, that no other course of action was really open to you? Wouldn't it be an attractive idea that your actions were determined by your genes and your upbringing or even by the way things were thousands or millions of years ago? (Jean-Paul Sartre once remarked that determinism was an endless well of excuses.) And it is immensely attractive to suppose that one is a member of a very small minority that has seen through an illusion that people have been subject to for millennia. The hypothesis has its unattractive aspects too, of course. For one thing, if it rules out blame, it presumably rules out praise on the same grounds. But, however attractive or unattractive it may be, it just seems to be false. If some unimpeachable source—God, say—were to tell me that I didn't have free will, I'd have to regard that piece of information as proof that I didn't understand the World at all. It would be as if an unimpeachable source had told me that consciousness did not exist or that the physical world was an illusion or that self-contradictory statements could be true. I'd have to say, "Well, all right. You *are* an unimpeachable source. But I just don't understand how that could be right."

I conclude that there is no position that one can take on the matter of free will that does not confront its adherents with mystery. I myself prefer the following mystery: I believe that the outcome of our deliberations about what to do is undetermined and that we—in some way that I have no shadow of an understanding of—nevertheless have a choice about the outcome of these deliberations. (And I do not believe that the concept of agent-causation is of the least help in explaining how this could be.)

I believe that if Jane has freely decided to speak then the following must be true: if God were to create a thousand perfect duplicates of Jane as she was an instant before the decision to speak was made and were to place each one in circumstances that perfectly duplicated Jane's circumstances at that instant, some of the duplicates would choose to speak and some of them would choose to remain silent, and there would be no explanation whatever for the fact that a particular one of the duplicates made whichever of the choices it was that she made. And yet, I believe, Jane had a choice about whether to speak or to remain silent. (It is important not to be misled by words here. From the fact that someone *makes* a choice, it does not follow that that person *has* a choice. If I am locked in a room and do not know that the door is locked, it may be that I *make* a choice *to* stay in the room even though I *have* no choice *about whether to* stay in the room.)

I accept this mystery because it seems to me to be the smallest mystery available. If someone believes that human beings do not have free will, then that person accepts a mystery and in my view it is a greater, deeper mystery than the one I accept. If someone denies the No Choice Principle, then that person accepts a mystery, and in my view it is a greater, deeper mystery than the one I accept. But others may judge the "sizes" of these mysteries differently.

It is important to be aware that we have not said everything there is to be said about the size of the mysteries. The most important topic that we have not discussed in that connection is the relation between free will and morality. In our preliminary discussion of the concept of free will, we said that it was a common opinion that free will was required by morality. If this common opinion is correct, then all moral judgments are false or in some way "out of place" if there is no free will. If that were so, it would greatly aggravate the mystery that confronts those who deny that there is free will. Could it really be true, for example, that those who believe that there is something morally objectionable about racism or child abuse or genocide or serial murder hold a belief that is false or in some other way defective? If an unimpeachable source were to inform me that there was nothing morally objectionable about child abuse, my dominant reaction would be one of horror. But I should also have a negative reaction to this revelation that was more intellectual or theoretical. I should have to say that, if that was so, then I didn't understand the World at all. I should have to say that I just didn't understand how it could *be* that there was nothing morally objectionable about child abuse.

It may not be, however, that those who reject free will must hold that all moral judgments are false or otherwise illusory. The "common opinion" that morality requires free will is not so common as it used to be. When almost all English-speaking philosophers were compatibilists, this opinion was held by almost everyone in the English-speaking philosophical world. It was the common assumption of the compatibilists and the few incompatibilists that there were. Now, however, compatibilism is a less common opinion, owing to the fact that philosophers are coming to realize that compatibilism requires the rejection of the No Choice Principle. Many philosophers are now inclined to reject compatibilism who would previously have accepted it. And because they are also inclined to reject the view that we could have free will in a way that required indeterminism, they are inclined to reject free will altogether. But most of them are not willing to say that morality is an illusion. It has, therefore, become an increasingly widespread view that morality does not after all require free will. It is because of this increasingly popular view that I have not included the thesis that morality is an illusion among the mysteries that must be accepted by those who reject free will. I myself continue to believe that morality is an illusion if there is no free will, but, since the issues involved in the debate about this question pertain to moral philosophy rather than to metaphysics, I shall not discuss them.

However one may judge the relative "sizes" of the mysteries that confront the adherents of the various positions that one might take on the question of free will, these mysteries exist. The metaphysician's task is to display these mysteries. Each of us must decide, with no further help from the metaphysician, how to respond to the array of mysteries that the metaphysician has placed before us.

Suggestions for Further Reading

Berofsky's *Free Will and Determinism* and Watson's *Free Will* are excellent collections devoted to the problem of free will and determinism. Fischer's more recent *Moral Responsibility* contains much useful material. My own book, *An Essay on Free Will* is a defense of incompatibilism. Large parts of it are accessible to those without formal philosophical training. The central argument of the book is attacked in Lewis's superb article, "Are We Free to Break the Laws?" (rather difficult for those without philosophical training). Dennett's *Elbow Room* is a highly readable (if somewhat idiosyncratic) defense of compatiblism.

12

Concluding Meditation

ON THE FIRST PAGE of this book, I said that when you had read the book you would have a tolerably clear idea of what metaphysics was. I expect that you now do. What you do not have (as I promised in the first chapter that you would not) is metaphysical information. If instead of reading this book you had devoted your time to a book about geology or tax law or music theory, you would have all sorts of information, but from this book you have got no information other than a little incidental information about what some people think or have thought. You now have a tolerably clear idea of what it means to try to get behind appearance and to investigate reality: the way the World really is and the ultimate reasons for its being that way. What we most often find when we try to do this are unresolved questions and mysteries. Part One was devoted mainly to unresolved questions. Metaphysical questions can often be answered, or, at least, individual metaphysicians are often confident that they have answered them. But these individuals, as I have repeatedly emphasized, are almost never able to induce the community of metaphysicians to share their confidence. In Part One, I have given answers to various metaphysical questions, answers that I have a great deal of confidence in. And I have explained why, in my view, the confidence that other metaphysicians have in their competing answers to these questions is misplaced. Parts Two and Three have been devoted mainly to mysteries. The mysteries seem to me to be far more interesting than the unresolved questions and generally more important. (But they are not in every case more important. Nothing in metaphysics is more important than the question of objective truth.) Let us conclude with a meditation on mystery.

The mysteries that metaphysics uncovers are, of course, mysteries relative to ourselves and to our ability to understand things. Nothing is a mystery *in itself*, whatever that might mean. Everything is as it is; everything has a certain set of properties and these properties must be consistent. (By definition, reality must be consistent, for inconsistency is a mark of unreality. That is how we know that round squares do not exist. They do not exist because they cannot possibly exist. The inconsistent is just that which cannot possibly exist.) If God exists, then nothing is a mystery to God. But perhaps God does not exist. Perhaps God *cannot* exist. Perhaps there could not be any being, divine or human, natural or supernatural, terrestrial or celestial, who was capable of understanding the way the World was and why it was that way.

This is a possibility that we must take seriously: that the World is unintelligible, not "in itself," but unintelligible to any being who could possibly be one of its inhabitants. However this may be, I do not expect any human being to solve any of the problems of metaphysics in the near future—or, if the truth be known, in the remote future. I shall try to explain why I am skeptical about the possibility of our solving any of the problems of metaphysics. Let us assume for the sake of argument that the problems of metaphysics are in some sense soluble, that it makes sense to speak of solving them. (If it does not, then, of course, no one is going to solve them.) We human beings have certain intellectual gifts. Other rational species might have others, and their gifts might be more impressive than ours or less impressive. It is very hard indeed to believe that a race of beings *less* gifted than we—even slightly less gifted than we—could solve all of the problems of metaphysics. (Could a species less gifted than ourselves succeed where we have failed miserably?) We can also imagine a race of beings possessing a considerably greater allotment of the intellectual gifts relevant to metaphysics than we. (At least I think I can imagine this.) Such a race would, clearly, be more likely to be able to solve the problems of metaphysics than we.

If we believe that we are able to solve the problems of metaphysics, then we must believe that we are *just barely* able to do this; we must believe that if our intellectual gifts were only slightly less impressive we should be unable to do it. We must believe that our ability to solve the problems of metaphysics is like the ability to run a mile in four minutes: something that we (that is, a few exceptional individuals among us) are just barely able to do. And isn't this a rather implausible thesis? Why should the intellectual abilities that we happen to have be just barely adequate to the task? Why should we expect such a stroke of luck?[1]

Let us suppose, unrealistically, that IQ tests really measure intellectual ability. Let us in fact assume, even more unrealistically, that they measure the intellectual abilities that are relevant to success in metaphysics. Why should we suppose that a species with a mean IQ of 100—our own species—is *able* to solve the problems of metaphysics? Pretty clearly a species with a mean IQ of 60 wouldn't be in a position to achieve this. Pretty clearly, a species with a mean IQ of 160 would be in a better position than we to achieve this. Why should we suppose that the "cut-off point" is something like 90 or 95? Why shouldn't it be 130 or 170 or 250? The conclusion of this meditation on mystery is that if metaphysics does indeed present us with mysteries that we are incapable of penetrating, this fact is not itself mysterious. It is just what we should expect, given that we are convinced that beings only slightly less intellectually capable than ourselves would *certainly* be incapable of penetrating these mysteries. If we cannot know why there is anything at all, or why there should be rational beings, or how thought and feeling are possible, or how our conviction that we have free will could possibly be true, why should that astonish us? What reason have we, what reason could we possibly have, for thinking that our intellectual abilities are equal to the task of answering these questions?

Notes

Chapter 1

1. Nor is information about the history of the word much help. For what it is worth, however, here is a brief account of how we got the word 'metaphysics'.

The word 'metaphysics' was invented by the ancient Greeks. It comes from two Greek words: *'meta'*, which means 'after' or 'beyond', and *'phusis'*, which means 'nature'. (There is a sound in Greek that used to be represented in our alphabet—the Greeks, of course, did not use our alphabet—by the letter 'y' but which is today usually represented by the letter 'u'.) One meaning of the word 'nature', not a very common one, is something like 'the universe'. Thus, the basic laws that govern the universe are called the laws of *nature*, and those scientists whose work most closely concerns the basic laws are called *physicists*. These facts suggest an obvious explanation of what the Greeks had in mind when they invented the word 'metaphysics': they meant this word to designate a study that *goes beyond* the study of nature, that investigates matters that somehow transcend those investigated by physics. Unfortunately, this obvious explanation is probably wrong. (For one thing, the word 'meta' was not used by the Greeks in the metaphorical sense of 'beyond' that this explanation requires.)

The correct explanation is probably the following. In the fourth century B.C., the Greek philosopher Aristotle wrote (among many other books) a book about nature called *Physics* (or *Ta Phusika*) and a book about what he called "first philosophy." The latter book was devoted to what we today call metaphysics. After Aristotle's death, his books came to be arranged in what students of his philosophy considered their appropriate order. In this conventional ordering, the book on "first philosophy" came immediately after the *Physics*, and students of Aristotle's philosophy began to refer to it as *Ta Meta ta Phusika*, or *Metaphysics*. They probably meant no more by this title than "the book that comes after the *Physics*."

2. The practitioner of metaphysics is called a metaphysician and not, as one might expect, a metaphysicist. This is because the words 'metaphysician' and 'physician' already existed (and meant what they mean today) when people first began to feel a need for a special word for those scientists we today call physicists. The best word would have been 'physician' (indeed, a physicist is called a *physicien* in French), but that was already taken. The word 'physicist' was therefore invented, but too late to affect the established use of 'metaphysician'.

3. The word 'philosophy' was, according to Plato, invented by his teacher Socrates. If Plato's story is historical, it records events that took place late in the fifth century B.C. In those days, there were men who made a living by teaching wisdom (in Greek, *sophia*), or so they claimed. The most successful made a very good living indeed. Because these men claimed to be wise, and to be able to teach wisdom to others, they were called "sophists." Socrates, however, believed that the sophists had no wisdom to teach and,

in fact, that what many of them taught—that morality is only a human convention, for example—was false and harmful. Socrates, interestingly enough, claimed that he himself was not wise. (Or not in the way the sophists claimed to be wise. He believed that the sum of his wisdom consisted in the fact that he realized that he did not possess *that* kind of wisdom.) But, he said, although he was not wise and realized that he was not wise, he would very much like to be wise. He proclaimed himself not a possessor but a *lover* of wisdom. If one loves what one does not possess, Socrates said, one will seek after that thing and *try* to possess it. It is this proclamation that is the origin of the word 'philosophy', for the Greek word *'philosophia'* means just exactly 'the love of wisdom'. The word was used by Plato, and by Plato's student Aristotle, for what they wrote their books about, and, since all subsequent thinking about these subjects is a continuation of the work of Plato and Aristotle, the word has come to designate the subjects that Plato and Aristotle wrote on. (It should be noted that this is an account of the origin of the word 'philosophy' and not of philosophy, for there were philosophers in Greece before Socrates—they are called, appropriately enough, the pre-Socratic philosophers. Moreover, philosophy arose independently of Greek philosophy in China and India.)

4. To say that there are no established facts in metaphysics is not to say that there are no facts, and to say that there is no information is not to say that there is no knowledge. Consider, for example, the proposition that was briefly argued for in the text that there is an ultimate reality (even if we can know nothing about it except that it exists). In my view the argument I presented shows that it is a *fact* that there is an ultimate reality (and if this is a fact, it is a metaphysical fact), and I believe that, because I am aware of and understand this argument I *know* this fact. Nevertheless, this fact—assuming that it *is* a fact—cannot be said to be an *established* fact, and the statement that there is an ultimate reality cannot be said to be a piece of information. It is an established fact, a piece of information, that the continents are in motion. We call the latter fact "established" because anyone who does not agree that the continents are in motion either does not fully appreciate the data and arguments that a geologist could put forward in support of the thesis that the continents are in motion or else is intellectually perverse. (There exists an organization called the Flat Earth Society, which is, as one might have guessed, devoted to defending the thesis that the earth is flat. At least some of the members of this society are very clever and are fully aware of the data and arguments—including photographs of the earth taken from space—that establish that the earth is a sphere. These people take great delight in constructing elaborate "refutations" of the thesis that the earth is a sphere. Apparently this is not a joke; they seem to be quite sincere. What can we say about them except that they are intellectually perverse?) It cannot be said that it is an established fact that there is an ultimate reality, however, because there are people who are aware of, and understand perfectly, the argument given earlier in this chapter for the conclusion that there is an ultimate reality and who, nevertheless, do not accept this conclusion. And these people cannot be called intellectually perverse. I think that the argument I have given is good enough to support my claim to *know* that there is an ultimate reality; I do not believe that it thrusts its conclusion upon the mind with such force and clarity that anyone who disputes it simply cannot be taken seriously—as people who say that the earth is flat cannot be taken seriously.

5. The thesis that there are no established results in philosophy should not be confused with the thesis that philosophy has no practical consequences. The latter thesis is demonstrably false. Even if we leave aside the question whether physics and the other natural sciences grew out of philosophy, a large number of examples of the practical consequences of philosophical thinking can be cited. Many features of the Constitution of the United States can be traced to the writings of the philosophers Thomas Hobbes and John Locke, and much of the misery of the twentieth century is rooted in the writings of the philosophers G.W.F. Hegel and Karl Marx. (Not all practical consequences

are good consequences.) Much of the theory that computer scientists use in their daily work has its origin in early twentieth-century philosophy of mathematics. In the 1960s, an ambitious project to write computer programs for translating scientific articles from one language to another was abandoned because of a philosophical argument (devised by the philosopher of language Yeshua Bar-Hillel) for the impossibility of such programs. At the present time, there is a good deal of fruitful interaction between philosophers of mind and psychologists.

6. We can see this happening with logic. About one hundred years ago, the study of logic began to undergo a radical transformation, and there began to be a body of established logical fact. (Or one might argue that there had been a body of established logical fact ever since the fourth century B.C. but that, until about one hundred years ago, this body of fact was too meager and obvious for there to be much motivation for thinking of logic as a science in the present sense of science.) As the effects of this radical transformation of logic have borne more and more fruit, logic has come to be regarded less and less as a branch of philosophy and more and more as either a science in its own right or as a branch of pure mathematics.

7. The nineteenth-century German philosopher G.W.F. Hegel unkindly cited an advertisement from an English magazine that promised a "philosophical" cure for baldness!

8. The calculus was independently invented by the physicist Isaac Newton.

9. In the nineteenth century, there were philosophers who called themselves *positivists* because they held that there was no knowledge but "positive" knowledge, which was their term for what we should call scientific knowledge. The twentieth-century logical positivists called themselves positivists because they agreed with this thesis about knowledge. They called themselves *logical* positivists not because they were claiming to be logical where the nineteenth-century positivists had been illogical but because they made extensive use of the discoveries and techniques of twentieth-century logic.

10. I once heard the linguist Noam Chomsky suggest this in a lecture.

11. And this comes down to facts about what *words* philosophers have written. There is often extensive disagreement about the interpretation of what philosophers have said. If you have read something by, say, Plato, and if your instructor (or the author of this or any book) says that Plato meant x and it looks to you as if Plato meant y, there is no law that says that you have to take anyone's word for it that Plato meant x. It would be a better procedure to see what sort of case can be made for each of the two interpretations and then to form your own opinion about which (if either) is right.

12. In this sentence, I have treated the beneficence of colonial rule, Freudian psychology, and Marxism as if they were things that all educated people *now* know it would be absurd to believe in. Notice how easy it is to do this.

13. Could it be that this is what is "wrong" with metaphysics? Should we say that a theory is valueless if it does not make predictions about how experiments will go or about what observations will reveal? This is a very attractive position. Variants on it were held both by Kant and the logical positivists. Unfortunately, every attempt to work out a carefully stated theory along these lines has turned out to be "just more philosophy."

Introduction to Part One

1. A particular metaphysical theory or position or system of beliefs is often called a "metaphysic."

2. It is a plausible thesis that the "Common Western Metaphysic" is also the Common Eastern Metaphysic—that it is common to the views of the World held by ordinary, unreflective people in India and other parts of the Far East. It would seem to be a doctrine of Hinduism and of at least one form of Buddhism that only a small minority of enlightened people—people who have been willing to subject themselves to a certain rigorous discipline—are capable of "seeing through" the illusions of individuality, space and time, cause and effect, and so on.

Chapter 2

1. In ordinary usage, the term 'substance' is often used in the sense in which we are using 'stuff'. Thus, someone who claims to have seen a flying saucer may report that it was made of "a silvery, metallic substance." But the word 'substance' has a special, traditional meaning in metaphysics, a meaning close to the meaning of our term 'individual thing'. We shall not use the word 'substance' in this traditional sense in the present book, but it would be inadvisable for us to use it in the ordinary sense of 'stuff', for that usage might sow the seeds of later confusion in those readers—I hope they are many—who go on to read other books about metaphysics.

2. The word 'nihilism' has several meanings in philosophy. It is often used for the thesis that morality is an illusion—that in reality there are no moral restraints on human conduct.

3. This is one way to interpret the metaphysical consequences of modern physics and chemistry. Another way would be this: today we know that no region of space *is* entirely filled with bronze (or any other stuff). On that interpretation, the thesis "Every region of space that is entirely filled with bronze is such that every smaller region contained within that region is also entirely filled with bronze" is not false but vacuous—that is, there are no regions entirely filled with bronze for it to apply to. It is like the thesis that all unicorns have pointed ears.

4. There is another kind of Nihilism, which was suggested to me by my colleague Jonathan Bennett. According to this view, properties can be "present" or "instantiated" in certain regions of space even if there is nothing (no individual thing and no stuff) in that region that has them. Thus, for example, it might be that redness is spread out through a certain region of space, even though there is nothing (neither individual thing nor stuff) in that region of space and, therefore, nothing there that is red. I am unable to pursue this fascinating suggestion, since the only way that I can see in which a property could be present in a region of space is for there to be a thing or stuff in that region that has that property.

5. The word 'monism' is sometimes used for the thesis that there exists only one *kind* of individual thing—that all individual things are material, for example, or that they are all mental. Used in this sense, it is opposed to 'dualism'.

6. It is customary in current philosophical writing to use the word 'part' in such a way that everything is, by definition, a part of itself. The Taj Mahal, for example, is said to be a "part" of the Taj Mahal—its largest part, the part that includes all the others. Philosophers who use the word 'part' in this way call the other parts of the Taj Mahal—its parts other than itself, its parts in the usual sense of the word—its "proper parts." Various technical advantages are gained by using the word 'part' in this way, but I think that this usage is likely to confuse beginners in philosophy, and I shall therefore in this book use 'part' in the usual way: a part of a thing will always be one of the "lesser" objects that together make up that thing.

7. In his book *Time and Eternity* (Princeton: Princeton University Press, 1952), W. T. Stace maintains, in effect, that although the poetic language employed in various

Hindu sacred texts often seems to imply the third version of Monism, it is really the second version that is the considered Hindu position (p. 162).

8. The *Ethics Demonstrated in Geometric Order* was published in 1677, shortly after Spinoza's death. The book was published posthumously partly because Spinoza continued to revise it throughout his life and partly because its monism was incompatible with Christianity and Judaism, a fact that could have caused considerable difficulty for Spinoza even in the relatively liberal religious climate of late seventeenth-century Holland. (Spinoza, a Jew, was expelled from the Amsterdam synagogue because of his religious views.) While the book, as its title indicates, deals largely with ethical matters, it begins with an extensive exposition and defense of Spinoza's metaphysic, on which his ethical theory is based. (As a matter of fact, the initial metaphysical part of the *Ethics* has attracted far more attention and commentary throughout the three hundred years that have elapsed since its publication than the later ethical part.) The perhaps puzzling allusion to geometry in the full title stems from the fact that the *Ethics* is arranged like a geometry textbook, with definitions, axioms, postulates, theorems, corollaries, and proofs.

9. This discussion of Spinoza's argument for Monism does not employ Spinoza's technical vocabulary.

10. I do not mean to imply that this premise is the only weak point in Spinoza's argument; it is simply the weak point that is relevant to our present topic. Almost all philosophers would agree that Spinoza's argument for the conclusion that there must exist an absolutely independent being is invalid, and almost every feature of Book I of the *Ethics* (which is where Spinoza's argument for Monism is to be found) has been disputed by some commentator.

11. It can be plausibly argued that Spinoza was an atheist, though he can hardly be described as a *typical* atheist. Philosophers have been reluctant to apply the word 'atheist' to Spinoza for two closely related reasons. First, he applied the word 'God' to his version of the One, and he regarded this label as both important and appropriate. Secondly, his emotional attitude toward the one absolutely independent being was very similar in many respects to certain emotions that theists feel toward God. Typical atheists have an aversion to the word 'God', and they regard the feelings that Spinoza had for the One as feelings that people should not have toward anything. My own opinion is that it is technically correct to call Spinoza an atheist (since Spinoza does not believe that there is anything to which the word 'God' applies, in what I regard as the proper sense of the term) but that it would be very misleading to do so.

12. Logic would seem to dictate that the term 'theism' be used for the thesis that some things, but not all things, are God (or gods); the term 'monotheism' would then be used for the thesis that there is one God, and the term 'polytheism'—from Greek 'poly', meaning 'many'—for the thesis that there are many Gods (or gods). In actual usage, however, the term 'theism' means the same as 'monotheism', the term 'monotheism' being reserved for contexts in which it is relevant to oppose it to 'polytheism', as, for example, when one describes the development of monotheism among the ancient Jews.

13. William James, *The Varieties of Religious Experience* (New York: Mentor Books, 1958), pp. 321f. The book is based on James's Gifford Lectures, which were delivered at the University of Edinburgh in 1901.

Chapter 3

1. In a footnote to the introduction to the second edition of his *Critique of Pure Reason* (1787), Immanuel Kant writes, "… it still remains a scandal to philosophy, and to human reason in general, that the existence of things outside us … must be accepted

merely on *faith,* and if anyone thinks good to doubt their existence, we are unable to counter his doubts by any satisfactory proof" (Immanuel Kant, *Critique of Pure Reason,* ed. and trans. by Norman Kemp Smith [2nd ed. London: Macmillan, 1933], p. 34n.).

2. At any rate, one cannot be mistaken about the "surface content" of one's own mind. I do not wish to dispute the notion that we have various "unconscious" beliefs and motivations that we are not only unaware of but would vigorously deny having if they were suggested to us.

3. But some proponents of the Common Western Metaphysic might partly agree with Berkeley: *certain* properties of things like snowballs cannot exist apart from the mind (colors are the properties that it is easiest to believe are dependent on the mind), but other properties do exist apart from the mind (shapes are the properties that it is hardest to believe are dependent on the mind).

4. In saying that Berkeley denies the existence of an external world, we do not mean to imply that he is what is called a solipsist. If one is a solipsist—from the Latin *solus,* "alone"—one believes that one is the only individual thing there is. Berkeley believed that there were many things besides George Berkeley and his modifications, but he believed that these things were other persons (we could also say 'the minds of other persons', for Berkeley identified a person and that person's mind) and their modifications and collections of their modifications.

5. This idea is summed up in what is perhaps the most famous sentence in all of Berkeley's works: '*Esse est percipi*'—that is, 'To be is to be perceived'.

6. The first is by Msgr. Ronald Knox. The second is by the prolific Anon.

7. For example, the Supreme Mind would certainly not need to be morally good. And it is far from clear whether that being would need to be all-powerful or to know absolutely everything. Is it even clear that there would have to be just *one* mind responsible for the order of our sensations? Wouldn't it be possible for two or more minds to cooperate to produce this order? One difficulty with this suggestion is raised by the question of how all of these minds would communicate. One mind cannot perceive another mind or its content "directly," and, unless one single mind coordinated all of the sensations present in the multitude of minds that were coordinating human sensations, those minds could not communicate and coordinate their activities by some indirect means analogous to the way in which human minds communicate. But if there were such a mind, then *that* mind would be the Supreme Mind.

8. More exactly, that we *could* perceive and refer to if we were in the right place at the right time: a dinosaur or a rock on some planet human beings will never visit is a common object.

By the ordinary business of life I mean just about any activity that human beings engage in together when they are not thinking about metaphysics. Thus, two physicists discussing the track left by some exotic particle are engaged in what I am calling the ordinary business of life.

9. Berkeley is perfectly well aware of examples of this type. He has constructed many of them himself, although not this one. What he takes them to show is that common objects cannot exist independently of the mind.

The thesis that beings who did not have the same color-sensations as we when they looked at the same physical objects would be *misperceiving* those objects is sometimes called Naive Realism. Or, at any rate, there is, or is supposed to be, a famous philosophical thesis called "Naive Realism" (it is presumably not called that by those who accept it, if there is anyone who accepts it), and this formulation of Naive Realism is the only one that I have been able to understand.

Introduction to Part Two

1. From a Samoan creation story. Quoted in Robert Shapiro, *Origins: A Skeptic's Guide to the Creation of Life on Earth* (New York: Simon & Schuster, 1986), p. 36.

2. Genesis 1:1–4. According to some scholars, the opening words of this passage could also be translated as follows: 'When God was first beginning to create the heaven and the earth, the earth was without form and void'.

3. See, for example, G. W. Leibniz's treatise (published in 1714; there are many editions and translations) *Principles of Nature and Grace*, particularly §7.

Chapter 5

1. The label 'ontological argument' seems first to have been applied to Anselm's and Descartes's arguments by Kant in the eighteenth century. The word 'ontological' is derived from the Greek word for 'being' or 'existence'.

2. What Kant actually says is that existence is "a logical but not a real predicate (*Prädikat*)." I believe that the idea he intended to express by this formula is more or less the idea I have expressed in the text by the words 'Existence is not a property'.

3. Or perhaps it would be better to say, "a complete specification of a way *a* World might have been," for it may be that the World is a full-fledged individual thing, as opposed to a mere collection, and that if things had been sufficiently different, that individual thing would not have existed at all, and some other individual thing—either a part of the World or some individual thing that does not exist at all—would have been the World.

4. What allows us to speak of *the* actual world here? Why can't there be *two* possible worlds that specify the way things really are? Well, those two possible worlds, being, by definition, completely specific, would have to agree in all details—otherwise at least one of them would get the way things really are wrong. If, according to one of the two possible worlds, the number of Douglas fir trees in Canada is odd and according to the other it is even, then it can't be that both possible worlds get the way things really are right, for, as things really are, the number of Douglas firs in Canada is either odd or even. But if the two possible worlds agree on *everything*, in what sense are they *two* possible worlds, two *different* specifications of how things are? Does it make sense to speak of two specifications of the features of, say, a house that are the same in every detail and yet are two different specifications? At any rate, I am going to make this true by definition: if x and y are possible worlds, and if x and y agree in every detail, then x and y are one and the same possible world.

5. Consider, for example, the sentence, 'If the Pythagorean Theorem has been proved, then it can't be false'. This could mean either 'The following is impossible: that the Pythagorean Theorem be proved and also be false' or 'If the Pythagorean Theorem has been proved, then the following is impossible: that the Pythagorean Theorem be false'.

6. The logically sophisticated will be aware that this premise must be read as saying that not only is the property of existing necessarily in fact a perfection but that this property would exist and would be a perfection no matter what. But few would want to deny that *if* there is such a property as necessary existence, and *if* the property of necessary existence is a perfection, then this property would exist no matter what and would be a perfection no matter what.

7. At any rate, it is possible for there to be animals that are shaped the way the unicorns of legend are supposed to be shaped. The American philosopher Saul Kripke has,

however, presented interesting and plausible arguments for the conclusion that no possible animal would really count as a *unicorn* and that unicorns are therefore impossible.

8. But it was by no means a recent invention. Hume, for example, wrote, "Whatever we conceive as existent, we can also conceive as non-existent. There is no being, therefore, whose non-existence implies a contradiction." (*Dialogues Concerning Natural Religion*, XI. The *Dialogues* were first published in 1779, three years after Hume's death.)

Chapter 6

1. G. W. Leibniz, with whose name the phrase "the Principle of Sufficient Reason" is primarily associated, states the Principle as follows: "now we must rise to *metaphysics*, making use of the *great principle* ... which holds that *nothing takes place without sufficient reason*, that is to say that nothing happens without its being possible for one who has enough knowledge of things to give a reason sufficient to determine why it is thus and not otherwise." (*Principles of Nature and Grace, Founded on Reason*, 1714, §7). The translation is taken from *Leibniz: Philosophical Writings*, trans. and ed. by Mary Morris (London: J. M. Dent & Sons, 1934), pp. 25–26.

2. The cosmological argument is usually classified as an argument for the existence of God; that is, of a unique, necessarily existent Person who is responsible for the existence of all other things. But the conclusion of the argument, at least as the argument is usually formulated, does not say either that there is one and only one necessarily existent thing or that any necessarily existent thing is a person. Indeed, the argument is often criticized on just the point that its conclusion cannot be read as 'God exists'. But for our purposes this is no defect in the argument. If there were a thousand and two necessary beings, none of which was in any sense a person, and if we knew this, we should know why there was something rather than nothing.

3. The proposition that Possible World Four is the actual world is a false proposition, but if it *were* true, it *would* necessitate all the truths that *would be*—in that circumstance— truths. It is only such "world propositions" (propositions asserting of a particular possible world that it is the actual world) that are capable of necessitating all truths.

4. The professional metaphysician will recognize that it has been assumed in this argument that if the proposition that A and the proposition that B necessarily have the same truth-value, then they are one and the same proposition. Or, at least, the argument assumes that if the proposition that A and the proposition that B necessarily have the same truth-value, and if they are contingent truths, the fact that A cannot be offered as an explanation of the fact that B. This assumption is controversial and it could be important. Suppose, for example, that God exists necessarily and is essentially omnipotent, and suppose it is possible for Him to decree the whole set of contingent truths. Then the proposition that God decrees that Possible World Two be the actual world is true in and only in Possible World Two. But it is not wholly implausible to suppose that the statement, "Because God decreed that Possible World Two be the actual world," is, if true, a proper answer to the question, "Why is Possible World Two the actual world." (No doubt there are non-theistic analogues of this objection.) This objection is serious and deserves a lengthy reply. Here is a short reply: Suppose the case imagined is actual. What is the explanation for the fact that God decrees that Possible World Two be the actual world? Is the fact its own explanation? Is its explanation, perhaps, the further fact that God decrees that God decree that Possible World Two be the actual world? Is its explanation that God desires the actual world to have a certain intrinsic property F, together with the fact that Possible World Two alone has F? All of these candidates for an explanation seem unsatisfactory. (Consider the third. If a possible world has some intrinsic property, then it is a necessary truth that it has that property. Now consider the

proposition that God desires the actual world to have F. This proposition is either necessary or contingent. If it is necessary, then the proposition that Possible World Two is the actual world will be necessary and Possible World Two will be the only possible world. If it is contingent, what explains its truth? The fact that God decrees that He desire that the actual world have the property F?) And what other candidates are there?

5. The translucent sphere and various other features of the following discussion are borrowed from the brilliant exposition of the cosmological argument in Richard Taylor's *Metaphysics*, 4th ed. (Englewood Cliffs, N.J.: Prentice Hall, 1992), pp. 99–108.

6. Quoted in an article that appeared in the Science Section of the *New York Times*, 12 March 1991.

7. Daniel Kolak and Raymond Martin, *Wisdom Without Answers: A Guide to the Experience of Philosophy*, 2nd ed. (Belmont, Calif.: Wadsworth Publishing Co., 1991), pp. 79–80.

8. *Ibid.*, p. 77.

Introduction to Part Three

1. Many people shy away from language like this these days because they believe that the use of such language implies that human beings have the right to hunt non-human animals for sport or to use them in medical experiments or to do just about anything else that it might occur to human beings to inflict on their fellow creatures. And many people are opposed even to eating the flesh of animals, much less engaging in wanton cruelty toward them. It is therefore natural that they would object to language that implied that human beings had the right to use their fellow animals in any way they liked. But the term 'rational being' has no such implication. One might as well say that to distinguish between animate and inanimate objects is to imply that I, being a living being, have the right to smash Michelangelo's *Pietà* with a hammer. If I am considering a course of action that will affect the welfare of dolphins, the fact that I am a rational animal and the fact that dolphins are not rational animals will no doubt often be facts that are *relevant* to the question of the morality of the proposed course of action. But these two facts by themselves could not settle the question.

2. Science-fiction writers have taken to using the word 'sentient' to express the idea that I express by 'rational'. This usage is incorrect, however, for 'sentient' means 'capable of sensation and feeling': dogs and cats are sentient beings.

3. It is wrong but apparently very natural. I once attended a lecture by a specialist in "artificial intelligence" that was devoted to the enormous difficulties that would face anyone who wanted to program a computer to be able to talk, like "Hal 9000" in *2001: A Space Odyssey*. A member of the audience asked afterward, in genuine puzzlement, "But why don't you just make the computer very smart; if it's smart enough, won't it be able to learn to talk?" He was thinking of intelligence and the ability to talk on an "automotive" model: intelligence and the ability to talk are related as are power and the capacity to go fast.

Chapter 7

1. See Robert Shapiro, *Origins: A Skeptic's Guide to the Creation of Life on Earth* (New York: Simon & Schuster, 1986).

2. This figure is taken from an article by the evolutionary biologist Ernst Mayr, "The Probability of Extraterrestrial Intelligent Life," in *Philosophy of Biology*, ed. by Michael Ruse (New York: Macmillan, 1989), pp. 279–285.

3. The mechanisms might require other factors to be present in the organisms and their environment, provided that these additional factors were ones whose existence was "natural" enough to require no particular explanation or "probable" enough that their existence could reasonably be ascribed to chance. The Darwinian mechanisms, for example, require not only that the configurations of matter be self-reproducing but also that the configurations make use of certain limited resources in order to continue to exist and to reproduce, that the configurations reproduce themselves not perfectly but with (random) variations, and that a significant proportion of the variations be such that a variant configuration will have a tendency to pass some of the variations it exhibits on to its "descendants." In the case of organisms that reproduce sexually, some versions of Darwinism require that it occasionally happen that small populations of organisms capable of interbreeding become isolated.

4. These examples are entirely made up. They are meant only to give the reader a "feel" for the sensitivity of the existence of life to changes in the actual values of certain numbers, according to modern physics and cosmology. The reader who is interested in some real information on this topic should consult John Leslie's splendid book *Universes* (London and New York: Routledge, 1989).

Chapter 8

1. One school of twentieth-century philosophers, the existentialists, held that it was contrary to the nature of a rational being—but existentialists would not use the term 'rational being'—that a purpose be imposed on its existence "from outside"; even an all-powerful Creator, the existentialists held, would be unable to confer on a rational being a purpose that existed independently of that being's free choices, for it is by freely choosing between alternatives that one creates one's own purposes. This is an interesting point of view, but we shall be unable to devote to it the attention that it deserves. I am simply going to assume that it is in principle possible for a creator to endow its creations with a purpose, even in the case—admittedly a very special case—in which those creations are rational beings.

2. A sailor notes a strange cloud formation that has suddenly appeared on the horizon. A spectroscopist regards a puzzling group of lines in the spectrograph of a certain star. A detective considers the fact that the murder victim, though otherwise fully dressed, was wearing no underwear. An archaeologist reading an ancient inscription comes upon a hitherto unrecorded hieroglyph. Each says, "I wonder what *that* means?" In each of their utterances, the word 'mean' has a different sense.

3. The importance of this principle in discussions of the implications of the fine-tuning of the cosmos has been pointed out by John Leslie in *Universes* and other publications. Leslie calls the principle the "Merchant's Thumb" principle, on the basis of the following story. A merchant, displaying an expensive silk robe to a potential buyer, consistently keeps a hole in the robe covered with his left thumb. When he is accused of dishonestly concealing the hole from the buyer, his defenders point out that everyone's left thumb has to be *somewhere*. And so it does; but one can think of a very good explanation for its having been over the hole, and it is therefore wrong to proceed on the assumption that its having been over the hole requires no more explanation than its having been at any other particular place.

4. One possibility would be that, although there are many cosmoi, they exist "one at a time": a cosmos has a finite "lifetime" (the heavens will wear out like a garment, as the Psalmist says), and, when it has passed away, another will somehow be born from its remains. And each cosmic "rebirth" has the effect of re-setting the dials.

5. *The First Three Minutes: A Modern View of the Origin of the Universe* (London: André Deutsch, 1977), p. 155.

Chapter 9

1. The word 'materialism' is often used as a name for the thesis I am calling 'physicalism', and it has stronger and weaker senses corresponding to the stronger and weaker senses of 'physicalism'.

2. It should be noted that not all theories pertaining to the relation of the human person to the human organism are either physicalistic or dualistic. We have noted that it may be that some idealists would want to say that there are no human organisms and that there is thus no problem about how they are related to human persons. Some "eliminative physicalists" and "behaviorists" and some epiphenomenalists might be understood as maintaining that there are no human persons—that there is nothing that the word 'I' refers to—and thus that there is no problem about how they are related to human organisms. And there are theories according to which human persons are what we earlier called "composites," that they have both physical and non-physical parts. (Saint Thomas Aquinas defended a theory that falls into this category.) We do not have the space to discuss all of these interesting theories. We shall simply assume that there are both human persons and human organisms—an assumption that leaves it an open question whether the persons *are* the organisms. And much of our discussion of whether human persons are physical things will be relevant to the question whether every *part* of a human person is a physical thing, although we shall not explicitly address that question.

3. Our explanation of what it is for a certain organism to be a certain person's body was introduced in connection with our exposition of dualistic interactionism. This definition presupposes that x can cause changes in x's body and that x's body can cause changes in x. The physicalist, who holds that the person and the organism are identical, might prefer to word the definition slightly differently. Perhaps the physicalist would prefer to say that x's body is that organism in which x can *bring about* changes without bringing about changes in any other organism, and it is the organism changes in which can *result in* changes in x without resulting in changes in any other organism. This way of wording the definition does not carry the implication that a person and the person's body are distinct things. And this way of wording the definition should be acceptable to the dualist as well, since it does not carry the implication that the person and the person's body are identical.

4. G. W. Leibniz, *Monadology* (1714), §17. The translation occurs in the note "Mill" in Jonathan Bennett and Peter Remnant's translation of Leibniz's *Nouveaux essais* (*New Essays on Human Understanding*, Cambridge: Cambridge University Press, 1981), p. lv.

5. What about *physical* simples? Could *they* think and feel? This question would not have troubled Leibniz, who believed that all simples were non-physical things. (But this is a rather misleading statement if it is read without reference to the whole of his metaphysic.) The Greek atomists, however, believed that what they called atoms were physical simples, and current physics strongly suggests that various physical things—electrons, for example—have no parts. Any dualist who accepts the thesis that there are physical simples, whether in its ancient or its modern form, will probably want to say that while being without parts is a *necessary* condition for the capacity for thought and sensation, it is not sufficient; no dualist, I would suppose, would be willing to say that an electron was capable of thought.

6. We have defined a physical property as a property that could be possessed by and only by a physical thing. Let us define a *non-physical* property as a property that could

be possessed by and only by a non-physical thing. It is important to note that just as there may be individual things that are neither physical nor non-physical, there may be properties that are neither physical nor non-physical: properties that could be possessed either by physical or non-physical things. For example—assuming that it is possible for there to be non-physical individual things—the property of being an individual thing and the property of being either physical or non-physical are both properties that are neither physical nor non-physical. Other examples would be more controversial: I think that mental properties are neither physical nor non-physical, but Descartes would say that they were non-physical, and some physicalists would say that they were physical.

These considerations show that we must qualify the explanation given in the text of what Descartes meant by saying that our essence was thinking: the only *non-physical* intrinsic properties that a human person has or could have are mental. (For Descartes would admit that, say, *being an individual thing* was an intrinsic property of human persons, and this is not a mental property.)

Chapter 10

1. These three terms were invented by Jonathan Bennett.

2. J. Z. Young, *An Introduction to the Study of Man* (Oxford: the Clarendon Press, 1971), pp. 86–87.

3. In the Hebrew Bible (Daniel 12:2) we read "And many of them that sleep in the dust of the earth shall awake, some to everlasting life and some to shame and everlasting contempt." The Christian "Athanasian Creed" speaks of the resurrection of the dead in these words: "all human beings shall rise again with their bodies and shall give account for their own works. ..."

Chapter 11

1. It should be evident from this discussion of "free will" that what we are calling by this name would be more appropriately called 'free choice'. 'Free will' is, however, the term that has traditionally been used to express this concept, and I use it out of respect for tradition.

Chapter 12

1. There is no mystery about the fact that our physical abilities are just barely adequate to the task of running a mile in four minutes. This is because the figure "four minutes" was not chosen *independently* of our physical abilities; the task "running a mile in four minutes" is of interest to us because it represents a challenge to creatures that have the physical abilities we just happen to have. But the task "solving the problems of metaphysics" is not interesting to us because of the challenge it presents; it is interesting because the problems of metaphysics are interesting to us. Suppose that there were a race of intelligent horses—like the Houyhnhnms in *Gulliver's Travels*. The task "running a mile in four minutes" would be of no interest to them because it is absurdly easy for a horse to run a mile in four minutes. But the task "solving the problems of metaphysics" might well be of great interest even to a species that found it absurdly easy to solve them simply because the members of that species wanted to know the solutions to those problems.

Bibliography

Alston, William P. "Yes, Virginia, There Is a Real World." *Proceedings and Addresses of the American Philosophical Association* 52 (1979): 779–808.

Ayer, A. J. *Language, Truth and Logic.* London: Gollancz, 1936.

Bennett, Jonathan. *A Study of Spinoza's Ethics.* Indianapolis: Hackett, 1984.

_____ . *Locke, Berkeley, Hume: Central Themes.* Oxford: the Clarendon Press, 1971.

Berkeley, George. *Three Dialogues between Hylas and Philonous,* ed. and with an introduction by Robert M. Adams. Indianapolis: Hackett, 1979.

Berofsky, Bernard (ed.). *Free Will and Determinism.* New York: Harper & Row, 1966.

Blackman, Larry Lee (ed.). *Classics of Analytical Metaphysics.* Lantham, Md.: University Press of America, 1984.

Bradley, F. H. *Appearance and Reality: A Metaphysical Essay.* Oxford: the Clarendon Press, 1893. Chapters II and III are reprinted in Blackman.

_____ . "On Appearance, Error and Contradiction." *Mind* 74 n.s. (1910). Reprinted in Blackman.

_____ . "Reply to Mr Russell's Explanations." *Mind* 77 n.s. (1911). Reprinted in Blackman.

Burrill, Donald R. (ed.). *The Cosmological Arguments: A Spectrum of Opinion.* Garden City, N.Y.: Anchor Books, 1967.

Dawkins, Richard. *The Blind Watchmaker.* New York: Norton, 1986.

Dennett, Daniel C. *Elbow Room: The Varieties of Free Will Worth Wanting.* Cambridge: M.I.T. Press, 1984.

Denton, Michael. *Evolution, A Theory in Crisis.* London: Burnett, 1985.

Descartes, René. *Meditations on First Philosophy,* trans. from the Latin by Donald A. Cress. Indianapolis: Hackett, 1979.

Edwards, Paul (ed.). *The Encyclopedia of Philosophy,* 8 vols. New York: Macmillan and the Free Press, 1967.

Ewing, A. C. *A Short Commentary on Kant's Critique of Pure Reason.* London: Methuen, 1938.

Fischer, John Martin (ed.). *Moral Responsibility.* Ithaca: Cornell University Press, 1986.

Hofstadter, Douglas R., and Daniel C. Dennett (eds.). *The Mind's I.* New York: Basic Books, 1981.

Hume, David. *Dialogues Concerning Natural Religion,* ed. by H. D. Aiken. New York: Hafner, 1955.

Hutchison, John A. *Paths of Faith,* 4th ed. New York: McGraw-Hill, 1991.

James, William. *The Varieties of Religious Experience: A Study in Human Nature.* New York: Mentor Books, 1958.

Johnson, Phillip E. *Darwin on Trial.* Washington: Regnery Gateway, 1991.

Körner, S. *Kant.* Baltimore: Penguin Books, 1955.

Kripke, Saul A. *Naming and Necessity.* Cambridge: Harvard University Press, 1980.

Leibniz, G. W. *Principles of Nature and Grace,* included in *Leibniz: Philosophical Writings,* trans. and ed. by Mary Morris. London: J. M. Dent & Sons, 1934.

Leslie, John. *Universes.* London: Routledge, 1989.

Lewis, David. "Are We Free to Break the Laws?" included in Lewis's *Philosophical Papers, Vol. II.* New York: Oxford University Press, 1986.

Mayr, Ernst. "The Probability of Extraterrestrial Intelligent Life," included in Michael Ruse (ed.), *Philosophy of Biology.* New York: Macmillan, 1989.

Monod, Jacques. *Chance and Necessity: An Essay on the Natural Philosophy of Modern Biology,* trans. by Austryn Wainhouse. New York: Vintage Books, 1971.

Nietzsche, Friedrich. *Thus Spake Zarathustra,* included in *The Portable Nietzsche,* ed. and trans. by Walter Kaufmann. New York: Viking, 1954.

Paley, William. *Natural Theology* (selections), ed. by Frederick Ferré. Indianapolis: Bobbs-Merrill, 1963.

Perry, John. *Personal Identity.* Berkeley: University of California Press, 1975.

Plantinga, Alvin. *God, Freedom, and Evil.* New York: Harper & Row, 1974.

———— (ed.), with an introduction by Richard Taylor. *The Ontological Argument: From St Anselm to Contemporary Philosophers.* Garden City, N.Y.: Anchor Books, 1965.

Plato. *Phaedo,* trans. and with introduction, notes, and appendices by R. S. Bluck. London: Routledge, 1955.

Polkinghorne, John. *The Particle Play: An Account of the Ultimate Constituents of Matter.* Oxford: W. H. Freeman, 1979.

Putnam, Hilary. *The Many Faces of Realism: The Paul Carus Lectures, 1985.* La Salle, Ill.: Open Court, 1987.

————. "The Meaning of 'Meaning'," included in Putnam's *Mind, Language and Reality, Philosophical Papers, Vol. II.* Cambridge: Cambridge University Press, 1975.

————. *Reason, Truth and History.* Cambridge: Cambridge University Press, 1981.

Rorty, Amelie O. *The Identities of Persons.* Berkeley: University of California Press, 1976.

Rorty, Richard. *Philosophy and the Mirror of Nature.* Princeton: Princeton University Press, 1979.

Rowe, William L. *Philosophy of Religion: An Introduction.* Encino, Calif.: Dickenson, 1978.

Russell, Bertrand. "Some Explanations in Reply to Mr Bradley." *Mind* 75 n.s. (1910). Reprinted in Blackman.

Schwartz, Stephen P. (ed.). *Naming, Necessity, and Natural Kinds.* Ithaca: Cornell University Press, 1977.

Shapiro, Robert. *Origins: A Skeptic's Guide to the Creation of Life on Earth.* New York: Simon & Schuster, 1986.

Spinoza, Benedict. *Spinoza: Selections,* ed. by John Wild. New York: Scribner's, 1930.

————. *The Collected Works of Spinoza,* ed. and trans. by E. M. Curley. Princeton: Princeton University Press, 1984.

Swinburne, Richard. "The Argument from Design." *Philosophy* 43 (1968).

Taylor, Richard. *Metaphysics,* 4th ed. Englewood Cliffs, N.J.: Prentice-Hall, 1992.

Thomson, Judith Jarvis. "Parthood and Identity across Time." *The Journal of Philosophy* 80 (1983): 201–220.

van Inwagen, Peter. *An Essay on Free Will.* Oxford: the Clarendon Press, 1983.

Watson, Gary (ed.). *Free Will.* Oxford: Oxford University Press, 1982.

About the Book
and Author

ACCEPTING THE TRADITIONAL DEFINITION of metaphysics as the study of ultimate reality, Peter van Inwagen builds this strikingly original textbook around three crucial questions: What are the most general features of the world? Why does the world exist? And what is the nature and place of rational beings in the world?

In the informal but precise style for which he is known, van Inwagen surveys the classical answers to these questions while teaching his readers through example how to think about them more clearly and deeply on their own. By the end of the book, he has introduced most of the perennial topics of metaphysics, including appearance and reality, identity and individuation, objectivity, necessary existence, mind and body, teleology, and freedom of the will.

Engaging and provocative, but always fair and reasonable, *Metaphysics* provides both a lucid guide to the study of First Questions and a paradigm of philosophical exposition. It will immediately take its place at the forefront of leading contemporary texts on metaphysics.

Peter van Inwagen is professor of philosophy at Syracuse University and author of *An Essay on Free Will* and *Material Beings,* editor of *Time and Cause,* and coeditor (with James Tomberlin) of *Alvin Plantinga* in the Profiles series. He has published many articles in leading journals on metaphysics and related topics.

Index

DATE DUE